D1542493

Connecting the Roots
of the Global Economy:
A Holistic Approach, Brief Edition

Dr. Denise R. Ames

Published in 2015 by Center for Global Awareness

Text copyright © 2015 by Dr. Denise R. Ames
Images are copyright © the respective owners as noted in each photo credit and are used under
    one of the following licenses:
Creative Commons License 3.0 *http://creativecommons.org/licenses/by-sa/3.0/*
GNU Free Documentation License
Uncreditied images are, to the best of the author's knowledge, in the public domain.
Figures created for this work are copyright © 2015 by Dr. Denise R. Ames

All rights reserved. No portion of this book may be reproduced, stored in a retrieval system, or
transmitted in any form or by any means, mechanical, electronic, photocopying, recording or
otherwise, without written permission from the publisher.

ISBN: 978-1-943841-00-4

Book and cover design by Jeanine McGann

The princpal text of this book was composed in Adobe Caslon Pro.

The Center for Global Awareness
Albuquerque, New Mexico, USA
www.global-awareness.org

Acknowledgments

This book, *Connecting the Roots of the Global Economy: A Holistic Approach, Brief Edition*, has been evolving for many years prior to when I started to actually sit down and write about the global economy. I would first like to thank Frank Beurksens for introducing me to the topic back in the 1970s. He patiently described options and futures trading to me until I finally grasped a semblance of the topic. I found that during a trip to the Soviet Union in 1989 with a group of agricultural economists, the global economy was not an exact science and I could hold my own in a discussion of the topic.

I continued my exploration of the global economy in the 1990s as part of my research and teaching in world history. I discovered that the economy changed through time, like other cultural elements. The current organization of the global economy is by far not etched in stone and certainly subject to continuous change. Special thanks to my thesis and dissertation advisor and friend, Professor Joseph Grabill, for helping to guide and mentor me through this exploration.

My teaching, research and interest in the global economy continued through the 2000s as I conducted workshops, lectures, and classes for the lay public and educators on the subject. I extend a thank you to all those who listened to my ramblings and insights on the global economy and to those who offered suggestions for improvement.

I started to write this book on the global economy in 2010. It was a formidable journey that I was nonetheless happy to embark upon. In this process I especially want to thank my partner in the Center for Global Awareness, Nancy Harmon, for her encouragement, remarks, and crisp editing. Without her unfailing support this book would not have been completed. I would also like to thank Margaret Govoni for her editing and input. Thanks to several readers who provided helpful comments, feedback, and editing: Cliff Wilke, Bob Riley, Sally Jacobsen, and Phil Fisk. And a final thanks to my husband, Jim Knutson, for his encouragement and listening.

Contents

Preface

My first immersion into examining different economic systems took place on a trip to the Soviet Union in 1989 with a group of agricultural economists. I accompanied my husband who was in the grain marketing business and had a good grasp of economics. I was perplexed by the site of an immaculate modern subway system, complete with chandeliers, in Moscow, while in the countryside horse-drawn wagons of elderly woman with hoes in hand went out to work the fields, as the tractors sat idly by in a state of disrepair in the rickety sheds. I was also stunned by the vibrant black market, where anything could be bought and sold at a reasonable price, even the coveted caviar, while the state-owned grocers showcased empty shelves, displaying a prized cow-tongue when available. The beautiful production of the classic ballet Swan Lake showed the system worked in some ways, but in others, such as the shabby tractors, it failed miserably. The American economists were unable to explain this discrepancy very well, except for a standard statement about the virtues of the capitalist system.

I continued my fascination about the global economy in the 1990s when I was teaching undergraduate U.S. and world history and working towards my doctoral degree at Illinois State University in Normal, Illinois. Since my students overwhelmingly liked current issues, I wanted to include more up-to-date information about both the world and the U.S. Globalization was the buzzword of the day and frequently in the news, so it was a topic that I investigated with gusto. At first glance, most of what was written referred to globalization in glowing terms. The increasing integration of economies and people around the world promised a rosy future of increased prosperity, not only for Americans but for those around the world who embraced innovation, an entrepreneurial spirit, and the desire to make a better life. If people were more connected through transportation and communication networks, it stood to reason that the world would be a more peaceful place. Communism had collapsed in the Soviet Union and Eastern Europe in the early 1990s and, therefore, the capitalistic economic system and democratic political system appeared to be victorious over their communist Cold War rivals. It all sounded great! After all, the newscasts of the day portrayed the newly-democratic Russians clamoring for American-style blue jeans or the rising middle class youth of China lining up for hours at McDonald's just to get a Big Mac. Globalization was often equated with the spreading of American style values and consumption habits. The closed system of communism had given way to open markets, free expression, and democratic ways.

Many in America thought that globalization meant that the rest of the world, especially the former communist world, had discovered the wonders of the American way of life and were eager to embrace it. Newscasts showed exuberant formerly communist youth dancing to western music in newly-formed night clubs, complete with strobe lights and pulsating rhythms. Others thought that the youth of China were willing to risk their lives for American-style democracy and freedom, as witnessed on cable television when a lone student demonstrator bravely faced a formidable Chinese military tank ready to crush him at any moment in the June 4, 1989, demonstration at Tiananmen Square in Beijing. The business section of any American book store in the 1990s portrayed globalization as a "win-win" proposition with untold profits for entrepreneurs to easily earn with a little initiative and little risk. New internet start-up companies, such as Netscape and Amazon, popped up almost daily and promised untold riches for the founders, as well as for those who invested in their companies. Bill Gates, who founded Microsoft in 1975, was the hero of the 1990s. He was the richest person in the world, and his entrepreneurial spirit and work ethic were the envy of all those who aspired to follow his path to fame and fortune. We were all exhorted to get on the globalization train, since it was an inevitable process that could not be held back by those fearful of change. It was an optimistic time.

As often happens with dazzling new trends, the globalization craze of the 1990s turned out to be too good to be true. I realize that many Americans and others were able to make a good living or even fortunes from high-tech start-ups and more expanded business opportunities. I acknowledge that the appeal of the "American way of life" is a dream many people around the world aspire to. But, I knew that globalization meant more than that. To understand globalization, I needed to dig a little deeper than a CNN newscast or an article written in the pro-business *Fortune* magazine. After the initial euphoria melted away, another side to globalization that hadn't been told began to emerge. Although some people were profiting from globalization, there were many more whose lives were adversely affected. Many manufacturing workers in the U.S. were losing their well-paid, secure jobs that were being outsourced to Mexico or China. Small farmers in the rural heartland of America, where I lived at the time, were being swallowed up by large corporate farming operations that had better political connections and enormous economies of scale and were able to fatten their bottom profit line with exorbitant agricultural subsidies funded by American taxpayers. There were also dire effects on the environment that were a direct result (and some indirect) from economic globalization. Tax cuts and new economic rules made it easier for the wealthy to profit from the system, while the middle and working classes were being squeezed by stagnant wages and higher living costs. As I dug a little deeper into the topic of globalization, I found that it was much more complex than was simply communicated in the media.

Another viewpoint about globalization burst into public consciousness in November 1999, when 40,000 "anti-globalization" activists converged in Seattle, Washington to protest against the World Trade Organization (WTO) Ministerial Conference, in what became known as the "Battle in Seattle." The protesters ranged from labor unionists to students to religious-based groups to anarchists who wanted to overthrow the government. The media lumped the groups together under the umbrella of anti-globalization protesters, although what they were protesting and the tactics they used varied considerably. Unfortunately, a small percentage of the protesters turned violent, and the police responded with force to quell the disturbances. Many Americans were glued to their TV as angry young protesters randomly smashed store windows, damaged cars, and immaturely taunted police. The public linked all those who questioned globalization with violent acts. The media helped to create this distorted message by continuously showing the violent acts committed by angry young protesters; the peaceful protesters, some sporting gray hair and sensible shoes, were of secondary importance. But the protests, despite their violent component, had the effect of raising awareness about the other side of globalization, and I and others became interested in finding out more.

My research into the global economy in the 1990s helped me refine my model for teaching world history. What became apparent was that at the turn of the millennium, a new force was emerging on the world stage that was a noticeable break from the past. In my book *Waves of Global Change: A Holistic World History*, I identify this evident break as the Global Wave. According to my holistic world history model, there have been four other waves or major transformations in our human history, and the Global Wave represents a fifth wave. The other four waves – Communal, Agriculture, Urban and Modern – all represent major discontinuities in our human story. The Global Wave is such a significant transformation as to warrant the distinction of representing a fifth significant change. Thus, the global economy that was changing in the 1990s was morphing into a momentous force shaping many aspects of world society and defining the Global Wave. Therefore, the phenomenon widely known as globalization was more than just a mere business craze or a way to sell more hamburgers around the world; it was a multi-faceted process that continues to be in the making.

Many of you have possibly observed the changes that are presently occurring or have actually experienced the changes yourself. Perhaps you or your family have lost a job as a result of the latest downturn in the economy, or perhaps your job has been outsourced to India or China. If you are a student, perhaps your teachers have admonished you to study harder, since millions of well-educated Chinese students are your global competitors for future jobs. Or perhaps you realize that almost all the clothing you buy is made in China, Indonesia, India, or other places besides the U.S. Or your house has declined in value to the point that you owe more than it is worth, a phenomenon known as being "underwater." Or you realize that our dependence on oil to fuel the economy contributed to British Petroleum's (BP) horrendous oil spill in the Gulf of Mexico in 2010. Or perhaps you are a member of the global elite, and you have made a fortune by expanding your national business into a global business that has tripled its profits. These events are signs of major and disruptive changes that are occurring today. So, you may ask, how is the global economy related to all these changes that are taking place in the Global Wave? That is the very question we will be exploring in this book.

A study of the global economy will not be an easy task. It holds many contradictions and uneasy tensions that challenge our way of looking at the world. This book does not offer easy answers or solutions listed 1 through 10. Instead, it is designed to be an examination of the global economy today as it really works. If you are reading this book, you most likely have experienced the benefits that capitalism has brought to your life: an education, the latest technology, communication devices, constant entertainment, plentiful food, medical care to extend your life, and a social safety net to keep you out of total destitution. But just because capitalism has had successes in the past, and many in the present, it does not mean that all is well with the system. We will uncover many of the failures of the capitalist economic system along with its successes.

Most of us know very little about the global economy. I certainly didn't until I started to concentrate on contemporary global issues in graduate school and my teaching career. Even then, it was hard to uncover the real workings of the global economy. It always seemed to be covered in a veneer of mistaken assumptions or by an intractable worldview that everyone seemed to accept as reality. But once I started to peel away the layers of veneer covering the real global economy, I was surprised to find that the reality was quite different from the commonly held assumptions. When President Clinton signed the North American Free Trade Association (NAFTA) in 1994, I thought free trade was good for everyone, just as our president claimed. We smugly laughed as a family when we headed to the malls in the mid-1990s to do our Christmas shopping, jokingly claiming that "we were helping the economy." When I first heard about global warming, I was confident that some kind of technological fix would be invented to cut emissions, or that we would have cheap solar and wind energy by the time my children reached adulthood. I had some rethinking to do as I learned more about the global economy and uncovered some of the deep-seated assumptions that turned out to be untrue. I also learned that our worldview (see chapter 1) has a lot to do with how the global economy is structured. This rethinking has led me to question our whole global economic system.

As I contemplated writing a book about the global economy as part of the Global Awareness Program series (GAPs), I struggled with how to organize this massive topic. I wanted to simplify the information and put it into an order that readers could grasp. It seemed to me that when discussing the global economy, many vague terms were used and many false assumptions were made without basis. I thought people's perception of the global economy is like a wad of hard-as-a rock taffy, all stuck together and difficult to pull apart. So my goal in this book is to pull apart the taffy-like global economy so that some of the sticky strands can be seen and identified. When I did this myself in order to write this book, I found that three dimensions to the global economy surfaced; each dimension is distinct but interconnected, as well. By organizing the global economy into these three dimensions – neoliberalism, economic globalization, and financialization – the wad of taffy is pulled wide apart.

I have found in my research that there are very few books that give a general, holistic overview of the global economy. They may concentrate on what is wrong with the economy or the disastrous financial crisis of 2008, but they fail to give us a firm grasp of why this turmoil all started in the first place. Blaming it all on greedy bankers or clueless homeowners doesn't seem to get to the roots of the issue. This book attempts to give an overview of the global economy today. What are the different roots of the global economy and how do they connect. Once we have a better idea of how the global economy is organized then we are better equipped to critique it, see the fault lines, and propose solutions.

I like to think that I am a fitting person to write and teach about the global economy. What gives me this confidence? My illustrious career as an investment banker on Wall Street? My PhD in global economics from Harvard College? My tenure teaching in "third world" countries? My career in the Treasury Department advising the Secretary of the Treasury during times of economic crisis? Well, none of these remotely apply. Compared to many who are writing about the global economy, such as Nobel Laureate Paul Krugman, my credentials are modest. But, before you slam this book shut or turn off your Kindle, I do have unique reasons for writing about the global economy. I do have the degreed credentials, I have taught in the classroom for many years, I have conducted ample research about the topic, I have personally experienced many of the wrenching economic changes that have taken place since the end of World War II, and I am able to place the global economy into an understandable framework.

Since I have witnessed many of the changes that have taken place over the years, I will chronicle some of my experiences and reflection in this book to give you a personal account of the changes. I encourage you to do the same. Ask others you know about what they experienced during the high unemployment era of the 1970s or the economic changes they witnessed during the Reagan era of the 1980s or the difficulty of finding a well-paying job in the 2010s. You are bound to get interesting insights and a wide reaction to the events. Everyone has his or her own story.

I searched to find an apt metaphor for the title of this book on the global economy. I came up with several different ones, such as a puzzle, a network, a tsunami, a stew, and even taffy. Even though I used some of them in explaining different topics in the book, none resonated with me as a subtitle. Then, in the fall of 2012, my husband and I visited a remote cabin in the mountains of Chama, New Mexico, for a few days of relaxation. We took long hikes along a mountain trail, and we felt a sense of awe and wonder as we gazed upon groves of majestic aspen trees clinging to the mountainous terrain, just about ready to turn to shimmering gold. It was then that it came to me in a flash; why not use the aspen trees as part of the cover and subtitle of the book. The roots, of course, are intertwined below the earth's surface, and the aspen roots are unique in that they are all connected. The global economy is like the aspen trees. The roots of the global economy form an interdependent system of connections below the surface, while supporting a maze of what looks like individual facets of the global economy above the surface. A global corporation, such as Bank of America, seems as though it is a separate entity, traded on the stock exchange with the symbol BAC as its identifying stock ticker. But below the surface, Bank of America is intricately connected to many parts of the global economy, such as money market funds, government regulations, foreign investments, debt, shareholders, CEO compensation, and so on. Thus, the title of the book was born: *Connecting the Roots of the Global Economy: A Holistic Approach, Brief Addition.* Thinking of the global economy as an interconnected system is the purpose of this book.

So please join with me in the adventure of examining the global economy. I hope you will find this holistic approach to the global economy a journey that is challenging but worthwhile.

FEATURES OF THE BOOK

Chapter 1, *The Global Economy: An Overview*, offers an introduction to the organization of the global economy along with a definition of important terms and concepts, such as state capitalism, core and periphery, West and modern, and others. It distinguishes between the various forms of capitalism, such as neoliberalism and managed capitalism. A brief overview of a systems thinking approach used in this book is given, along with a look at five worldviews – indigenous, modern, fundamentalist, globalized, and transformative.

Chapter 2, *Historical Roots of the Global Economy*, traces the roots of capitalism from 1500 onward. The first phase, commercial capitalism (1500-1750), evolves into industrial capitalism beginning in Britain around 1750. Capitalism expands and splinters in the tumultuous 20th century, yet survives. During the crisis of the 1970s, conservative business leaders steered capitalism to its neoliberal form. The various forms of capitalism are highlighted along with their repercussions on the world economy.

In chapter 3, *The Neoliberal Stew: A Dozen Essential Ingredients*, the turn to neoliberal restructuring that occurred in the U.S. in the 1970s is investigated through examining 12 essential ingredients in the "neoliberal stew." The 12 ingredients include free trade, privatization, deregulation, push for small government, supply side economics, lower taxes, reduce the deficit, faith in markets, support corporations and the financial sector, suppress labor, extol individualism, and spread neoliberalism.

In chapter 4, *The Impact of Neoliberalism in the United States: Ten Consequences*, the effects of neoliberalism are examined. The 10 consequences are reduction of the local economy, unbridled economic growth, rampant consumerism, increased commodification, concentration of corporate power, rise of externalized costs, build-up of debt, emasculation of labor, widening social inequality, and ascension of dollar democracy.

Chapters 5, *The Economic Globalization Puzzle: Ten Pieces*, looks at economic globalization from a interacting systems perspective. The 10 interacting pieces are a reduction of local communities and self-reliance, economic growth, a promoting network, rules of economic globalization, privatization, commodification, concentration of power, specialization, squeeze labor, and military hegemony.

In chapter 6, *Evaluating the Impact of Economic Globalization*, three criteria are used in the evaluation: the impact on the environment, the growing socioeconomic gap, and human well-being. A comparison between two economically different nations – the Democratic Republic of the Congo and Bhutan – rounds out the chapter.

Chapter 7, *The Financial Sector of the Global Economy*, begins with a brief overview and then highlights the financial sector's 10 fatal flaws: too big to fail banks, unchecked deregulation, the federal reserve, the real estate bubble, a mountain of debt, dicey financial products, speculation, moral hazard and lack of transparency, deceptive rating agencies, and bloated compensation plans.

Chapter 8, *The Financial Sector: Crisis and its Aftermath*, begins with a look at patterns found in financial crises and examines several different ones through history. Next, the chain of events of the financial crisis of 2007-2008 are studied. Finally the response to the financial crisis is looked at through five responses: revolt, restore, react, reform, and rebuild.

Accompanying the book are carefully designed supplemental resources for educators and students, for those using the book in a study group, or for whoever wishes to examine this topic more closely. Please visit the Center for Global Awareness website at www.global-awareness.org/global economy or email us at info@global-awareness.org for more information.

CHAPTER ONE

The Global Economy: An Overview

"Think not forever of yourselves, O Chiefs, nor of your own generation. Think of continuing generations of our families, think of our grandchildren and of those yet unborn, whose faces are coming from beneath the ground."

--- *Peacemaker, founder of the Iroquois Confederacy (ca. 1000 AD)*

THE FAIRLAND FAMILY: A STORY

John Fairland sat back in his easy chair before a blazing fire one gusty cold day typical of January on the flat prairie lands of central Illinois. John peeked over his spectacles to see the eager young faces of two students who were recording his oral history and that of his ancestors. He and his family had farmed the rich soils of central Illinois for generations. John smiled as he started to talk about his family's long and interesting history; he had a lot to share with the students.

He started the story …

"I can trace the history of the Fairland family back many centuries to peasant farmers in England during the Middle Ages. They didn't own their own land but worked it for the nobleman who gave them a plot of land to grow crops for their own survival and then they worked on the nobleman's large fields with other villagers. Their labor was a sort of tax paid to the nobleman in exchange for the benefit of living on his land. My ancestors also had a few cows and sheep that grazed on the commons, land that the nobleman held but which the peasants were free to use. They hunted in the forests for game and kept what they killed. Life was hard, but there were always feasts and church events that they all enjoyed.

In the 1600s, life began to change for my ancestors. One day the nobleman ordered my family to start to collect hundreds of stones. The nobleman told them to build stone fences along carefully marked lines that broke up the land into parcels. My family carried out the orders. Soon stone fences criss-crossed the wide-open common lands and forests. They heard the nobleman call these areas "enclosures," which meant that each section of land would be sold to investors in agriculture. Before enclosure the nobleman didn't care about producing a huge surplus, but rather only to grow enough to get by. But now, growing a surplus was important. The investors even asked some of our neighbors to leave the land they had worked for generations. They allowed my family to stay; however, life would not be like it was in the past.

The Fairland's soon found out that they needed to produce more grain than before, and it was sold to towns across England. Although they worked harder, their standard of living did not improve. Instead of just one crop per year, they now planted two crops. Soon my ancestors were growing more than ever before but because they didn't own the land, they had to give a greater share of their crop to their far-off landowner. When the landowner asked my ancestors if they wanted to buy the land they were farming or move to the city, they decided to purchase the land. They dreamed of having a better life.

By the 1700s, even though my family now owned the land, farming was uncertain. They had to sell their grain according to market prices, which would go up and down according to supply and demand of the market. In order to earn more money, the women decided to do piece work in their cottages for textile merchants. The city merchants brought raw wool to their cottages, and the women carded the wool into thread. Next, they wove the threads into cloth that the merchants picked up and paid them for. It was a good way to make some cash, which they now needed to pay extra expenses.

By the late 1700s, these cottage industries, as they were called, gave way to new textile factories in the cities. Cotton instead of wool was the new fabric of choice. Even though the income from the cottage industries was gone, my family was able to continue farming. Since the English population was growing, there was an increased demand for grain for food, so prices were good – for a while at least. My family learned that they were able to have high grain prices because of the Corn Laws.

These laws placed tariffs (a tax) on grains imported from outside England. This made the imported grains more expensive than English-produced grains. They were thankful for the Corn Laws and hoped parliament would not take them away.

My ancestors faced a real problem in the 1840s when the parliament decided to repeal the Corn Laws. Since the price of grain was now set according to the supply and demand of the market, it meant that without tariffs the grain they sold would have to compete with the price of grain from Germany, which was a lot lower. They wondered if they would be able to continue to make a living as farmers in England. Even more of their farming neighbors suffered economic ruin. Many of them sold their land and moved to the cities or to work in the dreadful factories sprouting up in the countryside, like their grain did before. It was a sad time for my family. While the livelihood of the English farmer declined, factories were producing more than ever. The English government had chosen free trade, as they learned it was called, which helped the factory owners but not the farmers. The new economy turned my family's lives upside down.

In the 1870s, rumors swirled that investors were buying up land in the nearby village to build a huge new sewing machine factory. My family decided to sell their land to the investors for a fair price. My great great-grand-parents thought they had no choice but to sell the land my family had worked for centuries. They decided to take the money and immigrate to America, where farm land on the prairies of the state of Illinois was for sale at a good price. They bought a much larger farm and had some money left over. They packed for their journey; it was the first time my ancestors had left their village home.

My family arrived in their newly-adopted country and found a busy farming community starting to form. They cleared the forested land, drained swamps, built barns and a house, and planted gardens, while getting the rich soil ready for planting. It was harder work than in England, but the rewards appeared greater at first glance. But my family had to produce greater quantities of grain to make ends meet, since grain prices were low. The market determined the price of grains according to the laws of supply and demand, but the farm machinery they had to buy was high-priced because tariffs protected these factory-manufactured goods, resulting in higher consumer prices. The Fairlands, like their fellow farmers, all produced huge amounts of grain, which increased supply and, thus, further lowered prices. Also, when they borrowed money from the local bank to plant the next year's crop, they had to pay high interest rates.

My family learned that money was so hard to get because the U.S., like Britain, was on the gold standard. There wasn't enough money in circulation because there wasn't enough gold to back up the money. They and their neighbors agreed that it would be a good idea to have more money in circulation, so they supported a gold and silver standard, which would also mean lower interest rates on loans. But the moneyed interests in the Northeast liked the fact they could get high interest rates when they loaned out money. Anger grew about the gold standard. My great-grandfather remembered when speakers came to the town's Grange Hall to tell about the failure of the gold standard. It got everyone fired up. But the anger eased in 1896 when miners discovered new gold deposits, which meant more money was in circulation. Prices shot up on their grain crop. Interest rates eased. My great-grandmother said life was good for the Fairland family.

The good times for my family continued until the 1920s. My great-grandparents bought new machinery and more acres of land because the demand for grain and prices had been high for decades. It looked like the good times would continue. But, as World War I ended in 1918, the demand for grain slid, since Europe started to produce its own grain again instead of importing it.

My family had less money from their crops with which to repay loans. Times were very lean. My grandmother remembered riding the train to Chicago, a short trip to the north, and was amazed to see a bustling city, but her small prairie hometown was stuck in despair. A depression settled over all of rural America, a forewarning of what was to come.

Things were bad in the 1920s for my grandparents, but it got worse with the Great Depression in the 1930s. The bank they had done business with for decades went out of business. It held the mortgages for many of the farmers who were unable to pay back their loans. My grandparents had long ago sold much of their machinery and some of their land, at reduced prices. They were able to survive the hard times by making a living as best they could. My grandmother took in laundry, opened up her house to boarders, and sold butter and cheese wherever she could. Some of the young men in the family joined the Civilian Conservation Corps (CCC), a depression-era government program to employ young men and preserve the environment, and had their wages sent home to help the family. Everyone pitched in. Since four generations lived under one roof, even my great-grandparents helped out by doing what they could.

The threatening signs of World War II were on the horizon in the late 1930s. My grandparents geared up their farm production to meet the growing demand, and higher prices followed. Through the war and into the early 1970s, farming was profitable. My grandparents passed on and my parents took over the farm. My parents were able to buy a few of the new modern appliances that came out in the 1950s, such as a refrigerator and a washer and dryer. They bought a car to drive to town in style. During the Cold War with the Soviet Union, it was a source of national pride to boast of farm efficiency, a well-fed population, and surplus grains shipped to areas of demand and need. My family was proud to be farmers. But the good times were about to come to an end.

The crisis of the 1970s brought hardship to about everyone, farmers included. I know because now my wife and I were in charge of the family farm. Since the whole farm ran on fossil fuels, the energy crisis of 1973 hit us very hard. It took a big bite out of our profits, which were shrinking because of lower prices and overproduction. Once again, many of our neighbors left their farms. Some of those buying up the empty farmsteads were corporate farms, bent on squeezing out the "little guy." Even though all farmers got subsidies, the generous government farm subsidies aided corporate giants more than the "little guy." From the 1980s onward, small farms continued to decline while giant agricultural corporations grew. We had withstood untold hardships in the past, but now we were unsure we could go on.

The farming family story fascinated the two young students. They asked John to go on, which he did with a look of sadness in his eyes. Our family worked hard to compete with the big farming corporations, but the trends were clear; corporate farming was the wave of the future, not small, independent family farms. The large corporations now held many of the cooperative grain elevators where we bought our fertilizer, sold our crops, and bought seed. Even the excellent, local school system consolidated and lost its high standards. The farm had shrunk to a fraction of its former size, only about 500 acres. Farming as we knew it could not continue as it had in the past.

The two students noticed that the look in John Fairland's eyes took on a new twinkle as his adult son and daughter walked into the room. They wore work overalls, which brought the smell of the earth floating through the room. John said that his way of farming had ended, but a new way of farming continued with the next generation. The two younger Fairlands happily told the story of how the family dealt with farming changes. Something had to change, or they could join their neighbors in the mad dash to the city for jobs in an office cubicle. Instead, they decided to change the farm from the mass production of one crop, corn, to an organic farm that produced a variety of vegetables, fruits, honey, eggs, butter, and cheese. It was hard work that required lots of research and trial and error. But, profits were up, and better yet, they were producing good, healthy food for their community and even some families in Chicago. They felt they were taking an ethical path to farming.

John Fairland said, "Starting the organic farm was like my ancestors selling their land and moving to America. It took a lot of courage to shed the past and start anew, and that is what my family is now doing." The two young Fairlands eagerly told of their plans for the organic farm. Even some of their neighbors were now exploring the possibility of starting up organic production and selling their products at farmer's markets. The future looked bright.

John's daughter, Lilly, painted a picture of how they were returning to the roots of their ancestors during the Middle Ages. "Our ancestors grew their own organic food, without chemicals and gasoline-powered machinery. They knew how to take care of the land for the next generations. I feel we are in close touch with the land, as well, even though we use scientific research to aid us in our efforts. We have gone full circle from the past to the present, in one continuous arc. It is a very comforting thought to all of us."

Although the Fairland family is imaginary, their story shows the economy changing from a locally based one, to a national economy, to a global economy, and back to a local economy. The global economy today is having a tremendous impact on people of all walks of life and in every corner of the world, including the imaginary Fairland family. As you read this book – *The Global Economy* – keep your family and the Fairland family in mind, as economic changes bring about many changes to everyone's way of life.

THE GLOBAL ECONOMY: AN INTRODUCTION

Our global economy represents a paradox. The spread of capitalism as the leading economic system today is the most successful system in world history in terms of providing for the comfort and luxury of a large population. It has solved the problem of feeding large numbers of people (but not all) in an efficient way. It has provided advances in health and medicine (but not for all), which allow billions of people to live longer lives than in the past. It has created technological wonders such as communication devices and transportation never seen before. In many ways it has united people in common interests as has no other economic system. It has promoted the dignity and worth of every individual as a universal value system. It has unlocked educational opportunities to billions of people who desire to learn about the world. It has opened up the mysteries of the universe through scientific research and remarkable discoveries.[1]

Here lies the paradox. It remains to be seen when the balance sheet is added up whether capitalism, despite its accomplishments, represents the height of "progress" that has been claimed in its honor. It has been creative, but it has also been destructive. Its failures are beginning to creep into our awareness, jolting us into a fear that perhaps our accomplishments are turning against us in a kind of hushed revenge. The environment is groaning under our huge and growing population who are demanding more and more of the earth's resources to satisfy the consumer life-style of a modern world. The industrial machine that has belched out products to make our lives easier and more comfortable is torturing the earth with its excesses. The signals are clear: our way of life is not agreeing with the earth, and she has the last word.

Yet with all the advancements, it is clear that the world's population does not share the earth's resources in an evenhanded way. This unequal divide of the world's resources remains one of the global economy's visible failures. For the vast majority of the world's population, jobs are scarcer for those in both the poor and rich countries, as wages decline as a result of global competition. Despite our material comforts and pleasurable activities, there is a deep gloominess that affects many of those who have made capitalism the centerpiece of their economy and culture. Could it be that our sense of well-being and desire for social connection have weakened in our pursuit of capitalism's bounty?

My thoughts about the global economy have led me to question our entire economic system. I see an economic system that is set up for a different period of time. It is outdated and no longer able to effectively deal with the global situation today. All of the economic systems that provide the foundation for today's global economy – from capitalism to communism – are from the 18th and 19th centuries. These economic ideas have served their purpose: they have provided a comfortable standard of living for many around the world. But these economic ideas have reached their effective limits. We already saw the fall of communism in the early 1990s, and the current capitalist economies are facing difficulties in the West. In 2008, the most serious financial crisis since the Great Depression took place. The state capitalist economy of China has high growth rates, but a population of 1.4 billion people, environmental problems, and a rigid communist party weighs it down.

What will replace these economic systems? My honest answer is "I don't know." Capitalism will probably not collapse as quickly as communism, but the signs of instability are everywhere. Below the surface is an unsteady American and global economy which is fueling political and social hatred. Different political parties have different ways in which they want to "fix" the economy, but it is just patching up the old economy with band aids used in the past. Perhaps the band aids will stop the bleeding of a wounded economy temporarily, but they are not a long term solution.

The present economic systems in place around the world are probably not able to adapt to the present situations: there are too many flaws in the different systems. I want to be clear, though: I do not support a revolution that overthrows the whole system. I imagine that to be a real tragedy, and I would be careless to support such an idea. However, change is needed, and if we are aware of the problems, it will help us to create an economic system that is more in keeping with real human needs and the needs of the earth.

You may ask at this point, "What is the old system you refer to?" That is the very question that this book hopes to answer. I will attempt to explain the global economy in understandable terms. I will do so through the lens that the present day global economy has serious flaws and needs to be changed. What kind of economic system will take the place of our current global economy is left for another book. Let me first describe further what

See the forest, not just the trees -- photo Denise Ames

this book is about and then what this book is not about.

What we learn in our classrooms is usually divided into separate subjects. The purpose is to learn as much as possible about a topic. Then a test is given to see if you mastered the subject. This way of learning has its place; after all, I want my heart surgeon to be an expert on every aspect of the heart! But there is also a place for "a big picture" approach to a topic. We don't want too many details to constantly overwhelm us. The same often happens in economics, when economists examine scenarios in ideal world situations but not the real world. In other words, we should be able to see the forest, not just the trees.

What this book is not is a "textbook" on the global economy. I will leave that to the economic experts. But it is a book about the real global economy and how it affects our everyday lives. The purpose of this book is to understand the global economy as an interconnected system rather than as a specific, separate topic. When we study a subject from a systems approach, we see how all parts of the system interact. Let's get started into understanding more about the global economy.

Questions to Consider

1. After reading this story and the brief introduction, what three questions come to your mind about the global economy?

Key Features of Globalization

1. **Integration** of humans across the globe, more so than at any time in the past. Instantaneous digital technologies change our relations with each other by breaking up former barriers of time and distance.

2. **Global Capitalism** is the dominant (but not the only) economic system in the world, with almost all nations pulled into its economic web. A globalized economy pulls national and local economies together, where multinational corporations and state enterprises make many of the rules.

3. **Environmental Pressures** and the health of the planet are a primary concern for global citizens. Solutions are needed at a cooperative international level.

4. **Nations** share their influence with world organizations, including the following: the United Nations (UN); regional organizations such as the European Union (EU); regional trade alliances like the North American Free Trade Association (NAFTA); human rights agencies such as Amnesty International; and environmental watchdog groups like Greenpeace.

5. **English Language** is the language of business, commerce and education, and is the world's unofficial universal language, since a common language acts as a unifying factor. The world's elites speak English in part because of the influence of the British in the 19th century and the U.S. in the 20th century.

6. **Consumer Culture**, a vast entertainment and advertising industry has pushed consumerism as a form of status, individual identity, and profit.

7. **Democracy** is promoted by the U.S. and others as a favored political organization in much of the world.

8. **Human Rights** are regarded as a universal cultural values system. Although not practiced in about half the world, social justice and equality for women, children, and non-elites, along with racial equality and protection from hate crimes, are becoming common moral standards to guide nations.

9. **Population Growth** is an urgent issue today. The carrying capacity of the earth is severely strained by our current population and its consumption levels.

10. **Globalized Conflict** is much different from past warfare. Conflict has become random, irrational, and volatile. When acts of violence are directed towards the West, it is often called terrorism.

11. **Social Inequality** has increased between the rich and poor, both within and among nations.

12. **Technological Marvels** have exploded since the 1990s. The Internet, television, high-speed travel, cell phones, and electronic social networks link the world.

13. **Identity Tied to Global Citizenship** has resulted in a growing awareness of connections, commonalities, and differences among people of the world.

14. **Recognition of Systems** means that an interconnected system links formerly separate events, people, and institutions together.

Globalization: A Definition

Simply put, globalization describes the dramatic changes that are taking place today. But it is a fuzzy word that has several different meanings for different people. It has been used in so many ways it is difficult to come up with a useful definition. But here goes.

Globalization is a complex, dominant, process that interconnects worldwide economic, political, cultural, social, environmental, and technological forces that go beyond national boundaries. On the rise since the 1980s, it reflects the many ways in which people are drawn together through the flow of goods, services, capital, labor, technology, ideas, and information. It refers to the world-wide shrinking of space and time and the reduction of the national government in importance. Globalization influences the way billions of people around the world carry out their everyday lives.

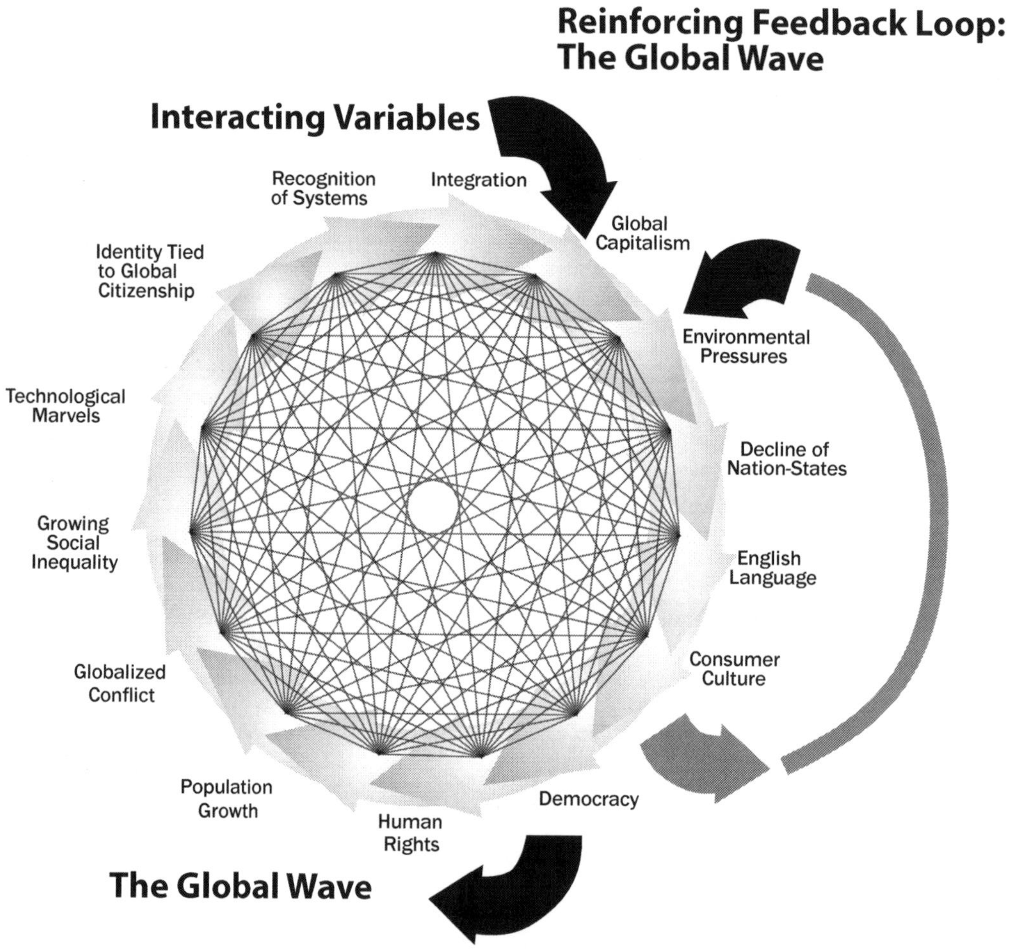

Reinforcing Feedback Loop: The Global Wave

Interacting Variables

Recognition of Systems · Integration · Global Capitalism · Identity Tied to Global Citizenship · Environmental Pressures · Technological Marvels · Decline of Nation-States · Growing Social Inequality · English Language · Globalized Conflict · Consumer Culture · Population Growth · Human Rights · Democracy

The Global Wave

Economic Globalization

From the above graphic, it is clear that globalization has many different and interacting dimensions. In fact, my book *Waves of Global Change: A Holistic World History* describes in the last chapter – "The

Global Wave" – the different dimensions of globalization. The dimension that we will study in this book is economic globalization. However, because it is difficult to separate economics from the globalization process and study it alone, we will look at the global economy as part of the whole system and one of its most important dimensions. We will study it holistically, meaning that we will look at the relationship of the economy to society, politics, culture, the environment, technology, education, and other dimensions. All these dimensions interact and shape each other; hence, the approach is called holistic. When talking about the global economy, the term economic globalization is often used. It is a term that we hear all the time, but it means something different to almost every individual. I tell people that I am writing about the global economy for students and they say that is a great idea because students need to know about economic globalization. I then ask them how they would define the term. Just about every person I ask gives me a different answer. The answers range from, "It is a way to make life better for people around the world" to "It is a conspiracy for corporations to get more money." Many say, "It is just the way the economy works today." Let's next turn to a definition of economic globalization.

Economic globalization means the increasing integration and expansion of the capitalist economy around the world. In this economic system, trade, investment, business, capital, finance, production, management, markets, movement of labor (although somewhat restricted), information, competition, and technology are carried out across local and national boundaries on a world stage. Economic globalization brings national and local economies into one integrated system. There is a growing concentration of wealth and influence of multi-national corporations, huge financial institutions, and state-run enterprises.

Economic globalization, as already mentioned, is just one dimension of globalization. But when we describe the whole global economy there is more to it than just economic globalization. This can get confusing because economic globalization is often the term used to describe the whole global economy. But it is our job in this book to get to the roots of the global economy, which is made up of different economic systems around the world. Let's first describe the different economic systems found in the global economy.

Questions to Consider

1. What does economic globalization mean to you?

AN OVERVIEW OF ECONOMIC SYSTEMS

The definition of economic globalization mentions that the economic system is capitalist even though capitalism is not the only economic system in the world today. In fact, it would be hard to find any two nations that have the same economic system. Rather than describe each individual nation's economic system, to simplify I have arranged the economic systems of the world into two divisions: capitalism and socialism. Within these two divisions, neoliberal capitalism is separated out from managed capitalism. Within socialism is its branch – communism. Emerging in the first decade of the 21st century is a fifth economic system that combines elements of socialism and capitalism – state capitalism.

State Capitalism

Communism   Socialism   Managed Capitalism   Neoliberalism

To explain the relationship of the five economic systems, I have placed them on a continuum. On the right end of the continuum are neoliberal economies. In these economies there is limited government regulation. Located somewhere in the middle right of the continuum are managed capitalism economies in which there is more government regulation and a social safety net that protects individuals who have fallen on hard times. The government plays an active role in socialist economies, located on the center left of the continuum. They have a social safety net to help individuals. On the left end of the continuum is communism, where governments run the economies, and there is no private enterprise or private property. In the middle are sandwiched state capitalist economies that follow capitalist principles, but overall the state runs the economy.

In Eastern Europe during the Cold War, this popular graffiti plastered the walls of Communist capitals: "Capitalism is the exploitation of man by man. Communism is the opposite: the exploitation of man by man." This simple riddle echoes the common roots of the world's economic systems. Aside from the small, isolated, local, domestic economies that still dot the landscape in remote areas of the world, the majority of the world has an economic system rooted in the modern ideas of the past 200 years. Paradoxically, communism and capitalism have the same underpinnings.[2]

Capitalism and communism came out of the same 19th century modern worldview. The capitalist corporation and the communist politburo were elevated above individuals and communities. They both favored the material over the spiritual – for example, the Soviet Union outlawed religion – and both tasked a rational government bureaucracy with carrying out their economic principles. In varying degrees, they both belittled traditions and long-held values and overlooked the stability of the family, friendships and relationships. They both scorned those hostile to change.[3] In the name of progress, both economies have exploited the environment. Both economic practices sought to undercut the domestic and local economy and bring it into either the communist or capitalist system. They both pushed industrialization as the preferred method for production of goods. But they advanced different systems of ownership and distribution.

Questions to Consider

1. Compare and contrast the communist and capitalist economic systems.

Capitalism

Capitalism is an economic system in which private parties make their goods and services available on a free market and seek to make a profit on their activities. Private parties, either individuals or companies, own the means of production – land, machinery, tools, equipment, buildings, workshops, and raw materials. Private parties decide what to produce. The centerpiece of the system is the market in which individuals or corporations compete, and the forces of supply and demand, not the government, determine prices. Businesses may make profits, reinvest the profits gained, or suffer losses.

Capitalism has no one way in which it operates. When we hear people talk about capitalism or hear about it in the media, it seems as if there is just one type of capitalism, but this is not the case. As an economic system, it can operate with little government regulation or with government taking an active role in guiding and regulating it. Under capitalism, the elites can make laws and regulations that favor them or, on the other hand, laws and regulations can spread out wealth to a greater number of people. A capitalist economy can be in a democracy, such as the U.S., and even in communist China. China is politically communist but part of its economy runs according to the rules of global capitalism, while another part follows a command or state economy. Where the dividing line is between the two is anyone's guess. Some European countries have socialist aspects of their economies, but they are also connected to global capitalism. Parts of India are tied to the global economy, while parts of its rural areas continue with local exchange. There is no clear cut line drawn between the economic systems of different countries, and even within countries, each one has an economic system that suits its needs. Thus, capitalism takes on different forms, such as neoliberalism and managed capitalism.

1. Neoliberalism

Neoliberalism has been expanding in the U.S. since the early 1980s. Other terms describe the same economic concept: free market capitalism, free trade capitalism, market capitalism, supply-side economics, laissez-faire capitalism, or classical capitalism. Sometimes people say capitalism but really mean neoliberalism. Nevertheless, it is important to understand the different types of capitalism. I found it difficult to select a term to use throughout the book because neoliberalism is not familiar as a term in the U.S, but I will use the term because it is more commonly used around the world.

The "neo" in neoliberalism means new, since it is a newer version of the economic system that Great Britain developed and promoted in the 19th and early 20th century. **Neoliberalism** favors free trade, privatization, little government intervention in business and reduced public spending on social services.[4] It got a boost in the early 1980s when two world leaders were cheerleaders of the neoliberal agenda: Margaret Thatcher, prime minister of the United Kingdom (UK) and Ronald Reagan, president of the U.S. They thought neoliberalism was the best system for their countries.

Ten Principles of Neoliberalism[5]

1. Free trade (remove protective tariffs).
2. Deregulate industries (remove government oversight).
3. Cut taxes for the wealthy who will then invest in business.
4. Wealth will "trickle down" from the wealthy to the poor.
5. Government support for some infrastructure.
6. Privatize publicly held industries and services.
7. Continued economic growth is the way to prosperity.
8. Rapid commodification of every remaining aspect of life.
9. Wages tied to supply and demand, eliminate minimum wage and unions.
10. Globalization benefits everyone.

2. Managed Capitalism

With the crippling effects of the Great Depression in the 1930s hurting Western nations, many economists thought that governments should take a more active and responsible role in planning national economies. To these economists, government planning would soften the "boom and bust" cycles of laissez-faire capitalism found in the 19th century. These boom and bust cycles were hard on workers when employers laid them off from jobs during the bust cycles, and they had to survive without any help. Business owners also had to endure the bust cycles when demand for their business products declined. The British economist **John Maynard Keynes** (1883-1946) said that the government must accept responsibility for regulating capitalist economies. He thought regulation should be through a number of controls, such as running government surpluses or deficits when necessary and creating public works projects, such as the Civilian Conservation Corps for the unemployed during economic downturns. The purpose of these plans was to make capitalism work better through government action. The U.S. tried some of Keynes' ideas during the Depression, but Western nations more fully adopted his ideas after World War II.

In **managed capitalism** the government regulates the financial sector to prevent wild speculative swings and insures the system operates smoothly. Tariffs protect manufacturing jobs in the home country; therefore, wages and prices are set according to supply and demand at the national level rather than the global level. For the most part, services such as education, health care, the military, and prisons are government-run and paid for through taxes. The state sometimes owns large service providers, such as utilities and transportation, or closely regulates them. Private enterprise exists, but the government regulates it. The wealthiest individuals pay high taxes, for example, the highest tax bracket in the U.S. was 90 percent during World War II and the 1950s. Corporations pay a larger share of taxes than in the neoliberal model. Labor unions have a say in wages and benefits. There is a more equal circulation of wealth with managed capitalism than with neoliberalism, resulting in vibrant middle and working classes.

Socialism and Communism

Economic alternatives to the laissez-faire capitalist system arose in 19th century Europe in response to labor's horrible working conditions and low wages in the newly industrialized factories. Alternatives to capitalism – communism and socialism – arose during this time to help suffering industrial workers. One of the leading critics of capitalism was **Karl Marx** (1818-1883) who thought the state should run the economy for the benefit of all people. Under **socialism** the government owns and controls the means of production and distribution of goods and services. There is more emphasis on government planning by state officials than in capitalist societies and less response to supply and demand. Workers in state enterprises have little risk of unemployment and labor unions have more say than in capitalist countries.

Karl Marx in 1875

Communism is a branch of socialism that is based on the holding of all property in common, with actual ownership held by the state. As much as possible, forms of distribution based on social needs replace market exchange. It provides a safety net for those unable to participate in the workplace. Supposedly, a socialist or communist system will eliminate poverty and reduce economic inequality, both of which are part of neoliberal societies. Communism has declined after the collapse of the Soviet Union in 1991. Perhaps, North Korea and Cuba are the only hold-outs.

In many countries today, economies are a combination of some large state owned enterprises (socialism) with private capitalism. For example, Canada has socialized its medical system in order to provide health care for all of its citizens. The government provides this medical care that all citizens pay for through taxes. No profit is made in this system since the purpose is to provide good medical care, not enrich individual businesses or shareholders in private insurance companies. About half of the medical care in the U.S. is socialized: Medicare for its senior citizens (over 65 years), veterans, Medicaid for the very poor, and some programs for children not covered by private insurance. These figures may change with "Obamacare" or the Patient Protection and Affordable Care Act passed in 2010. Private medical insurance is available for purchase at a substantial cost. Some workplaces offer medical insurance to their employees, who usually share in the cost. This leaves approximately 52 million people in 2010, who "fall through the cracks" and do not have either type of insurance. They are left to their own means.[6]

State Capitalism

The neoliberal version of capitalism was popular around the world in the 1990s, but another economic system surfaced in the 2000s: state capitalism. **State capitalism** is where the state is the leading economic actor and uses markets mainly for political gain. The nations that support this system believe that public wealth, investment and enterprise offer the surest path toward economic development. These governments control entire sectors of their economies to promote national interests and to protect their own political standing.[7] Over the past decade, the governments of several countries have made sure that valuable national assets remain in state hands. In some cases, they have used state-owned energy companies to build up national wealth. Among the world's leading state capitalist countries are China, Russia, and Saudi Arabia.[8]

Over the past several years, state-owned companies are on the lists of the world's largest companies. Between 2004 and

Bank of China headquarters in Beijing, China. Founded in 1927, in 2010 it had 389,827 employees and $1.723 trillion in assets. Once 100% owned by the Chinese state, now 26% is privately owned.

the start of 2008, 117 state-owned and public companies from Brazil, Russia, India, and China (BRIC countries) appeared for the first time on the list of the world's largest companies. A total of 239 U.S., Japanese, British, and German companies fell off the list; their market value dropped from 70 percent to 50 percent over those four years. For example, in 2009, three of the world's four largest banks were state-owned Chinese firms – Industrial and Commercial Bank of China (ICBC), China Construction, and Bank of China. And ICBC, China Mobile, and Petro China were among the world's five largest companies by market value. Energy giants like China National Petroleum Corporation, Petro China, Sinopec, Brazil's Petrobras, Mexico's Pemex, and Russia's Rosneft and Gazprom are among the world's richest companies.[9] State capitalism is a powerful economic system.

Questions to Consider

1. From these brief descriptions of the various economic systems, which one do you prefer? Explain.

THE GLOBAL ECONOMY: DEFINITIONS, TERMS, AND CONCEPTS
The Core and Periphery

Economic inequality exists among individual nations, within nations, and even among people. Several different terms describe this inequality, but which terms are the best ones to use? After World War II, the terms first, second, and third world were used; the first world was the U.S. and Western Europe, while the second world was the Soviet Union and its allies, and the remaining nations were lumped into the third world. As you can imagine, this ranking was insulting to those in the third world. Other terms, which basically mean the same, are now used. Today "developed" and "developing," or even "less-developed" nations are common terms. Sometimes critics call the U.S. "overdeveloped." "Emerging" often refers to countries that are becoming more economically developed. Sometimes the terms industrialized or non-industrialized are used, as well. Also, the geographically incorrect terms, "the global South" or "the global North" are used, but once again the meaning is the same – the South is the poor region, and North is the rich region. But I find that it gets confusing when referring to a country like Australia that is geographically in the south but is economically in the "global North." Is China in the global North or South? Are you confused? To simplify this confusion I am using the more handy terms "core" and "periphery."

The core and periphery concepts show the unequal relationship among nations and also the unequal status of people within nations. These fluid terms describe more than one experience. **Core areas** have modern advancements in technology, military, society, politics, culture, and especially the economy. These areas are where wealth is concentrated and also where they make and enforce the rules for the system. For example, Detroit, Michigan, in the U.S. was a core area in the 1950s when it was an automobile manufacturing center; sadly, it is no longer a core area. New York City is a core financial city, along with London, UK, Shanghai, China, and Singapore. Core areas often draw **periphery areas** into a dependent relationship; commercial wealth is taken from the periphery in the form of cheap raw materials produced with cheap labor – or, more recently, manufactured goods produced with cheap labor. The wealth from this relationship flows to core areas where it builds up or is used to make more wealth. **Middle areas** fall somewhere in-between core and periphery status and have characteristics of both. **External areas** are outside of the core-and-periphery world system. Core, middle, periphery, and external areas are not fixed but shift over time.

Today the major core nations include the United States, the world's largest economy; parts of China, the world's second largest economy; individual nations of the European Economic Community (EEC) that have strong economies – Germany, France, and Netherlands; Japan, the third largest economy; United Kingdom (UK), Canada, Australia, and other smaller nations, such as South Korea and Singapore.

Middle status nations such as Brazil, Russia, India, Argentina, Indonesia, Saudi Arabia, Turkey, China, and Union of South Africa are members of the G-20 nations. They are sometimes called the developing world or emerging economies.

Other nations and peoples live on the periphery, separated from core regions by a wide economic gap. The periphery supplies core areas with cheap or relatively cheap raw materials such as oil, mineral resources, agricultural products, and timber. Many people within the periphery nations labor for low wages to mine, grow, and manufacture raw materials into finished goods that are then shipped to core areas as consumer items. Many barely make a living growing crops for the global market. Today about 80 percent of the current world population either lives in periphery or middle areas or has periphery status in core nations. External areas lie within countries, such as large parts of Afghanistan, Somalia, or Burma.

Elites and non-elites live in core, periphery, and middle nations. In the periphery countries, the wealthy elites are large land and mine owners, business owners, government officials, and other professionals. Their numbers are small, with an undersized middle class, while there is a large periphery population. Elites also reside in core countries. Core nations have a sizable middle class if government policies are in place to support them, such as laws that favor home ownership and funds for education. As the government in core nations reduces the policies to support a middle class, such as in the U.S., this group has fewer members.

A number of periphery-status people live in core nations, as well. For example, in the U.S. some estimate the periphery population or the "underclass" at 25 percent. They are unemployed or labor for minimum wages, lack health insurance, do not own homes (or lost their home in foreclosure), live in poor neighborhoods and are increasingly pushed to the margins of society. This group also includes undocumented workers from other countries who labor for minimum wages at low-skilled jobs.

All these labels, including the core and periphery, show that economic measurements are used to judge a nation. Using the economy as an evaluation tool determines that the core areas are superior to the periphery areas. It further says that the periphery must copy the economic policies of the core areas or they will remain in the periphery. Rather than using an economic measurement, perhaps we should judge a nation's well-being according to its environmental practices or family relations. Perhaps we should use a happiness index. According to a happiness survey, Denmark ranks as the happiest nation, Switzerland is second, Austria ranks third, and Iceland and the Bahamas round out the top five "happily developed" nations. The United States, which ranks 23rd on the index, would be judged as "developing happiness"![10]

Eight Interest Groups

Since around 1500, when capitalism started to develop, there have been different interest groups who have sought to benefit from the wealth creation of capitalism. Which interest groups have profited the most has changed over time, depending upon economic circumstances and which group has been able to shape governmental policies that benefit them. Over the past 500 year time span, eight conflicting groups have created untold dramas and sometimes armed conflict. Sometimes the groups overlap; for example, a consumer can also be part of the middle class or a small business owner. Usually the government or state decides which group to favor through its policies. Keep this chart in mind as you read the history section in the next chapter.

Questions to Consider

1. What interest group(s) do you associate yourself with?

8 Interest Groups in Capitalism

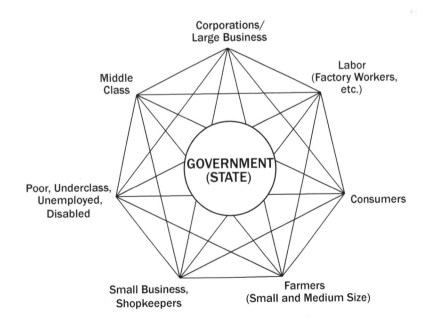

Corporations/Large Business
Labor (Factory Workers, etc.)
Middle Class
GOVERNMENT (STATE)
Poor, Underclass, Unemployed, Disabled
Consumers
Small Business, Shopkeepers
Farmers (Small and Medium Size)

Understanding the Global Economy: Two Approaches

Tsunami waves are shifting events in our world today. We live in an interdependent world, and we are struggling with rapid changes that are affecting our lives. We are trying to sort out what paths to follow today and into the future, while also trying to make sense of the changes affecting our fragile planet. Global problems are battering us at such a frequency that they often paralyze us into fear and inaction. These problems require a collective effort to solve, something that we have never had to undertake in the past and for which there is no guide to follow. The question begs: where to begin? Perhaps one way to better understand the issues and the consequences of our actions is to draw upon different approaches to problem solving. I would like to introduce two approaches that I will use in this book, and I hope you will use when thinking about and discussing the global economy.

1. A Holistic Approach

"Holistic" is an approach to understand and think about the global economy. **Holistic** in this context means that all a society's cultural traits – political, economic, technological, cultural, religious, and social, as well as the arts, values, attitudes, and the environment – reinforce and support each other. A change in any cultural trait changes the others. This means that a society's economy reflects its political policies, its treatment of the environment reflects the values of its citizens, its technology reflects its economy, and so forth. For example, in the U.S. a brown smog from car emissions hangs over a large city, such as Los Angeles, California. This brown smog is unhealthy, and if the government outlawed cars, the smog would be gone. But the U.S. economy depends upon fossil fuels and, therefore, the smog is a necessary by-product. It would be impossible to simply outlaw cars, since all parts of the economy depend upon cars as a means of transportation, a cultural symbol, and source of economic growth fueling the economy.

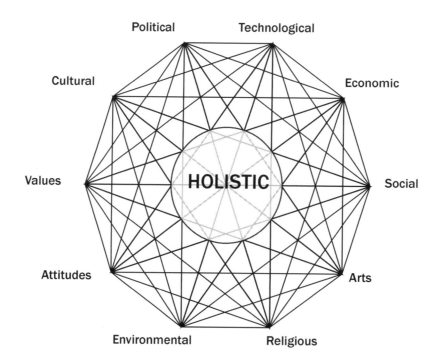

2. A Systems Approach

The increasing complexity and interdependence of the world today calls for a new way of thinking. Our global community faces a long list of problems – climate change, running out of resources, poverty, wars, terrorism, inequality, population pressures, political corruption, and others. Although the list hasn't changed much over the past few decades, the problems have gotten worse, and we have not solved them. The current mode of thinking, which looks at only parts of issues and problems in isolation, will not move us forward to create a more livable, stable, and hopeful future. Instead of looking at each isolated part of the global economy, we need to understand the whole economy as a system.

Systems thinking is an approach I will be using in this book. In **systems thinking**, individual elements of the global economy are part of a puzzle that, when pieced together, create a whole picture. A **system** is something that functions as a whole through the interaction of its parts. To put it another way, a system is a collection of parts that interact with each other to function as a whole and continually affect each other over time. Systems are organized around a shared purpose. For example, the human body is a system; each part of the body affects another. A school is a system. Systems can be simple or complex.[11] Systems thinkers look beyond what appears to be isolated and independent events to see deeper structures within the system. The whole system and the interrelationship of the parts to the whole are the focus, not just the isolated basic building blocks. In other words, as the saying goes, "See the forest, not just the trees."

WORLDVIEWS: THE WAY WE LOOK AT THE WORLD

The question remains that if we all know what the problems are and we have known about them for decades, why haven't we been able to solve them? Why isn't systems thinking within our radar screen as a problem solving method? Quite simply, I would say, because these global problems are caused in large part by the ways we think, communicate, learn, and understand! Our way of thinking or worldview heavily determines the kind of political, economic and social systems that we create.

An Iceberg

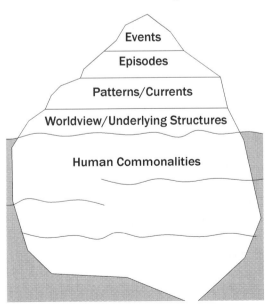

Systems thinkers often use an iceberg as a comparison for looking at a problem. At the tip of the iceberg, the 10-20 percent seen above the surface represents events. These events are reported on the television news, headlined in the newspaper, or featured on the Internet. Looking beneath the surface level of the iceberg's events are episodes. These separate events are linked together to create episodes that have common, unifying features. In turn, when examined closely some episodes have common patterns. The iceberg's patterns – political, economic, technological, social, environmental, and cultural (I call these "currents" in my holistic world history) – create these problems. Many scientists say that such violent and extreme weather conditions, such as the event called Hurricane Katrina, are the result of climate change caused by burning fossil fuels. Events, such as Hurricane Katrina and Sandy and massive flooding in Britain, are linked together as episodes of extreme weather. These extreme weather episodes are linked to the modern economic system, a pattern, which is based on burning fossil fuels for energy consumption to drive our modern way of life.

Farther down towards the base of the iceberg lies what I call the worldview, which, in turn, influences the events, episodes, and patterns.[12] Our worldview is fashioned around the pattern that unlimited economic growth is the unquestioned path to prosperity and well-being. Finally, at the very base of the iceberg are our human behaviors, the universal human commonalities that shape who we are as a species, such as the universal human need for acceptance and belonging. If we want to change the events, episodes and patterns, we must change the worldview that creates them; this means to change the way we think, learn and communicate.

A **worldview** is an overall perspective from which one sees and makes sense of the world, a set of beliefs about how the world works and what we see and don't see. It is a collection of assumptions held by an individual or a group that they firmly believe to be true. These assumptions shape an individual's beliefs, ideas, attitudes, and values, which, in turn, affect behaviors and actions. A worldview acts as a filter. It admits information that is in keeping with our beliefs about the world while guiding us to ignore information that disproves these beliefs. When we look through a filter we usually see through it, rather than seeing it – so it is with worldviews. A worldview acts as a built-in "operating system" that filters how we see things. We rarely bring worldviews into the light of day, so people are not usually aware of them. But our worldview influences every book we read, class we take, vote we cast, as well as the way we raise our children, the way we solve problems, what we believe about religion, and our opinions about the global economy, more than any data or analysis.[13]

Contemporary Worldviews

A unique period of human history is occurring today, a fifth turning – the **Global Wave** – that is changing our human story. Within the Global Wave there is not just one way of thinking. Instead, I have identified five different worldviews with five diverse ways of understanding the world. In the U.S. and throughout the world, I have found that most people identify with one or a combination of these worldviews. The following is a brief summary of the five major worldviews: indigenous, modern, fundamentalist, globalized, and transformative.

1. An Indigenous Worldview

Very few people today hold an indigenous worldview. **Indigenous peoples** share a similar ethnic identity and usually inhabit a geographic region with which they have had an early historical connection. "Indigenous" means "from" or "of the original origin." They are usually an underprivileged group that has an ethnic identity other than those ruling the nation. Other terms used to describe indigenous peoples are aborigines, first people, native people, or aboriginal. However, different international agencies, such as the United Nations, seem to prefer the term, "indigenous peoples." The world population of indigenous peoples is hard to estimate, but recent counts range from 300 million to 350 million. This would be just under 5 percent of the total world population. This number includes at least 5,000 distinct peoples in over 72 countries.[14]

Indigenous peoples today live in groups ranging from only a few dozen to hundreds of thousands or more. Many groups have declined in numbers and some no longer exist, while others are threatened. Modern populations have assimilated some indigenous groups, while in other cases they are recovering or expanding their numbers. Some indigenous societies no longer live on their ancestral land because of migration, relocation, forced resettlement or having their land taken by others. In many cases, indigenous groups are losing or have lost their language and lands, and have experienced intrusion and pollution of their lands and disruption of their traditional ways. For example, in the U.S. the Navajo language is undergoing a renaissance and is a popular subject in Navajo schools.

2. A Modern Worldview

The **modern worldview** traces its history back more than 500 years to the expansion of Western European power and influence around the world. The modern worldview has been especially powerful over the last two centuries and has today expanded to the farthest reaches of the world. A description of the economy according to a modern worldview has already been presented in section 3.

Indigenous peoples, the Kung. Their village in Namibia, Africa. They have survived for over 50,000 years as hunter/gatherers in the Kalahari Desert.

A modern worldview continues today as a way of understanding the world and solving problems. It has ushered in a host of astonishing achievements such as the equality of women, medical breakthroughs, technological successes, educational progress, a high material standard of living for some, and the advancement of human rights. But it has also promoted terrible failures, such as values of rampant consumerism, cut-throat competition, unlimited economic growth, the use of punishment as a way to correct behaviors, military force to resolve conflict, and individualism over

Modern Worldview
upholds scientific reasoning
praises individualism
treats nature as a commodity
promotes liberal political traditions
separates church and state
encourages industrial production
places faith in technological solutions

community. One of the challenges of the 21st century is how to draw on the achievements from a modern worldview and cast off the darker elements.

3. A Fundamentalist Worldview

Fundamentalism is a strict belief in a set of principles that are often religious. Many who hold to these ideas wish to defend what they see as traditional religious beliefs of the past. Although fundamentalists believe they are following the exact traditions of the past, this would be impossible in a modern society. Instead their beliefs have grown out of a rejection of modern ideas along with a response to the unsettling effects of globalization. They see their religion as true and others as false. There are fundamentalist sects in almost all of the world's major religions, including Christianity, Islam, Hinduism and Judaism. Across cultures, fundamentalists share several common characteristics including a factual reading of scripture, a mistrust of outsiders, a sense of separation from modern culture, and a belief in the historical correctness of their religion. Some religious fundamentalists are

33

politically active, trying to shape the political and social order in line with their beliefs. Many feel that the state should be run according to religious principles.

Fundamentalists see the choices for organizing their nation as limited to a Western/modern society or a traditional society. Since they reject a modern society, the only other choice they see is the continuation of their traditional ways. Also many people in modern nations find that their traditional values give comfort and security in a rapidly changing and complex world. Many have strong opinions about social and political values and voice their opinions in a forceful and sometimes violent manner. Although the fundamentalist worldview is very diverse, these beliefs continue today and are held by millions, if not billions, of people.

Fundamentalist worldview: Women in traditional dress by mosque in Iran -- photo Denise Ames

4. A Globalized Worldview

A fourth worldview, a globalized worldview, is sweeping the world today. It has grown out of the modern worldview and has many of its characteristics. But one of the differences is that in the globalized worldview "time has speeded up" and the pace of growth and development has spread to the farthest reaches of the earth. Although the U.S. has heavily influenced the globalized worldview, it has taken hold in intensely industrialized areas of Canada, Europe, Japan, and Australia and reaches across the world into parts of China, India, Southeast Asia, Latin America, and parts

McDonald's Mega Big Mac and Coke in Malaysia. Everything is bigger according to the globalized worldview.

Descriptors of a Globalized Worldview

interconnections, blurred boundaries, approximation, speed, networks, diversity, differentiation, specialization, productivity, consolidation, mergers, acquisitions, interdependence

of the Middle East and Africa as well. A globalized worldview affects all aspects of society and individuals' daily lives.

In a globalized worldview, global capitalism is the dominant economic system. One global economic system governed by capitalist principles has enveloped national and local economies that governments have regulated and protected in the past. A global economic marketplace conducts business, currency exchanges, and trade policies that ignore national boundaries. Global multinational corporations make many of the economic rules and conduct the business of the world marketplace. They promote a consumer-focused economy and support a powerful financial sector. As we will find out, the globalization process, and in particular economic globalization, has both negative and beneficial aspects.

5. A Transformative Worldview

At this point in time, diverse people are actively challenging the negative parts of the four other worldviews. These people say a different worldview or a different story is needed to make sure our human species and life as we know it on earth continues. Leaders from diverse fields – religious leaders, students, entrepreneurs, international political leaders, indigenous farmers, political activists, environmentalists, entertainers, scientists, working people, artists, writers, academics, educators, economists, concerned citizens, and others – are contributing to the creation of what I call a **transformative worldview**.

Critics say that none of the other worldviews are able to meet the challenges of the 21ˢᵗ century. For example, some think that fundamentalist beliefs will not help build a more culturally tolerant atmosphere in an increasingly interracial world. Yet, they admire the sense of community fundamentalists support. Some people advancing a transformative worldview admire the sense of local place and the importance of the environment that many indigenous people have connected with for millennia but don't want to lose a shared awareness as global citizens. Some people say that we need to move beyond the modern worldview without losing the value of scientific inquiry and rational, logical thought. Many people supporting a transformative worldview admire the advances in technology, transportation and communication, while rejecting the despoiling of our planet. They draw upon the globalized worldview idea that we are all global citizens yet want to limit the dominance of the world's economy by giant, multinational corporations and large state enterprises.

Descriptors of a Transformative Worldview

embraces cultural diversity, resists corporate dominance, questions consumer-driven values, supports collective efforts, advocates for more equal distribution of wealth and power, encourages sustainability, emboldens progressive education, lobbies for worker owned businesses

Wind farm in UK represents the transformative worldview. Royd Moor Windfarm in the United Kingdom (UK).

Even though the modern and globalized worldviews are the dominant ones at this point in time, the transformative worldview is challenging their sway and offering choices for a sustainable, more equitable future. Which worldview or combination of worldviews will we as global citizens choose for our future? We all have a voice and a critical stake in the future outcome.

Questions to Consider

1. Which worldview do you most closely indentify with? Explain.

CONCLUDING INSIGHTS:
AN OVERVIEW OF THE GLOBAL ECONOMY

Let's stop to reflect a moment about why you are taking the time to read this book about the global economy. Since you are reading this book, chances are the workings of the global economy have puzzled you. Why are so many people, especially young people, unemployed? If they are employed, why are many of them looking for better jobs? Why are so many people angry and taking it out on politicians? In the U.S. we are still experiencing the effects of what has been termed the "Great Recession" of 2007-2008. Why did so many people buy houses that they could not afford? Why did banks loan them the money to do this? Why didn't politicians step in to stop these abuses? Why did financial speculation bring untold riches to some and misery to others? These are questions we will be examining in this book.

Our Global Economy

1. has been leading to a shift of wealth from the middle class to the wealthy since the 1980s.

2. is built upon endless growth with little regard for the natural environment which sustains all life on earth.

3. encourages overconsumption of both food and other items for the sake of profit (as opposed to human well-being).

4. has bled periphery countries of natural resources, often with no real benefit for the majority of the people.

The foundation of our global economy has historically profited from addictions. The early global economy profited from sugar, tobacco, and addictive caffeine drinks, such as coffee and tea, alcohol derived from either corn or sugar and cotton to make clothing. Today these addictions continue as new ones are added to the list: playing video games, compulsive texting, consumer shopping for unnecessary goods, prescription drug abuse, eating addictive fast foods that have high fat and sugar levels, obsession with social networks such as Facebook and Twitter. Although creating more addictions for consumers is a good way to create more wealth for some, is it a good way to structure an economy and society?

It is important that we dig deep to better understand the underlying forces of the global economy and the problems they have created. Only if we understand these driving forces will we be able to propose solutions. Our job in this book is to get a better understanding of the global economy.

In this book I will question our current global economy. I do not have all the answers. But I do realize that something is wrong today, and I feel it is important to think about, discuss, and act upon the problems that we all encounter. I hope you all will keep up your study of the global economy in order to think about and act upon solutions that will be beneficial to a majority of the people in the world and to the health of the earth.

CHAPTER TWO

Historical Roots of the
Global Economy

"Written into the long history of our planet, in one form or another, is the record of what is coming our way."

— Julia Whitty writer and filmmaker

THE WESTERN ECONOMY PRIOR TO 1500

Our global economy did not magically start overnight. It has a long history. To get a clear picture of the global economy today and the changing nature of capitalism, we need to travel back in time to around 1500, the beginning of what I call the Modern Wave (see *Waves of Global Change: A Holistic World History*). Among other changes, this date signaled the expansion of capitalism.

Western Europe was an unlikely future core area, since it remained on the periphery of world history from 500 to 1500, in what is called the European Middle Ages. Peasants made up the vast majority of the European population, with a small elite noble class and a very small merchant class. A self-sufficient, domestic economy in the countryside and city guilds made up a simple economy. The household was the center of the economy. Almost everyone lived in a household – family, servants, and apprentices – and everyone worked: men, women, and children. The market economy was on the fringes of society, but as cities grew, trade and commerce increased. The merchant class slowly began to become more powerful.

The urban economy, especially in the later Middle Ages, was based on a guild system. A **guild** is where artisans who had a common business or trade banded together to regulate the production and distribution of their products. For example, bakers, blacksmiths, and hat-makers formed guilds. They limited membership, regulated quality and price, discouraged competition, and stopped technological changes. Guilds charged a just price, not a market price, for their products. A **just price** covered the guild member's expenses and a small profit. But the guilds did not seek huge profits; instead they wanted to protect their market share and keep their members' livelihoods. They did not follow capitalist principles.

Western Europe was the seedbed for the sprouting of capitalism. Beginning in the 1200s, **cottage industries** began to grow. Textile merchants seeking profits found the guild system limited their efforts. Thus, they moved textile production to the countryside, away from the prying eyes of the city guild masters. Merchants set up shops in rural cottages; hence, the name cottage industries. The merchants took raw wool to rural households where men and mostly women spun wool into yarn, wove the yarn into cloth, cut the cloth into patterns, or sewed the pieces into clothing. The merchants paid workers a piece work wage for their services, picked up the finished goods, and then sold them in the market place for a profit. This production system continued until Britain started to industrialize around 1750.

By 1400, Western Europe had an unfavorable balance of trade with Asia. They imported valuable spices, silk, sugar, perfume, and jewels from the East, while they exported less valuable wool, tin, and copper. Faced with a desperate need for new markets, Europeans launched a search for trade and profit. Portugal and Spain forged the way in finding new trade routes, getting colonies, and spreading their influence across the world. But Britain, France, and the Netherlands snapped at their heels as they sought to overtake the leaders. Accidentally, the explorer Christopher Columbus blew into the Western hemisphere, which Spain claimed and began its search for treasure. The chance "discovery" and conquest of the Western hemisphere provided the wealth for Western Europe to create the capitalist economic system.

Questions to Consider

1. Would the use of just price work in a capitalist economy? Explain.

To better understand the historical roots of the global economy, I will divide it into three sections:

COMMERCIAL CAPITALISM IN THE EARLY MODERN ERA (1500-1750)

Capitalism, as an economic system, burst onto the world stage around 1500, largely because Western Europe folded the riches from the Western hemisphere into its economy. At this time **mercantilism**, one of the versions of capitalism, took shape. It was based on the economic relationship between a European country, called the "mother country," and its colonies. The colonial rulers imported cheap raw materials from their colonies and exported back to them the more profitable manufactured goods that they produced. This system favored the mother country. Western European commercial cities were the core areas and the colonies were the periphery. Some European governments, like the British and the Dutch, supported mercantilism by passing favorable laws.

Mercantilism needed a form of control called **colonialism**: a powerful country's control over a weaker country, territory, or people. The colonial periphery supplied natural resources to the colonial rulers: silver from Mexico, Bolivia, and Peru; furs and skins from North America and Siberia; sugar and cocoa from the West Indies and Brazil; tobacco, rice, and indigo, and later cotton from the American South; coffee and rubber from Southeast Asia; and jute and spices from India. Low-paid native laborers, indentured servants, or slaves labored to provide these raw materials.

Wealth built up in the core Western European cities. Money poured into their treasuries and entrepreneurs reinvested profits in other businesses. The vast wealth from Spain eventually flowed to British bankers and investors or to private shippers, financiers, merchants, and manu-

Potosi: A Mountain of Silver:
The former Spanish colonial city of Potosi, in Bolivia lies in the shadows of the famed "mountain of silver." To dig out the prized ore, the Spanish from 1540 to 1640 forced local indigenous men to labor in the mines for weeks on end; some never saw the light of day. Indigenous miners died by the thousands due to exhaustion, horrible working conditions, and mercury poisoning from the mining method. The Spanish in the end replaced disease-ridden indigenous workers with slaves from Africa, who were called "human mules," since they replaced mules who could not survive the horrible conditions.

facturers. This shift of wealth from Spain signaled its decline from core status and the rise of the Netherlands and Britain to that station. Because the economic wealth was from commerce, it is often called commercial capitalism.

Agricultural changes also spurred the growth of commercial capitalism. European peasants for centuries practiced an **open field system**, where they produced food for their own needs. They paid a certain amount of their crops as a tax to the landowner. In this system efficiency and productivity were not very important. With the advent of capitalism the **enclosure** of open fields gave way to farming according to capitalist principles, where efficiency and productivity became the most important. Farms and shared areas called "the commons" were first enclosed and made into privately owned plots of land marked with clear boundaries and individual ownership. Privatization first took off in England where large landowners, who benefited from this capitalist move, welcomed it.

39

Uprooted, small peasant farmers unsuccessfully protested their troubles, since many of them lost the land they had farmed for centuries.

Trade

In the 18th century the **Triangle Trade** started up between Africa, Europe, and the Americas. Slavery was a common practice in earlier civilizations, but with the expansion of capitalism, the buying and selling of slaves increased. African chiefs, who dealt in captured slaves, exchanged them with European slave traders who carried guns, knives, manufactured items, beads, colored cloth, and liquor on ships to the West African coast. The slave traders shipped their slave cargo to the Americas and traded them for sugar, tobacco, furs, metals, and raw cotton that Europe made into finished goods. Traders either shipped these finished goods back to the American colonies or to Africa to begin the trading cycle again. The slave trade made huge profits; in fact, it generated one-third of English wealth in the 17th century.[1]

African slave traders gained power for themselves by trading slaves for European firearms. They used their additional firepower to raid neighboring tribes and villages to capture even more slaves for trade and profit. Slaving sparked conflict between local tribes as deadly competition increased. African slave traders sold their human commodities to European buyers at port cities along the Atlantic seaboard who, in turn, transported their human cargo to slave dealers in the Western hemisphere. Misery, starvation, or early death awaited many of the captured victims. On average, 25 percent of the slaves transported to the Western hemisphere in what was known as the Middle Passage suffered a horrible death.[2]

Using a systems approach to examine the slave trade, all the actors – both African and European traders and buyers – were connected in this profitable line of work. The slave trade contributed to the collapse of previously stable and prosperous African villages. It also pitted Africans against each other as they competed for captured slaves in the horrible era of enslavement and genocide. Eventually, concerned activists became horrified at the immorality of slavery and they worked tirelessly to stop it.

Indigenous people also participated in the expansion of commercial capitalism. In the rich fur-producing areas of North America, indigenous peoples trapped animals and exchanged the pelts with traders for goods, such as wool blankets, iron pots, firearms, and liquor. The animal hides shipped to Europe supported a fashion industry showcasing beaver skin hats and fur coats. Beaver numbers declined so rapidly that trappers had to push further inland to capture more. When the trapping grounds dried up, the trappers had to go into a neighboring tribe's territories. This often led to conflict or war, which caused invaders and defenders to get more guns to capture more furs or to defend their territory. This cycle of violence, like the slave trade, created instability but also helped add to European wealth and power.

With a capitalist economy came the creation of corporations. British and Dutch merchants formed joint stock companies in the 16th century when the European monarchies issued royal charters to companies for trade with their colonies. Now one individual did not need to raise all the capital for a business; instead, investors could pool their capital. These companies, the forerunners of the modern corporation, were supposed to make a large profit for their shareholders with little interest in the social, environmental, or moral consequences of their actions. For example, England's Queen Elizabeth I chartered the British East India Company in 1600, which held monopoly trading rights with India until 1858.

40

Core Areas of Commerical Capitalism

By the 1540s, Spain was the world's most important power. But paradoxically, easy money flowing from its colonies hurt Spain's real economy based on wool and steel manufacturing. Costly wars in the early 1600s forced the government to borrow money, leading to huge debt. Peasants, artisans, and merchants paid most of the taxes, since laws excused the elites from their tax obligations. Spain ended up as a country with a few rich people, lots of poor and a tiny middle class. All these factors led to its decline. Half of the Spanish population fled from the decaying cities to make a living as farmers in the countryside.[3]

Independent Holland started its climb to core status while Spain was still strong. The era from 1648 to the 1670s was a time of economic openness and Dutch expansion. Holland had the world's largest merchant fleet in 1669, including 6,000 ships, and lots of capital (money) from its investments in technology, textiles, shipbuilding, agriculture, and fishing. But by the 1700s, the Dutch free-trade system declined because a wave of mercantilism swept Europe. Trade barriers went up, weakening the Dutch open trading system and profits weakened. By the late 1700s two costly wars further hammered the Dutch economy. As in Spain, town populations fell, and food and tax riots spread. As in the U.S. today, the Dutch elites turned to finance instead of commerce. They passively held onto bonds and securities instead of actively producing real products or services. A shift in core status from the Dutch to the British took place in the 18th century.[4]

The early modern era marks the appearance of Western Europe as a core area, but its influence had not yet reached around the world. It is not until industrialization began in the mid-1700s that capitalism spread around the world.

Questions to Consider

1. What similar problems did Spain and Holland face as they declined from their core status?

INDUSTRIAL CAPITALISM IN THE MODERN ERA (1750-1914)

The expansion of capitalism continued into the modern era with industrialization as a new source of wealth. **Industrialization** is a change from an economy based on home production of goods to one based on large-scale, mechanized factory production with a wage-based labor force. This change, called the **Industrial Revolution,** moved rapidly from Britain to neighboring countries.

Early Industrialization in Britain

Britain was the first country to industrialize, and the first industry was cotton textiles. The British government aided the infant textile industry by adding tariffs to the cheaper and higher quality imports from their colony, India. India had a centuries-old, hand-loomed textile industry. **Tariffs**, an import tax, made India's imported textiles more expensive than British-made cotton goods. Consumers chose the tariff-protected and cheaper British-made product, and, thus, its textile industry flourished.

As demand for textiles grew, a factory system

Cottonopolis, early painting of cotton mills in Manchester, England.

produced greater quantities of goods. Before the 18th century, a guild member or cottage worker made textiles at what we would consider a leisurely pace. But a more rushed work environment existed in the new **factories**. Factory workers earned a standard wage, divided tasks into parts, and worked under the close supervision of the owner or manager. The workers merely performed boring and repetitive tasks in an unfriendly work environment. The small guild owners went out of business as they were unable to compete with this cheaper, factory form of production.

The strong demand for American cotton links to British industrialization. Consumer demand for popular cotton textiles spurred a rush of new inventions to process cotton more rapidly, such as Eli Whitney's cotton gin in 1793. The cotton gin separated seeds from raw cotton, work which was previously painstakingly hand-done by slaves. The demand for raw cotton grew, and farmers in the South responded by growing more of it on larger cotton plantations. Slaves worked longer hours to produce more cotton, cotton farming expanded into new U.S. territories, more slaves were needed as farm laborers, and the price of land, slaves, and cotton skyrocketed as demand swelled. This demand helped spark the terrible conflict over slavery, the American Civil War (1861-1865).

Introduced in this modern era was a new form of capitalism, as opposed to mercantilism. English economist **Adam Smith** championed this different form of capitalism. He said that a free trade economy was better than mercantilism. He explained that the law of **supply and demand** directs an economy, and these two factors determine price. As demand for an item increases, prices rise. Government laws or regulations that get in the way of the free market economy – or, as he called it, the "invisible hand of the marketplace" – should be overturned. Smith did not like the governments' trade regulations and protective tariffs. He said that home or domestic industries should compete in the marketplace without government interference. The term **laissez-faire** capitalism describes these principles of free trade and deregulation.

By the 1820s, British manufacturers viewed mercantilism as harmful to them and pushed for free trade. Those against mercantilism wanted to repeal the **Corn Laws**, which were taxes on imported grain, or "corn" according to the British. Tariffs had been in place for years to protect British farmers from outside competition. Without the tariffs, the domestic price of grain was higher than imported grain. Of course, British farmers favored the tariffs, since this meant the law protected higher prices for their grain. They rightly said that repeal of the Corn Laws would doom British farming. They made the point that self-sufficiency in food was important to the security of the British people. Nonetheless, free traders won out, but only after a long and bitter struggle. In 1846-1847 Parliament repealed the Corn Laws. [5]

Tariffs Illustration*

Sewing Machine (in $)	U.S.	Britain
Cost to manufacture	10.	5.
Profit	2.	2.
Cost to consumer	12.	7.
US tariff added		+ 6.**
New cost to consumer	12.	13.

* not historically accurate, for illustration purposes only

** tariffs were deposited into the U.S. treasury

The British industrialists were eager to push for their free market form of capitalism and remove tariffs protecting domestic industries. At the time British industries were well established and able to sell their products at a lower price than their nearest competitors in the U.S. and France. The U.S., which was starting to industrialize in the early 1800s, wanted to protect its infant industries from cheaper British products and, thus, had tariffs. Although American consumers had to pay more for the tariff-protected products, the factories that made these products were able to grow and provide employment. The revenues from tariffs went directly into the U.S. treasury, which had a large budget surplus.

Corporations

With industrial capitalism, many small family businesses and guilds gave way to the modern corporation. A **corporation** is a formal business association with a publicly registered charter saying it is a separate legal unit. During this time, corporations branched out globally in order to gain cheap or hard-to-find raw materials and more markets. Commercial expansion needed additional capital for investments in factories, ports, warehouses, and transportation. A stock market, partnerships, banks, and government programs raised investment funds for new corporations. Britain and the U.S. established a national banking system, and this banking system regulated the money supply. But instead of corporations, often national governments took the greater financial risks and built railroads, canals, harbors, roads, and dams. In 1914, the British invested three-fourths of their funds in the U.S., Canada, Australia, South Africa, India, and Argentina. They used most of the money for railroads, ports, power plants, and other projects.[6]

A new class of entrepreneurs ably figured out risks, raised capital, and thought up new ideas for making a profit. Although they came from varied backgrounds, and rags-to-riches stories were not unknown, most industrialists came from an artisan or manufacturing background. For example, the father of the American steel tycoon Andrew Carnegie was a linen weaver in Scotland. Connected to the rise of capitalism, these new entrepreneurs adopted personal habits and beliefs that made it acceptable to display materialistic, aggressive behaviors.

The industrial capitalist economy produced a dizzying range of manufactured goods and some services. The government and private business built railroads, harbors, and roads, telegraph and telephone lines, and huge naval ships. Other industries emerged, such as chemicals, petroleum and coal-fired electricity, machines that made machines, and the steel and construction industry, which employed engineers, architects and carpenters. An infant service industry provided education, medical care, retail, entertainment, organized sporting events, leisure activities, publishing, and the news.

Labor

A wider population in Western Europe enjoyed the wealth made from an increase in economic productivity from machines, although certainly not everyone. Greater economic surplus for some meant they were able to have a more lavish standard of living. Factory workers labored long hours for low wages, while factory owners gained from their labor productivity. It would not be until later into the 20th century that workers pocketed more of the productivity gains from their labor.

Men, women and children entered the ranks of a growing industrial work force. They had limited options for earning a living as they made their way into factories where their unskilled wage labor was in demand. Factory workers received slightly higher wages than farmers, servants, or cottage workers, but they also were dependent upon others for employment. With the mechanization of spinning, many rural women lost income from their cottage industries as factories absorbed their jobs. Artisans' standard of living declined, as well, since the higher cost of their handcrafted items could not compete with lower-cost, mass-produced goods. For example, linen weavers in Scotland experienced high unemployment and the collapse of their craft in favor of cheaper, machine-loomed linens. One of those craft workers was the father of Andrew Carnegie, the steel tycoon I introduced earlier and one of the world's richest men.

Dreadful factory conditions and low wages generally marked the experience of most industrial workers. The wages of the lowest paid workers improved only slightly in comparison to higher middle class incomes. By the late 1800s, small groups of workers tired of their miserable working conditions and low wages, banded together to form unions. One American union, the Knights of Labor, formed in 1869. It lobbied politicians for reforms: higher wages, accident insurance, unemployment benefits, reduced working hours, medical insurance, regulation of child labor, and better working conditions. Businesses fought back by encouraging immigration and rural migration to make sure they had enough low-wage workers. Even though the government did not aid their plight, workers did gradually gain slightly better wages and working conditions.

Labor union demonstrators held at bay by soldiers during the 1912 Lawrence textile strike in Massachusetts, USA.

In many countries, such as Britain, labor unions and socialist parties strongly supported free trade, since more trade meant more work for them. Many in the labor movement backed socialism, since workers would, in theory, own the means of production and benefit economically. However, socialism was not a large scale movement in the 19th century.

Labor migration from the countryside to cities and even across continents took place in the late 1800s as workers moved to find employment. Millions of people from Europe and other nations sought work elsewhere. Approximately 12 million people left their homelands in Europe to immigrate to the U.S. from 1870 to 1900. Immigration uprooted peasants and artisans from their traditional occupations as they had to cope with the shock of starting a new life in a factory town while living in crowded, unsanitary tenements.[7] Alcoholism, domestic violence, and family desertion accompanied these shattering changes.

The flow of people from low-wage Europe and even lower-wage Asia lessened wages in high-wage North America and Australia. The result of an increased labor supply in industrializing nations was a lower wage scale than would have occurred without immigration: lower by one-third in Argentina, by one-fourth in Canada and Australia, and by one-eighth in the U.S. This fact drove labor movements in these countries to favor limits on immigration. There were many examples of immigration restrictions, yet in a global sense, they were relatively rare.[8]

Questions to Consider

1. What problems did labor face during this time? Are they similar to issues facing labor today?

The Gold Standard and the Long Depression

From 1815 to its decline, Britain was the leading industrial economy of the world, and it championed the gold standard. Centuries of tradition that used both gold and silver as currencies came to an end in the 1870s, when most industrial countries joined the gold standard. When a country's government went on gold, it promised to exchange its own national currency for gold at a fixed rate. The country's currency was then exchangeable with the money of any other gold standard country. In 1871, Britain was on gold, but others gradually joined, such as the U.S in 1879. Gold was the common global money, but each individual country had its own currency under different names – marks, francs, pounds, dollars, and so on. The gold standard was predictable, and bankers and investors could be certain that debtors would pay back what they owed in gold-backed currencies. It favored the investor but not the debtor or consumer.[9]

The countries on gold committed to making their national economy fit the currency. The most common way to fit an economy to the gold standard was to push wages down. Since countries on gold were not able to **devalue** their currencies (make them worth less), they used wages as the variable with which to reduce prices on their goods. Employers were able to force wages down by paying their workers less; this meant that an employer could charge less for his product. Industry used this as a way to reduce prices. All this was important to the functioning of the gold standard. If a country needed to restore its trade balance, it would increase the exports of the cheaper goods that businesses produced by cutting wages and reducing prices.[10]

It would be difficult today to force workers to accept such harsh wage reductions as in the past. But such reductions were common during the time. If business conditions worsened, the solution was to cut wages. But a big drop in wages might have only a slight impact on living standards since prices dropped too. A growing labor movement voiced its unhappiness with the unfairness of stabilizing the economy on the backs of labor; they demanded change.[11]

The **Long Depression of 1873-1896** contributed to dissatisfaction with free trade and the gold standard. This was generally a period of deflation and low growth, especially in Europe and the U.S. The financial problems starting in 1873 revealed that with global integration, economic events in one part of the globe echoed those in other parts. The Long Depression showed that global capitalism and its drive for unending growth can continue only as long as there is a ready supply of raw materials and an increasing demand for goods. Farmers' overproduction of wheat on the Great Plains of the U.S. was one example of another problem – what to do with overcapacity and increasing global competition. Along with labor demands, increasing competition and overproduction were squeezing business profits. Given the situation described, if you were an American or European investor after 1873, where would you look for economic expansion?

Hypothetical Example of a Country Using Wages as the Variable in Adjusting Prices for Export.*

Cost of Sewing Machine	U.S.	Germany
Fixed Costs (factory costs, etc. can't adjust)	$20.	$20.
Raw Materials (fixed can't adjust)	$10.	$10.
Labor (can adjust)	$20.	$20. $10.
Profit	$10.	$10.
Price of Sewing Machine	$60.	$50.

*In this example, since the other costs are fixed, Germany adjusted the only variable it could - wages. Those on the gold standard cannot adjust their currency. If Germany is experiencing a trade imbalance and wants to sell more goods abroad it has to lower the wages of labor to make their goods more desirable abroad.

Imperialism

Businesses answered the question posed above by expanding overseas, particularly into external areas untouched by capitalism. From 1873 to 1914, the West set out on a period of imperialism, which was somewhat different from colonialism in the early modern era. **Imperialism** is a more powerful nation's political and economic control over a less powerful territory or country. During this imperialist era much of Asia, the Pacific islands, the Middle East, and sub-Saharan Africa were the objects of a land-grab by the nations of Europe – particularly Great Britain and France, and to a lesser extent the Netherlands, Belgium, Russia, Portugal, Spain, and Germany – and the United States, Japan, and Australia.

The roots of imperialism can be found in the search for markets by the core countries whose industries faced declining profits and increased competition. The old core nations – Britain, France, Netherlands, and Belgium – were facing increasing competition from newly industrialized core nations – the U.S., Germany, Japan, Russia, and parts of central Europe. This increasing competition drove down prices and ate into profits, and increasing demand for raw materials squeezed profits even more. Investors, with visions of untold profits dreamed about bringing the world into the capitalist fold.

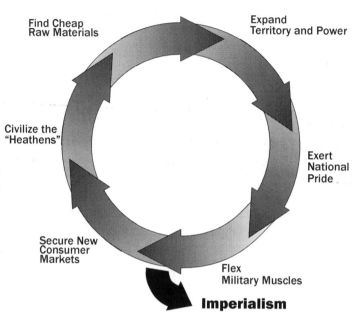

Reasons for Imperialism

Find Cheap Raw Materials

Expand Territory and Power

Civilize the "Heathens"

Exert National Pride

Secure New Consumer Markets

Flex Military Muscles

Imperialism

Using a systems approach, several interconnected factors contributed to imperialism. First, Westerners thought that a nation must expand its territory and power in order to have international respect. Second, nations wanted to flex their military muscles. Oceangoing steamships in the 1860s carried huge cargoes long distances and needed refueling bases. Controlling key harbors as refueling stations showed a nation's command over a far-flung empire. Third, industrial output in the last half of the 1890s was more than consumer demand, and stagnation resulted. Industrialized nations were anxious to find new consumer markets to peddle their surplus products in the periphery and buy cheap raw materials for their industries. Fourth, many misguided but well-meaning people believed that Western culture, European people, and Christianity were superior to non-Western culture, people, and religions. They thought it was their duty to "civilize the heathens." All of these factors provided a reason for imperialism.

A key element of economic globalization is integration, and in the late 19th and early 20th centuries the world was becoming more economically integrated than ever before. In the 45 years after 1870, colonial powers took over an average of 240,000 square miles each year, compared to an average of 83,000 square miles a year for the first 75 years of the 1800s. In 1815, Britain and France controlled over one third of the earth's surface, and by 1878, they controlled over two thirds. By 1914, Britain, France and the U.S. together controlled 85 percent of the earth's surface. As a result of their expansion, the world generally became – and remains today – a world economic system. The integration and expansion of capitalism landscaped the highly uneven ground on which that economic game is played. [12]

Cecil Rhodes, a British Businessman and Colonizer of Africa.
Rhodes, known for making a fortune in diamond mining in Africa, firmly believed imperialism was necessary for keeping peace at home. In 1895 he stated ... "I was in the East End of London yesterday and attended a meeting of the unemployed. I listened to the wild speeches, which were just a cry for 'bread,' and on my way home I became more than ever convinced of the importance of imperialism.... My solution for the social problem is in order to save the 40,000,000 inhabitants of the United Kingdom from a bloody civil war, we colonial statesmen must acquire new lands for settling the surplus population, and to provide new markets for the goods produced in the factories and mines. The Empire, as I have always said, is a bread and butter question. If you want to avoid civil war, you must become imperialist."[13]

During the 19th century, the European colonies shifted from external status to a dependent periphery status. For example, small farmers and plantation owners in the periphery grew **cash crops,** such as coffee, tea, fruits, tobacco, cotton, and sugar that they sold on the world market. Small farmers in the periphery relied on growing cash crops for the market economy in order to earn income to purchase necessities and pay taxes. As the world capitalist economy folded them into the world market, they grew fewer crops for their own needs and more for the world market. The market price small farmers received for their crops depended on supply and demand. At the time, overproduction usually kept prices low. In addition, colonial authorities forced small farmers to pay taxes on their land, which required cash payment. The limited options to earn cash were to work on a plantation or in a mine owned by the colonists or grow cash crops. This further brought the farmer into the capitalist economic web. Because of high taxes and low prices for cash crops, many small farmers in the colonies were unable to make a living and sold their farms to large landowners eager to add to their holdings. As a result of this shift to commercial agriculture, farmers in the colonies suffered the same economic consequences as small farmers in Europe. They could not make a living when farming became part of the global economy.

Most colonial powers cruelly interacted with their colonies but contributed to modern developments as well. Tensions flared between those who held to their traditional culture and those who liked Western culture. A modern, consumer-driven way of life, along with Western law and culture, tempted many colonized people. Others violently resisted the West's domination and modern ways of life. Integration of a colony into the world economy required certain political and legal conditions, especially secure property rights and judicial authority. Also, there needed to be an infrastructure – railroads, roads, and port – to get products to market. For their own benefit, the imperialists pulled their colonies into the global economy.[14]

The Golden Era of Global Capitalism

The years from 1896 to 1914 were the high point of global economic integration. The world had never seen such an open market for goods, capital, and labor. It would be another 100 years before the world returned to that level of integration. For those who benefitted from this early economic globalization, it worked beautifully. Those who were able to capture the comparative advantage of their country benefitted. Labor and capital moved around the world from where they produced less to where they produced more. Profits were astonishing.[15]

But not everyone benefited from global economic integration. On the destructive side, small farmers in Europe were unable to compete with large farmers in the U.S. and Argentina and were driven out of business. Many traditional societies fell apart as imperialists ravaged their homelands. For example, the Belgians exploited their African colony – the Belgian Congo – by forcing the colonists to collect quotas of rubber from wild rubber plants. Estimates are that 10 million Africans died as a result. A few of those on the losing side of specialization and economic integration included European grain farmers, Chinese artisans, and Indian textile weavers. Opening markets, paying back debts, and following the gold standard all involved sacrifices, which the poor and weak paid for.[16]

The very poorest periphery countries tended to favor free trade. They had little manufacturing to protect and made money by exporting raw materials and agricultural goods. For example, the southern and western regions in the U.S. supported free trade, since the South's main export was cotton, a raw material in demand by textile mills, and the West's main export was wheat, which was a staple around the world. These regions had little manufacturing, and thus, no need for protective tariffs

Fifty million visitors thronged the Paris International Exposition of 1900, a dazzling showcase of technological progress. They may have noticed the clues showing that industrial leadership was slipping away from the British to the new industrial titans – Germany, the U.S., and surprising to fair-goers, the island nation of Japan. The homeland of the Industrial Revolution was being left behind. In 1870, Britain, Belgium, and France together produced nearly half of the world's industrial output, but by 1913, they were producing barely one-fifth. German industrial output was more than Britain's, and America's was more than double Britain's. The U.S. introduced methods of mass production, while the Germans made advances in electrical engineering and chemicals.[17] A shift in core areas was underway.

Wheat farming in America, early 20th century. Farmers favored free trade.

The British had held their core status since the 1700s. Their golden age stretched from 1846 into the 1870s, during which international trade jumped fivefold. But from 1870-1900, the U.S. and Germany overtook the world leader. After 1900, the U.S. and Germany made exports from Britain more expensive for consumers by adding tariffs. The decline in British exports affected the wages of its workers, which dropped by about 10 percent. By 1914, women in Britain constituted 41 percent of the workforce because families needed two incomes to make ends meet.[18] The U.S. would experience this trend in the late 1970s.

As the British continued their decline, more wealth went to the top 1 percent. Their share of wealth peaked in 1911-1913 at 69 percent. The lifestyle of the upper class was a whirl of showy consumption, as the elite purchased huge yachts, attended pheasant shoots, and vacationed in luxury hotels. Although declining, by 1914 Britain still held 43 percent of all global investments. Similar to the situation in the U.S. today, some British wanted to revive manufacturing, but instead finance and the concentration of wealth continued. Having to pay for two costly world wars in the 20th century, the British sold most of their overseas investments. Along with the collapse of British world economic leadership, the share of wealth in the hands of the top 1 percent declined from 69 percent in 1914 to 33 percent in 1960.[19]

Questions to Consider

1. Do you see any similarities between the decline of Britain as a core economy in the early 20th century and the situation in the U.S. today?

THE EARLY TWENTIETH CENTURY ECONOMY (1914-1945)

Before 1914 the benefits of international economic growth were available only to some of the people some of the time. But almost everything from 1914 to 1945 was bad for almost all the people all the time. During this time the world staggered around a vicious circle in which global economic collapse caused national crises, and national hardships drove domestic groups to extremes.

As the warring factions in World War I battled in the trenches, there was a need for U.S. capital and manufactured exports. But the Allies, especially the British, had to pay for their purchases by selling what they could: goods, gold, and foreign investments. For example, Europe had the most interests in Latin America for centuries, while U.S. interest was limited. But after the war, the U.S. stepped up influence over its southern neighbors. As the U.S. took over Britain's core economic position, it began to find that the gold standard and free trade looked much better.[20]

At the Treaty of Versailles in Paris in 1918, the negotiations between the war's victors and the defeated took a nasty turn. The victors demanded that Germany admit guilt for causing the war and pay them compensation. The victors refused to renegotiate the large war debts, eventually contributing to the collapse of the fragile German democracy and the rise of the extreme Nazi Party and Adolph Hitler.

One notable event during World War I was the decisive German defeat of the Russian army. The weak Russian monarchy gave way to a Communist uprising in 1917. Those favoring the monarchy and victorious communist's supporters battled each other in a brutal civil war. The Union of Soviet Socialist Republics (USSR) or Soviet Union formed in 1922. The Soviets championed a command economy, which continued until its collapse in 1991. After the revolution, the country industrialized and collectivized agriculture. The heavy boots of the communist elites stamped out the infant free market.

With the end of World War I, an uneasy peace settled upon Europe, and economic turmoil prevailed. In an attempt to control the unrest, governments printed more money, causing inflation to spiral out of control. It was the worst in Germany where it was best to get paid in the afternoon because the morning pay would be worthless by the afternoon. It was common to see people pushing wheelbarrows full of cash just to buy a loaf of bread. This was inflation at its worst, wiping out the life savings of millions of people. Despite hardships, by 1924 most of Europe had recovered from inflation and the war. But to the German middle class, who lost most of their savings because of inflation, the chaos of the early 1920s showed that the liberal democratic elites were unfit to rule. In light of this backdrop, Hitler's anti-democratic message was appealing to them.[21]

The European middle class was squeezed again as large corporations came to dominate industry, and farming was modernized. Almost every European extreme right wing movement found its main base of support among small business people and small farmers. Fascism had an anti-corporate, anti-labor,

Berlin 1931, the army feeding the poor. Depression was felt severely in Germany.

and anti-foreign message. Farmers and businessmen in some nations where there were many Jewish-owned businesses or merchants identified with the European extreme right wing anti-Semitic views, since they saw Jewish competitors, creditors, or middlemen as part of the problem.[22]

The U.S. economy roared, especially in the late 1920s. Wall Street in New York City replaced London as the world's financial center and the U.S. was the world's leading creditor. Even though the U.S. was the world's largest economy, it continued its protectionist trade policy. One of the high profile industries was automobiles. The assembly line installed in Henry Ford's Highland Park, Michigan plant in 1913, reduced the time necessary to make a Model T chassis from over 12 hours to 90 minutes. Labor's strength grew as industry shifted to large corporations and factories, such as Ford Motors. The new corporations were friendlier to unions than older, smaller firms. Labor was a higher part of production costs in older, labor-intensive industries than in the newer, larger factories. In the newer factories, owners invested more capital in machinery, research and development, and marketing than in labor. Also, tariff policies meant that prices would not face competition from imports; thus, labor costs were passed on to consumers in the form of higher prices. The growth of unions and large corporations went hand in hand.[23]

The 1929 financial crisis started with a decline in growth outside North America. In 1928, farm conditions worsened because production outpaced demand. Much of Europe and Asia began to fall into recession, but the U.S. stock market continued to boom. On Black Tuesday, October 29, 1929, the U.S. stock market finally collapsed. It was a clear signal that the Great Depression was at hand.

The economic collapse of 1929-1934 was severe. The industrialized world crumbled for over five years as unemployment went above 25 percent almost everywhere. In the U.S. farm prices fell by 52 percent between 1928 and 1933. In response, conservatives in core countries said that governments should do nothing; inaction, they said, would speed recovery. "Don't just do something, stand there." However, the U.S. Congress raised tariffs with the passage of the Smoot-Hawley Tariff Act in 1930, and within a few months other countries also began raising tariffs.[24] The high tariffs put a further damper on international trade.

Deflation, a decline in prices and wages, was a major problem in the Great Depression. A country's commitment to the gold standard blocked attempts to combat deflation. Gold ruled. Countries on gold had to let prices take their course, for national prices were a local expression of world prices, and world prices were low – very low. Lending nearly stopped as credit markets tightened. The British government took its currency off gold in 1931. President Franklin Roosevelt took the dollar off the gold standard when he came into office in 1933. As a result, the dollar declined in value, causing the prices of agricultural products and other primary commodities to soar. With more money in circulation, prices rose continually, and deflation eased.[25]

The Depression left its mark everywhere, and it pointed away from laissez-faire capitalism and toward government involvement in the economy. The Western countries had become more democratic since the classical era, and labor, the middle class, farmers, and the poor, who bore the burden of earlier policies to stabilize the economy, were no longer willing to make that sacrifice.

Questions to Consider

1. Why didn't laissez-faire policies work to end the Depression?

The Rise of Economic Nationalism

While Western democracies sought to rebuild global economic integration in the face of economic collapse, the fascists and much of the world looked to protect themselves from it through a policy of economic self-sufficiency. The democracies worked with organized labor, while the fascists destroyed their labor movements and ties to socialism. Germany cast off global capitalism after 1929, and instead, the government built public works projects. Its plans needed a strong government, and the Nazis and their supporters gladly turned away from the weak governments of classical, global laissez-faire capitalism.[26] Many middle status, semi-industrial, debtor countries moved along an economic path that was often at odds with that of the core countries. They, like the fascists, followed a new economic nationalism and rejected the gold standard, levied high protective tariffs, and controlled foreign investment. They built urban industries that produced goods for their domestic market, although not for export. Their previous areas of specialization, such as agriculture, funded sectors of the economy that the market had not developed because of foreign competition, especially national industry.[27] For example, Argentina taxed its well-established agricultural sector to fund its infant national industrial growth policy.

Harzburger Front of 1931, a coalition of nationalist conservatives and the extreme right in Germany.

After 1928 in the Soviet Union, Joseph Stalin and his communist supporters consolidated their power. They began pushing the country toward rapid industrialization, with resources squeezed out of the agricultural and consumer sectors. The Soviet regime forced peasant farmers into government controlled collective farms. The small-to medium-sized farmers resisted forced collectivization. Rather than surrender their animals to the collectives, farmers slaughtered their herds and ate or sold what they could. Grain production dropped, and millions of peasants died in the famine years of 1932 and 1933. The government forced collective farmers to sell their crops at artificially low prices, providing cheap food for workers. On the other hand, the prices of consumer goods were high, and availability was limited. Although Soviet industrialization was a success in many ways, the government's supporters – urban workers and Communist Party members – received most of the benefits, while farmers suffered.[28]

Africa, Asia, and Latin America were economically cast aside from the global economy from about 1929 to 1953. In this period, the middle nations broke from their open economy of the past to a model based on **import substitution industrialization** (ISI). Under ISI a country manufactures its own products and reduces its dependency on foreign trade. Many Latin American countries adopted ISI from the 1930s until the 1980s, and some Asian and African countries followed from the 1950s until the 1980s. Cities and industries grew in areas of Latin America and the Middle East. For example, Egyptians, who had exported raw cotton to

An example of ISI projects. Argentina production line at the state military industries facility in 1950; on line since 1927. Populist President Juan Perón's modernized and expanded the complex.

51

Britain for decades, used their own cotton to make clothing textiles, and soon a busy, tariff-protected industry sprouted up.[29]

Building a Social Democracy

In the middle 1930s, the Western democracies began to shift the elite-favoring policies of laissez-faire capitalism to social democracy. It was a clear alternative to fascism and communism, which were firmly in place in various parts of the world by the late 1930s. A **social democracy** is where a country has some government management of the economy, safety net provisions, such as social insurance and social security, and labor rights. Every industrial nation developed similar social plans. Even the U.S., a country that boasted of rugged individualism as its core principle, turned to a limited social democracy. These benefits freed people from the worries of a modern, capitalist society and cushioned the cruel booms and busts of the market place.

Corporations in the social democracies of the 1930s largely backed the democratic reforms. Known as **welfare capitalism**, they quickly realized that their contributions to unemployment, pension programs, and social insurance did not affect their competitive advantages, since other Western nations were doing the same, and there was limited global competition at this point. Especially during the 1930s, many corporate leaders came to support, or at least not to oppose, social reform.

The **classical economic order**, based on the gold standard and limited government, was swept away on all fronts during the 1930s. The British economist John Maynard Keynes (1883-1946) helped shape the shift from laissez-faire capitalism to social democracy and managed capitalism. He disagreed with the classical economic order that said free markets would automatically provide full employment as long as workers were flexible in their wages. Instead, Keynes said that consumer **demand** for goods and services determined economic activity and that not enough demand could lead to long periods of high unemployment. He thought governments should take action in the economy to soften the boom and bust cycles of capitalism. Keynesian policies were important in the Western democracies, and these countries adopted them from the 1930s to the 1970s. For example, the American government's expenditures for building the interstate highway system in 1956 helped national commerce and indirectly fueled worker demand for goods and services.

The economic systems of the world – social democratic capitalism, communism, and fascist self-sufficiency – clashed on the global battlefield of World War II (1939-1945). The world had never seen a war of such global scope and horror. At the end, the defeated fascist economies lay in ruins, while the Allied victors promoted their favored economic forms: communism and social democratic (managed) capitalism. Even though devastated after the war, the Soviet Union was not about to submit to the economic lead of the U.S. and its managed form of capitalism.

Questions to Consider

1. What were the alternatives to laissez-faire capitalism in the 1930s? Why did they emerge?

THE POST WORLD WAR II ECONOMY (1945-1970s)

In the spirit of wanting to avoid another Great Depression and world war, the major world economies met to discuss the post-war economic order. In July 1944, nearly 1,000 delegates from more than 40 countries gathered at Mount Washington Hotel in the New Hampshire resort of Bretton Woods. Over the next three weeks, under the leadership of Keynes, the delegates made plans for a postwar economic order, simply called Bretton Woods. The delegates forged three long-lasting institutions to stabilize the post-war order: the International Monetary Fund (IMF), General Agreement on Tariffs and Trade (GATT) and the World Bank (all discussed later). Some delegates talked of a return to the gold standard; instead, they settled for a modified dollar/gold standard. Fixed at $35 to an ounce of gold since 1934, many felt the dollar was a good monetary anchor for international trade, finance, and investment. The compromise brought stability to the world economy for 25 years. It also meant that labor was a powerful force in shaping policies that benefitted them. During the post-war era, prices would not be adjusted on the backs of labor.

The post-war years turned out to be a golden age for nations across the globe. Prosperity increased for many, and economic progress appeared to be limitless. Aside from an over-hanging shadow of nuclear self-destruction, it was generally a time of optimism and confidence in the future.

1. The Golden Age of Capitalism

In the classical era of global capitalism, the elite generally had little concern for social or moral issues but hailed the market as a solution to all problems. In fact, they were against policies to lessen poverty. After the war an ethical shift occurred. The West's policies aimed to integrate market economies with more equal social policies in a new social democratic state.[30] Although imperfectly realized, this ethic continued until the 1980s, when a turn to a neoliberal philosophy and ethic took place.

Managed capitalism reigned during the golden age in the 1950s and 1960s. Some state-owned enterprises, usually large public services, such as energy, electricity, and transportation, coexisted with small businesses and free markets. Government was involved in the economy, offering a broad social safety net and supporting powerful labor movements. The result was a blend of active markets, strong governments, big business, and organized labor. This order oversaw the most rapid rates of economic growth and the most economic stability in modern history.[31] All prospered in this arrangement, but labor made the greatest strides. In contrast to the despair of the 1930s, the golden age was a time of order and optimism.

Soviet Union Premier Nikita Khrushchev and United States Vice President Richard Nixon debate the merits of communism versus capitalism in a model American kitchen at the American National Exhibition in Moscow in July 1959. Unlike the Soviet Union, consumerism fueled growth in the U.S.

2. The Golden Age of Communism and Socialism

The communist and socialist nations made the case that central planning needed to replace global and national markets. They thought that the needs of poor people and poor countries for equality and a better standard of living could not be met by integration with world markets but by getting rid of markets and adopting a command economy. From 1948-1973, the centrally-planned economies, such as the Soviet Union and Cuba, did quite well, and the results impressed many unhappy with the inequities of capitalism. Illiteracy dropped, and education improved. Medical care was free, and many socialist countries had more doctors and hospital beds per person than did core capitalist nations. Infant mortality dropped, often below that of wealthier countries. Communists and socialists ruled one-third of the planet and had millions of devout followers.[32]

3. The Golden Age for the Middle and Periphery Countries

There were two economic approaches for the middle and periphery nations to take. Most countries turned toward the inward economic development of Import Substitution Industrialization (ISI). Others turned outward and promoted exports, such as in South Korea. The decision to adopt one or the other approach differed among countries.

The ISI countries largely closed themselves to foreign trade and either continued or started to industrialize. They met with general success. The newly independent colonies, likewise, kept out foreign goods and often foreign capital to build up their independent national economies. Latin American countries continued the ISI policies of the 1930s, and India and some African countries also restricted trade. ISI governments' aim was to make domestic manufacturing more profitable, and they provided tax breaks to investors in the favored industries, as well as cheap credit from government banks. These policies resulted in remarkable industrial development, but it was at the expense of the primary exporting sectors, such as farming and mining. Farmers and miners paid much more for the tariff-protected manufactured goods they consumed, but they had to sell their own products without government assistance at world market prices, which were usually low. Taxes on the primary exporting sector, in effect, subsidized favored national industries. ISI policies shifted resources and people from farming and mining to manufacturing, from the countryside to the cities, in an effort to help industry flourish.[33]

Designed and manufactured in Argentina, the Justicialist was part of President Juan Perón's effort to develop a local auto industry as part of ISI policies.

In the mid-1960s four East Asian countries, the so-called "Asian tigers" – South Korea, Taiwan, Singapore, and Hong Kong – tried a different form of ISI: they pushed exporting their manufactured goods to core countries. The East Asians turned to **export-oriented industrialization** (EOI) in part because they had few natural resources to export, and the only way to earn foreign currency was to export manufactured goods. They specialized in exporting labor-intensive goods, using their hard-working and large pool of cheap labor as their comparative advantage. To encourage exports their governments got involved in the economy, giving help to export industries. Government involvement created plenty of jobs, and low wages kept exports cheap. Their exchange rates were also undervalued to make their exports more competitive on the world market, which also resulted in depressing consumers' purchasing power.

For capitalists, communists/socialists, ISI and EOI nations, the early 1970s was the high-water mark of the postwar world economy. Almost all core industrialized nations, centrally-planned economies rich and poor, middle-developing countries, and former colonies grew rapidly and consistently. Prosperity reigned. But things were about to change.

Questions to Consider

1. Why did different economic models exist during the post-war years?
2. Why wasn't there a return to the classical era of laissez-faire capitalism?

THE CRISIS OF THE 1970s

The 1970s, like the 1930s, proved to be an important era in the world's economic history. Looking at all the following factors as a holistic system we can see how all contributed to the 1970s crisis, it is hard to pin-point the major one. The 1970s crisis revealed serious problems in the post-war economy. They all created a significant crisis of managed capitalism and the other economic models of the post-war era.

The United States' position as the superpower of the capitalist world was suddenly hit from all sides, and the Bretton Woods system lay in disorder. Would the ruling powers be able to patch together the old Bretton Woods order again? Or would the old order be overturned and a different one established? The answer in the turbulent 1970s was not clear. [34]

U.S. social movements

Debt and poverty in middle and periphery nations

Decline in U.S. international authority

Oil

Dollar and gold

Low labor productivity

International financial flows

Stagflation

Overcapacity

Crisis

1. The Dollar and Gold

Since 1944, the U.S. had been committed to the Bretton Woods system – the post-war international economic order. It was about to be undone. After 25 years of stability, the collapse of Bretton Woods unleashed a host of problems. Confidence in the dollar declined. Holders of dollars wanted to exchange them for gold, which led to a run on U.S. gold reserves. The dollar's fixed rate of $1= 1/35oz. of gold needed to be undone and the dollar devalued. In August 1971, the U.S. decided to take the dollar off gold, meaning that no longer was the dollar exchangeable with gold. The dollar dropped compared to other currencies by about 10 percent and devalued again by 10 percent in 1973. [35]

2. International Financial Flows

When the dollar/gold standard was undone, currencies were allowed to **float**. This is when a nation's currency value varies according to the foreign exchange market. One side effect of floating currencies was the growth of currency speculation and the return of international finance. It had been inactive since the Depression years, with governments managing their own domestic monetary policies. For example, if international financial markets had been active in the 1950s and 1960s, lower interest rates in France compared to Germany would have seen a stampede of investors to withdraw their money from their French investments to invest in Germany. Governments had capital controls to prevent currency speculation that could cause economic instability but because of the collapse of the Bretton Woods order, speculators could now move money around the world in search of profits. [36]

3. Overcapacity

By the mid-1970s, a key problem for the core economies was **overcapacity** or overproduction of goods. There is a tendency for capitalist economies to build up more capacity to produce goods and services than the population's ability to consume them. Overcapacity was a result of vigorous production in the U.S. and Europe and added production from industrial powerhouses Germany and Japan that quickly recovered after the war. Also, newly industrialized countries like Brazil and South Korea added to overproduction. Yet, incomes limited the demand for all the consumer items produced. Thus, overcapacity resulted in a steady decline in profitability for business.[37]

4. Stagflation

Inflation picked up in the U.S. in the late 1960s, going from about 3 percent in 1966 to nearly 6 percent in 1971. These rates were considered high at the time. Inflation spiked to over 10 percent in 1974 and again from 1979 to 1981. Adding to the economic misery, the unemployment rate topped 8 percent in 1975 and reached nearly 10 percent in 1982. Taxes needed to go up and federal spending needed to be reduced to cool down an overheated economy. But neither happened.[38]

Growth in the core countries slowed. Governments tried to stimulate their economies by increasing spending, but then inflation raged. The economy seemed trapped in the new, cleverly-termed nightmare of "**stagflation**:" a combination of low economic growth and high unemployment (stagnation) with high rates of inflation. Policymakers seesawed back and forth between trying to solve high inflation and then trying to solve high employment. Nothing seemed to work.

5. Low Labor Productivity

Another problem was that the combined effects of rising wages and declining productivity growth resulted in large increases in labor costs per unit of output. While unit labor costs were constant in the first half of the 1960s, they grew at nearly 2 percent per year from 1966 to 1967, and at over 6 percent per year from 1968 to 1969. These rising labor costs, in turn, ate into business profits and added to inflation.[39]

6. Oil

The increase in the price of oil contributed to economic uncertainty and inflation. Some estimates show that the increase in the price of oil accounted for 25 percent of the inflationary surge of the period. To some, the world price of oil had lagged behind inflation for decades, and was merely "catching up" in the 1970s.[40] I remember paying only 25 cents a gallon to fill up my car in the late 1960s. My Mustang's mpg (miles per gallon) was not a concern to me since a couple of dollars would fill up the tank! But the situation

Line at a gas station in Maryland, USA, June 15, 1979. The oil embargoes in the 1970s contributed to the crisis of the 1970s.

changed in the mid-1970s when I had to wait in line to fill up my car. By the 1960s, the major oil producing nations were tired of supplying cheap oil to the core nations and formed the **Organization of Oil Producing Countries** (OPEC) that regulated the price and production of oil. Since oil supplied half to three-fourths of the industrial world's energy, oil importing countries were at OPEC's mercy.

7. The Decline of U.S. International Authority

The U.S. continued to be a major superpower in the world through the 1970s but it no longer enjoyed the dominance it had once experienced. The recovery of manufacturing in Western Europe and Japan meant more competition for U.S. firms in industries like steel and automobiles. Also, U.S. decline in the periphery undermined U.S. companies' easy access to cheap materials and energy resources. For example, the 1973 OPEC embargo of Western buyers and the following oil-price hike was during a low point in U.S. power, just after its defeat in Vietnam.[41]

8. Social Movements in the United States

Mass social movements of the 1960s and 1970s – civil rights, women's liberation, anti-war, gay rights, anti-nuclear, consumer rights, Native American rights and environmental concerns – contributed to the crisis of the 1970s. Increased pressure for social reform gave rise to greater government regulation of private business. Before, government agencies had just regulated specific industries such as railroads, trucking, telecommunications, utilities, and banks, but new social regulations, including environment, consumer-protection, occupational safety and health, and anti-discrimination laws, affected all companies. Although corporations were against the new regulations, it was a way for the government to respond to demands for reform without more government spending.[42]

9. Debt and Poverty in the Middle and Periphery Nations

With the return of international finance, middle and periphery nations could borrow money from private international bankers. And borrow money they did. Tens of billions of dollars a year flowed from banks and bondholders in the core nations to the borrowing middle and periphery nations. Inflation exploded. Their debts and interest payments soared.

ISI national economies were breaking under a number of problems. ISI nations favored industry over agriculture, which worsened rural poverty in countries that were heavily rural. Farmers migrated to the cities to look for jobs in the new industries. But ISI growth was very capital-intensive, and industrialists did not need much labor. Poverty awaited farmers who flooded into the cities seeking non-existent jobs in factories. ISI countries often ended up as dual economies. On one hand, skilled workers earning fairly high wages worked in industries; while on the other hand, government policy froze out a majority of struggling farmers and urban poor from the modern economy.

The socialist economies primarily relied on the export of natural resources – petroleum, gold, timber, minerals– but these would not be enough to pay for necessary imports. Although the socialist countries were not in crisis in the 1970s, signs warned of problems ahead. Socialist reform programs had stalled, and the central planners struggled with poor living standards, lagging technology, and declining growth rates. The 1970s signaled that the glory days of socialism would soon be over.[43]

The Uncertainty of the 1970s

The postwar order (1948-1973) had achieved its goals. The capitalist countries got economic integration, coupled with a welfare state and a well-managed economy. Some of the middle and periphery countries built their industrial base, along with protection from foreign influence. The socialist countries got rapid industrial and economic growth and a somewhat equal distribution of income. But by the late 1970s, these goals had become more difficult for all three groups. Global economic integration prevented a core nation's management of its own national economy, ISI nations experienced periodic crises and inequality, and central planning in the socialist nations slowed economic growth. The way forward was not clear.[44]

The late 1970s and early 1980s looked like the 1930s. Different interest groups fought each other over how to restructure national and global economies. There were the nationalists and globalists, free marketers and managed capitalism supporters; there were leftists who wanted socialism and rightists who wanted less government. Compromise appeared impossible. When the dust settled, it was the political right, the free-market supporters, who had gathered political and popular support. It wasn't an over-night victory, the right had been working on its agenda throughout the 1970s and even before, but its victory was decisive and shaped the economic and political landscape to the present day.

THE SHIFT TO THE RIGHT

The crisis of the 1970s marked the end of the "Golden Age" and the rise of neoliberal capitalism. Neoliberals wanted an end to social welfare programs, deregulation, and labor unions. The right drew on currents in U.S. political thought of an imagined past of individual independence and freedom. It blamed government regulation, taxation, and social programs for what it thought to be the economic and moral decay of society. It tapped into and fueled a backlash against the civil rights and women's movements. It also drew on the power of patriotism, since many Americans thought that their country was in decline. The right promised to restore the country to its rightful place of global supremacy.[45]

Even though many Americans supported the turn to the right, it was largely a movement of the powerful. Some of the very largest corporations organized a campaign to make sure that they settled the crisis in a way that favored them. First, they set up "think tanks" which outlined a conservative economic agenda. Second, they stepped up their lobbying efforts of friendly government officials and put money into supportive business organizations, such as the U.S. Chamber of Commerce. Third, they financed conservative candidates for public office. These efforts in the 1970s played a big role in bringing about the "turn to the right."[46]

A leader of the conservative revolution was President Ronald Reagan (1981-1989).

A new economic era dawned at the beginning of the 1980s. Driving the economy into two deep recessions and raising unemployment to nearly 11 percent, the conservatives tamed inflation but shifted the balance of power from the working and middle classes to investors and the financial sector. They gradually displaced the managed, social democratic form of capitalism followed for over four decades in the U.S. with an agenda similar to the classical era just under 100 years ago. It would fall to Republican Ronald Reagan, elected president in a decisive showing in November 1980, to forge a new economic agenda in the U.S. The new economic agenda had a new leader and a new name, "the Reagan Revolution."

CONCLUDING INSIGHTS: HISTORICAL ROOTS OF THE GLOBAL ECONOMY

The crisis of the 1970s had ended with the emergence of a neoliberal version of capitalism. It was a well-planned change to a system that benefitted specific groups of people. As we have seen in history, different groups of people have clashed with each other over who gets government support to pass policies and laws to benefit them. The golden era of post-war capitalism in the U.S. was a time when there was a balancing act among government, labor, the middle class, and business interests. Although not perfect, all groups generally profited from the cooperation. Yet, many business groups felt they were limited in their ability to make more profits. Big business interest groups organized and funded an agenda to take the lead in shaping the future economic system. For them, their hard work and investments paid off.

As the world's leading economy, the U.S. had a more significant role in shaping the global economy than other countries. Three dimensions to the global economy took shape out of the disorder of the 1970s – neoliberalism, economic globalization, and financialization. All three are intricately connected. It will be our job in this book to pull apart these three economic dimensions and see how each one functions and what its impact is. These three dimensions will be the subject of the rest of the book.

CHAPTER THREE

The Neoliberal Stew:
A Dozen Essential Ingredients

"Hear me, people: We have now to deal with another race – small and feeble when our fathers first met them, but now great and overbearing. Strangely enough they have a mind to till the soil and the love of possession is a disease with them. These people have made many rules that the rich may break but the poor may not. They take their tithes from the poor and weak to support the rich and those who rule."

--- *Chief Sitting Bull*

Chief Sitting Bull (1831-1885) was a Hunkpapa Lakota Sioux holy man who led his people as a tribal chief during years of resistance to U.S. government policies.

Today is a confusing time. We are often puzzled about the economy because different events, such as the shortage of well-paying jobs, seem unconnected to economic globalization; the manufacturing boom in China seems unconnected to the financial crisis; and the hollowing out of factories in the U.S. seems unconnected to neoliberalism. But they are all connected. All three dimensions of the global economy – neoliberalism, economic globalization, and financialization – are happening today and are interconnected.

Let's now turn to the first dimension of the global economy – neoliberalism – the subject of this chapter and the next. In these two chapters we will look at neoliberalism primarily in the U.S. In this chapter, we mix the 12 essential ingredients of neoliberal capitalism into a neoliberal stew.

THE PHILOSOPHY OF NEOLIBERALISM

Here is a refresher of the definition of neoliberalism. It is a version of capitalism favoring free trade, privatization, deregulation, and limited government. Conservative think tanks were hard at work during the 1970s drawing from past events and coming up with new ideas about neoliberalism. They called their ideas the free market or free trade, since the term free is appealing to most Americans. The conservatives certainly don't call it neoliberalism. But I will use the term neoliberalism since it is used more in academic circles. The first step in understanding neoliberalism is to describe its philosophy.

Neoliberals draw upon the works of free-market thinkers such as Frederich Hayek and Milton Friedman. Neoliberal commentators put their ideas into a language that made Americans think that the old system of managed capitalism was broken, and neoliberalism would benefit them. The backers of neoliberalism were extremely lucky to have the gifted communicator President Ronald Reagan to do the honors of explaining these new ideas. In the UK, the forceful Prime Minister Margaret Thatcher won over many supporters in her country and around the world to the neoliberal cause. It seemed a sensible solution to the failed policies of the 1970s. As Reagan exclaimed, "It was morning again in America."

In the 1970s, neoliberals framed managed capitalism with its business regulations and policies supporting the working and middle classes as a failure. They pitched neoliberalism as the solution to all economic woes. Even though neoliberalism dated back to the classical era of the late 19th century, alongside some of the failing economies of the 1970s, it looked like a practical alternative. The economies of the world encountered difficulties in the 1970s and early 1980s – socialism, communism, Import Substitution Industrialization (ISI), and managed capitalism. Neoliberals glowingly promoted their system as much more efficient and democratic than other systems. But there needed to be more to it than merely saying the other economic systems didn't work anymore. Neoliberalism needed a founding theorist, like Karl Marx was to communism/socialism and John Maynard Keynes was to managed capitalism.

Milton Friedman, an economics professor, rose to the occasion and provided the intellectual underpinnings of neoliberalism. Born in New York City, Milton Friedman (1912-2006) was a well-known supporter of what he called free markets. As a professor at the University of Chicago (1946-1977), he headed the "Chicago School" of economics, known for their rejection of Keynesian ideas. In his books, Friedman made the case for free markets to a general audience. In keeping with the 19th century classical era's economic principles, he opposed government regulation. In 1976, he was awarded the Nobel Prize in economics. He served as an adviser to President Ronald Reagan in the 1980s. His weekly columns for *Newsweek* magazine (1966–84) were well-read and were influential among political and business leaders and the general public. Throughout the 1980s and 1990s, Friedman continued to write editorials and appear on television championing the neoliberal cause. Among other places, he advised the government leaders of Eastern Europe, Chile, and China on the benefits of neoliberalism. He was a much-admired and influential economist who was active in his profession until his death at the age of 94 in 2006.

Alan Greenspan and the Federal Reserve

Alan Greenspan, 13th chairman of the Federal Reserve, a supporter of neoliberalism.

Alan Greenspan, the chairman of the Federal Reserve from 1987-2006, was influential in financial circles and a supporter of Friedman's ideas. He used the powers of the Fed to advance the neoliberal agenda. Born in New York City in 1926, he became a talented clarinet player and a professional jazz saxophonist in college. He graduated New York University before heading an economics consulting firm in New York City in 1954. Early on, Greenspan was a friend and follower of writer Ayn Rand, a noted free-market libertarian of the 1950s and 1960s. By the 1970s, he advised presidents Richard Nixon and Gerald Ford on economic issues. In 1987, President Reagan named Greenspan Chairman of the Federal Reserve where he directed national monetary policy. He kept inflation at low levels but allowed the boom-and-bust of the so-called "dot-com" era of the 1990s to happen. He stepped down from the post in January 2006.

A brief history of the **Federal Reserve** at this point helps to show Greenspan's role as a neoliberal promoter. A comparison of Greenspan's policies with a former Federal Reserve Chairman during the Depression era, Marriner Eccles, shows the shift from managed capitalism to neoliberalism under Greenspan's watch. The Federal Reserve (called the Fed or central bank) is the central banking system of the United States. Created in 1913 under the administration of Woodrow Wilson, it was a response to a series of financial panics, in particular a severe panic in 1907. The roles and responsibilities of the Federal Reserve System have expanded and evolved over time. Its duties today are to conduct the nation's monetary policy, supervise and regulate banks, and keep the financial system stable. The Fed has, in theory, been an independent institution, staying above politics; the President appoints the chairman.

Marriner Eccles, the Fed chairman during the Great Depression of the 1930s, was a Republican, Mormon banker from Utah. He attended Brigham Young College but did not graduate and then served a Latter-Day Saints mission to Scotland. After the untimely death of his father, he took over the family's banking business; he became a millionaire by age 22. In 1932, the newly-elected President Franklin Roosevelt noted Eccles' business skills and appointed him to serve as Fed Chair (1934-1948). He was a leading architect of New Deal reforms and worked to have the Fed apply Keynesian principles. The Fed, when necessary, stimulated the economy to encourage faster growth and full employment. At other times it stabilized the economy by putting the brakes on economic activity to avoid inflation. Eccles basically invented the modern Federal Reserve, which had followed the inflexible gold standard during the 1920s.[1]

Eccles and Greenspan are like historic bookends on the shift in economic thinking from managed capitalism to neoliberalism. Greenspan cast aside Eccles and Roosevelt's managed capitalism and instead brought back classical era economic principles which held that markets can run the economy better than the government. Going against Keynesian ideas, Greenspan said the marketplace should determine wages and the consuming power of workers. He believed that the government should not get involved in the market to stimulate demand. This was the era of business, and its rules triumphed.[2]

Questions to Consider

1. Which Fed Chair's economic philosophy do you most agree with? Explain.

The Neoliberal Stew: A Dozen Essential Ingredients

You may have already gained a glimpse into what the principles of neoliberalism are all about. In order to see these principles interacting together, I have explained them as separate ingredients that when all simmered and mixed together result in a stew – a neoliberal stew. The rest of this chapter explains the 12 ingredients in more depth. Let's turn to this neoliberal stew and see if you think it is a tasty and satisfying stew or one that is a distasteful mixture that is no longer edible to Americans today.

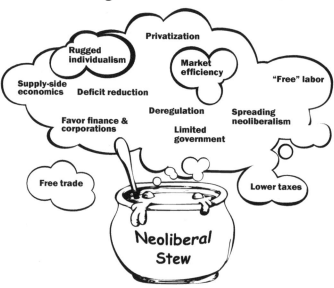

Ingredients in the Neoliberal Stew:

1. Free Trade – removal of trade tariffs, quotas, and subsidies.
2. Privatization – sale of state-owned enterprises, goods and services to private investors.
3. Deregulation – removal of many government regulations on business.
4. Limited Government – scale down the size of government; let the market make decisions.
5. Supply Side Economics – stimulate supply side of economy instead of demand side.
6. Lower Taxes – especially for the wealthy, who will invest their extra money to create jobs.
7. Reduce the Deficit – reduce budget deficits and overall government debt.
8. Markets Know Best – markets are better than the government in making economic decisions.
9. Support of Corporations and the Financial Sector – through favorable government policy.
10. "Free" Labor – the market determines wages and employment; destroys unions.
11. Rugged Individualism – let individuals shine, rather than create a shared community.
12. Spread Neoliberalism – it is the best system, so spread it around the world.

INGREDIENT #1: FREE TRADE

Free trade is the first ingredient in the neoliberal stew and one of its cornerstone principles. When we think of free trade, we imagine that there are no restrictions to trade, and any country can decide who it wants to trade with and who it does not. However, free trade really isn't free; it has rules – and lots of them. **Free trade** is the removal of import and export quotas and tariffs by the government. A reminder: the government places tariffs, duties or customs, on exports or imports. Free traders have also removed regulations on the flow of capital, which now moves from country to country at lightning speed. However, the U.S. and most countries control labor migration. With these policies in place, countries specialize in their comparative advantages, which free traders say helps everyone and is more efficient. Because of the removal of checks on trade, businesses can expand their markets around the world.

Free traders say that with the removal of tariffs, each country will produce specialized goods. A country that has plenty of capital will specialize in industrial goods because to set up a factory requires lots of money or capital, while a country that has lots of agricultural land will specialize in agricultural products. Today, for example, China specializes in producing labor-intensive manufactured goods because it has an abundant supply of labor willing to work long hours for low wages. When China started to industrialize, it did not have enough capital to set up manufacturing plants. It brought in profit-seeking investors from the West to take advantage of its cheap labor and lack of regulations.

Since an important ingredient in neoliberalism is free trade, it will help to briefly look at the debate in U.S. history. This debate is similar in other parts of the world as well. The debate between free trade and tariffs has often been a bitter one in U.S. history. It might be hard for you to imagine that in the past, different groups in the U.S. almost came to blows over the issue. Who benefits under free trade and who benefits under tariff policies is a hot topic in U.S. history.

A Brief History: Tariffs and Free Trade in the United States

The brilliant Alexander Hamilton (1789-1795) was the first U.S. Secretary of the Treasury. He said that competition from abroad hurt the creation of new industries. In order to build up new or infant industries, he explained, the government needed to protect them by adding tariffs on imported goods that competed with national industries. He pushed for high tariffs to protect the infant industries of the Northeast, which meant the country was less dependent on manufactured goods from Britain. Tariffs also added almost all the revenue to the U.S. Treasury. Thomas Jefferson opposed high tariffs and complained that tariffs raised the price of manufactured goods for consumers like his farmer supporters.

The infant industry argument shows how tariffs, quotas, and other regulations benefit new industries. This tariff protection allows industries to grow until they can compete on an equal footing with foreign competitors. For example, when the U.S. first started to industrialize in the early 1800s, Britain was ahead of the pack in the industrialization race. Since Britain was the world's leading economic power in the early 19th century, Britain liked free trade because it benefitted its economy. It was efficient in manufacturing and knew how to keep costs low. Thus, Britain could produce industrial goods more cheaply than the U.S. or, for that matter, anyone else in the world at the time. The U.S. wanted to protect its infant industries from British competition so the U.S. could grow and provide jobs for its citizens. The U.S. placed a tariff on imported goods from Britain. The tariff made

Britain's goods more expensive, which would steer U.S. consumers into purchasing American made products. Although this helped U.S. manufacturers, provided jobs, and added money to the treasury, consumers had to pay more for the tariff-protected goods.

In the U.S., the clash between free traders and protectionists carried over into the decades leading up to the Civil War (1861-1865). The debate pitted the industrialized North against small farmers in the West and the slave-holding plantation owners of the South. The free traders said tariffs only helped the manufacturers, while the protectionists said that by helping manufacturing, the tariffs were benefiting the country as a whole. Essentially, they were both right. The tension surrounding the tariff issue, as well as slavery, continued. The tension finally broke out in the Civil War.[3]

With the second Industrial Revolution in high gear in the late 1800s, the U.S. was beginning to close in on Britain's industrial lead. The U.S. continued its tariff policy which still split the country. The Republicans, the party of business, supported protective tariffs. Meanwhile, farmers and miners remained bitter towards tariffs and supported the Democrats, the party of free trade.

Democratic President Woodrow Wilson supported the passage of the Underwood Tariff bill in 1913. Tariffs on manufactured goods dropped from 44 percent to 25 percent. Since tariffs were a large part of the government's budget, the government needed additional revenue. The passage of the 16th amendment and a federal income tax solved this problem. With the onset of the Great Depression, Republicans passed the Smoot-Hawley Bill in 1930, once again raising tariffs.

By the end of World War II, it was clear that free trade would be in America's best interest. The U.S. had the world's strongest economy, accounting for 50 percent of all world production. With production continuing to grow, the U.S. needed new markets for its goods. Since the U.S. essentially controlled the global marketplace, free trade would help it. In the 1970s, the U.S. economy started to slip from its century of economic dominance. In 1971, the U.S. had its first trade deficit (imported more than exported) since 1893. Growing trade deficits in the 1980s were the first signs that free trade might not be in the country's best interests. Import tariffs dropped from a 1973 average of 12 percent to today's average of around 2 percent. Low tariffs resulted in lost jobs and declining tax revenues.[4]

Yet, in the 1980s, the neoliberal agenda was gaining ground and supporters said that instead of less free trade, there needed to be more. They promised that more free trade would speed up

A Systems Approach to Examining the Tariff Issue.
A shoe manufacturer provides a good example for this systems exercise in deciding who benefits from tariffs and who does not. A tariff on imported shoes makes those shoes more expensive, which benefits national shoe manufacturers because they can charge higher prices. Yet, the shoe-wearing consumer pays more. So the public assumes that free trade is best for them. But the free traders fail to measure the impact of tariff protection on the shoe manufacturing plant, which affects the whole community in which the plant is located. Without shoe-making jobs, many people in the community are unemployed, which hurts businesses, the tax base, and the community. If the unemployed live in the 21st century, many would draw on unemployment insurance financed through taxes and fees. Although the consumer might pay more for the tariff-protected shoes (since the shoes would probably be priced somewhat higher than a tariff-free import), what the above example shows is that the extra "tax" that the consumer pays for the shoes is off-set by other indirect taxes that citizens must pay as a result of the loss of well-paying jobs at the local manufacturing plant. Also, the U.S. and other countries have anti-trust laws to prevent the formation of monopolies. In addition, the tariff revenues go into the U.S. Treasury, easing the budget deficit. Thus, using a systems approach, tariffs on selected items most likely would be beneficial to workers, the community, state, and nation, and to consumers in the long run.

economic growth because business would have more entry into overseas markets and resources. Free traders point to two negative results of tariffs. First, tariffs raise the prices of goods for consumers. Second, tariffs make protected industries, in effect, artificially profitable. Tariffs benefit corporate monopolies because tariffs protect their industries from outside competition.[5]

This brief history on tariffs sheds some light on the debate today. Different groups argue for policies that benefit them. Today labor unions want tariff protection because competing products from low-wage countries undercut their wages and eliminate jobs. In the 1950s and 1960s, though, unions favored free trade since they were eager to have their products sold on the world market, which meant more jobs and higher wages for them. Today, many businesses favor free trade since it is profitable for them to ship production overseas to take advantage of a foreign country's lower wages and lower environmental standards. They turn around and import these foreign-made goods into the U.S. without tariffs. Consumers like the lower prices resulting from free trade, but if they lose their jobs because of free trade policies they might have a different opinion.

Questions to Consider

1. Do you favor protectionism or free trade? What are the benefits and drawbacks of each one?
2. Today, who benefits under protectionism? Under free trade?

North American Free Trade Agreement

There are many free trade agreements between nations. I have selected one, NAFTA, as an example to show the impact of free trade in North America. The governments of Canada, Mexico, and the U.S. signed the **North American Free Trade Agreement (NAFTA)** on January 1, 1994. The goal of NAFTA was to eliminate tariffs and regulations on investments and trade between the three countries. The agreement created the world's largest free trade area at the time, which linked 454 million people producing over $17.2 trillion worth of goods and services in 2010.[6]

Critics of NAFTA say it has benefitted business owners and elites in all three countries. But it has hurt farmers in Mexico, who saw crop prices fall because of cheap imports from the U.S. It has also hurt U.S. manufacturing workers, who have lost jobs to factories across the Mexican border. In addition, critics say that NAFTA has contrib-

NAFTA signing ceremony, October 1992 in Mexico.

uted to the rising levels of social inequality in both the U.S. and Mexico. Supporters of NAFTA say that it has been positive for Mexico, which has seen its poverty rates fall and income rise.[7] However, in Mexico in 2002, half of the people were living in poverty and 20 percent in extreme poverty, about the same level as before the passage of NAFTA in 1994.[8]

NAFTA rules have displaced over 2 million Mexican farmers from the countryside.[9] The farmers have fled to cities to try to get work or migrated either legally or illegally to the U.S. to find jobs. In a 2007 trip to the farms and villages of Mexico, I saw small villages hurt by the effects of NAFTA. Larger farmers or corporations bought up farms, while the displaced farmers looked for work elsewhere. Women, children, and the elderly often remained in the villages; some men returned, but many did not. Family and village stability bore the grim effects of these absences. One of the purposes of NAFTA was that it would spur economic development in the three countries and reduce poverty in Mexico. It does not appear that NAFTA has met these goals.

INGREDIENT #2: PRIVATIZATION

Have you ever gone to a state or national park and bought something to eat at one of its concession stands? Or have you driven down a major highway and suddenly realized that you had to pay a toll? Or have you noticed that the big garbage truck that picks up your garbage each week no longer has the name of your city on the door panel but the name of a private business instead? All of these examples have to do with privatization, our second ingredient in the neoliberal stew. **Privatization** is the sale of state-owned enterprises, goods and services to private investors. Put another way, it is a transfer of assets from the government to the private sector. This includes the sale of key industries, railroads, toll highways, electricity, schools, hospitals, prison management, fresh water, mining rights and many others. Although carried out in the name of greater efficiency, privatization has had the effect of concentrating wealth even more in the investor class and making the public pay even more for its services and needs.

This is a good time to introduce two different economic sectors. The **private sector** is businesses owned by individuals or corporations, and the **public sector** is ownership held by the government for the people. For example, all the people of a nation collectively own national, state and local parks. Privatization runs a very broad range, sometimes leaving very little government involvement and at other times creating partnerships between government and the private sector.

Privatization accompanied the expansion of capitalism around 1500. John Locke (1632-1704), an English Enlightenment thinker, wrote about property rights in 1688. He stated that ownership was lawful if men would use their own labor to make "unproductive" land into "productive" land.[10] Thus, the principle of private ownership became a central part of the Western tradition.

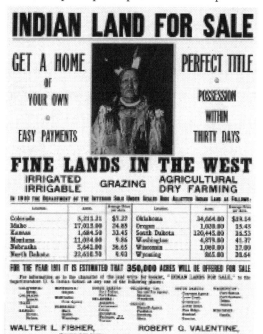

A 1911 ad offering "allotted Indian land" for sale as a result of the Dawes Act.

This act of converting unproductive land to productive land by one's own labor helped to justify the American conquest of lands held by indigenous peoples. The American settlers claimed they were taking "unused waste land" and working it into productive farm land, which they felt made their ownership legal. An example of early privatization of Native American land was the 1887 **Dawes Act** in Oklahoma. The act divided commonly held tribal lands into individually-owned parcels for the native people, while settlers and the railroads took ownership of the remaining "surplus" lands.

Fast forward to after World War II in 1945. At this time, many countries in Europe and some in the U.S. had a variety of public services, which the government provided for its citizens. These services generally included electricity, highways, public transportation, telephone, water, sanitation, broadcasting, fire protection, police, prisons, courts, military, research and development (R&D), education, health care, and social security. Since these services were essential to a certain standard of living, and it was difficult to make a profit without compromising the services, they did not fit very well into a capitalist system. Thus, the people decided the government should carry out these essential services for their benefit. These public services also required an initial large capital investment – railroad tracks, electric power grids, highway construction, sanitation facilities and others – which does not encourage private sector investment or competition. That is why the government took on the role of providing these public services to as many people as possible in order to improve their standard of living at a reasonable cost.[11]

The 1980s marked a sweep of neoliberal changes. One of these changes was the privatization or attempt to privatize many of the public services that the government provided for its citizens. Neoliberals pressured nations with managed capitalist, communist, or socialist economies to privatize, or sell to the private sector, many of their large state-owned enterprises. Neoliberals frame government as too inefficient and corrupt to provide these valuable services and promise the private sector would do a better job at a lower cost. They claim that customers will have a choice in deciding for themselves which service provider to use.

Those on the other side of the debate say that privatization is not more efficient or cost effective but is simply a scheme to shift wealth from the public treasury to private hands. The neoliberal message says only the private sector can deliver a quality product at the lowest possible price. However, privatization is more complex. Whether to have certain public services and how to deliver them has

False Assumptions about Privatization

1. Neoliberals say governments are broke because public services and tax dollars are mismanaged. Actually governments have lost major sources of revenue from lower tax rates, particularly from wealthy individuals, an economic downturn, and increased spending on wars, the military, and Medicare.

2. Neoliberals argue that privatization would do away with government waste and fraud. This statement assumes that the private sector is free from these problems. Waste and fraud will happen when the private sector provides services to the public. In fact, there are more chances for waste and fraud since there is less government oversight.

3. Neoliberals assert that market forces and competition make sure that the private sector delivers a higher quality service at a lower cost than the public sector. Simple math should tell us it's impossible for the private sector to deliver the same service for less and make a profit, as well. Private companies must make a profit for their investors, and they subtract this profit from the money available to provide the service.

4. Neoliberals maintain that it is impossible to get rid of bad public employees that don't care about their jobs. Public employees are not necessarily bad workers. If public workers don't do their jobs, employers can fire them.

5. Neoliberals hold that private corporations are more efficient and eliminate waste. However, the rate of corporate bankruptcy is high, and if it does occur, the services will stop.

6. Neoliberals proclaim that money paid in taxes would make us all richer if spent in the private sector. We get a lot of services for our tax dollars: public schools, street cleaning, sanitation, police and fire protection, animal control, public parks and zoos. Every time we take an elevator, buy food, or eat a meal in a restaurant we can feel safer because of government inspectors. The list of services governments regulate goes on and on.

7. Neoliberals state that all the studies show that privatization is better. But where do these studies come from? Privatization supporters have spent a lot of time and money telling the public that privatization is better. Yet, they rarely publicize their failures.

an impact on all of us. As the U.S. and the world move towards increased privatization, it's helpful to look at the other side of the issue. The textbox on the previous page shows some commonly held false assumptions that neoliberals hold about privatization.

Privatization of Water

A study in 2009 found that privatizing municipal water systems threatens jobs and hurts local economies. It found that while multinational corporations often claim to reduce operational costs, they do so by cutting corners, downsizing jobs and lowering wages. Corporate utility take-overs lead to an average job loss of 35 percent and workers earn 7.4 percent less at private utilities and accrue fewer benefits than their public sector counterparts.[13]

Questions to Consider

1. Would you support the privatization of your municipal water supply? Why or why not?

INGREDIENT #3: DEREGULATION

Deregulation is the removal or reduction of government rules and regulations that regulate market forces. Neoliberals say that fewer and simpler regulations will lead to more competition, higher productivity, more efficiency, and lower prices. They are against regulating wages, working conditions, business operations, and the environment. Neoliberals say laws protecting workers, consumers, or the environment should be left to the market. In the global marketplace, they believe that weak labor, consumer, or environmental standards are a country's competitive advantage.[14]

Crowd gathering on Wall Street during the stock market crash of 1929.

The history of deregulation goes back to the 1920s. During this time, large investors repeatedly manipulated the unregulated stock market. Shady investors purchased a good stock, such as the popular Radio Corporation of America (RCA), and then they put out favorable rumors about it. After the stock went up in price, investors sold it and collected huge profits. Today, this is illegal. The stock market just kept going up in the late 1920s. Of course, we all know what goes up must come down, and down the stock market came with a crashing thud in October 1929, marking the onset of the Great Depression.

Because of financial excesses in the 1920s, government officials recognized the need for large-scale financial reform. They saw terrible banking abuses in the 1920s and passed a number of regulations to prevent repeated abuses. They regulated commercial and investment banks, brokerages, stock exchanges, and the accounting profession, as well as public services. The most significant of the Depression-era regulations was the **Glass-Steagall Act** of 1933. The act prevented a single company from offering investment banking, commercial banking, and insurance services. It set up a "firewall" separating these services because of possible abuses and fraud. Aimed at maintaining a stable economy, the **Securities Exchange Act** of 1934 regulated the trading of stocks and bonds. Reforms continued after World War II.

The deregulation craze of the 1980s sparked a series of acts carried out by neoliberals. Deregulation of the transportation industry in the 1970s marked its first steps. A notable banking deregulation law, the **Riegle-Neal Interstate Banking and Branching Efficiency Act** of 1994, allowed interstate mergers between banks. The 1996 Telecommunications Act deregulated the broadcasting industry. The act amended the Communications Act of 1934, which did not allow cross-ownership of media outlets. Now a radio station could own a television station or both could own a newspaper or internet company. A wave of mergers followed deregulation, which resulted in a decline in the number of commercial radio stations. Although it was supposed to increase competition, this act actually decreased competition. One of the most significant deregulation acts, as we will find out in chapters 7 and 8, was the **Gramm-Leach-Bliley Act** of 1999, which repealed the long-standing Glass-Steagall Act. This act allowed commercial banks, investment banks, securities firms, and insurance companies to consolidate.

Enron

The energy giant Enron is an example of the dire effects of deregulation. Formed in 1985, Enron grew in 15 years to become America's 7th largest company, employing 21,000 people in more than 40 countries. Enron started with two gas pipeline companies and grew under the management of Kenneth Lay. The business magazine *Fortune* named it the most ground-breaking company of the year for five consecutive years. It even bought the name of the Houston Astros' ballpark. Company revenues peaked in the year 2000 at $100 billion and a share price of $90.[15] In 2001, however, the public exposed Enron's success as a fraud. The scam included lying about its profits, hiding debt, and being part of a range of shady deals.

Enron's management found ways to scam the public and mislead federal regulatory agencies. One of the scams was the special-purpose entity (SPE) it created. The SPEs appeared profitable because they were unregulated, offshore business accounts that avoided taxation and sold assets to each other at much higher prices than the market price. They also hid a company's losses in unofficial accounting balance sheets. Enron's officers carried out trades to show that they were making billions of dollars in profits, while the company was actually losing money.

One of the most deceptive and costly of Enron's practices was the California electricity crisis of 2000 and 2001. Enron, through illegal means, caused the state to have a shortage of electricity and large-scale blackouts. Enron's energy traders took power plants offline for maintenance in days of peak demand to increase the price of electricity. They sold power at high prices, sometimes up to 20 times its normal value. But these measures caused rolling blackouts that affected everyone. Ordinary California taxpayers picked up part of the Enron tab – $40 to $45 billion – as a result of electricity deregulation.[16]

Enron's scheming deals finally caught up with the company and it entered bankruptcy in December 2001. In 2002, its shares traded at 11 cents, a far cry from their $90 a share high. On May 25, 2006, the courts convicted CEO Kenneth Lay on ten counts of fraud. Arthur Andersen, once considered a respected accounting firm, was in on the illegal accounting practices, and surrendered its accounting license in 2002. Along with Enron's bankruptcy went millions of dollars in investors' savings, pensions and thousands of well-paying jobs.[17]

INGREDIENT #4: SMALL GOVERNMENT IS BEST

"Government is not a solution to our problem, government is the problem."
-- President Ronald Reagan First Inaugural Address, January 20, 1981.

President Ronald Reagan's simple sentence sums up the neoliberal view towards government. Neoliberals believed the economic problems of the 1970s were a result of big government: high taxes and too much regulation. To them the solution to economic problems was clear: downsize government, lower taxes, and deregulate.[18] Neoliberals strongly support limited government. They framed the debate about downsizing government as a way to "free private enterprise from government chains." Instead of the federal government, they sought to shift power to the states and the people. In 1981 Reagan made it clear that "we are a nation that has a government – not the other way around." Grover Norquist, a neoliberal adviser, once famously said: "Our goal is to shrink government to the size where we can drown it in a bathtub."[19]

President Ronald Reagan delivering his first inaugural address January 1981.

Small government supporters want to cut taxes. They want to do away with or reduce social service programs that have been added over the 20th century, such as providing allowances for housing, health care, education, the safety net for the poor, disability, social security, Medicare, and unemployment. Their purpose is to turn over these public social services to the private sector or state governments.

Neoliberals even want to stop government support for new infrastructure projects, such as high speed trains and maintenance of roads, bridges, and water pipes. For example, the U.S. Transportation Department had in the planning stages a high-speed rail network connecting the Midwest's largest cities, with the purpose of promoting commerce and rebuilding the hard-hit economy. After the 2010 mid-term elections, I heard on the radio that some neoliberal governors in Ohio and Wisconsin did not want a high-speed rail network in their states and were refusing federal funds for its construction. At first I was surprised to hear this, and then I thought that this is part of the neoliberal agenda: limit the size and role of government.[20] But neoliberals refuse to reduce or eliminate government spending for defense and security. They, however, generally don't oppose government subsidies and tax loopholes for business.

Despite Reagan's pledge to curb the size of government, he was not successful. In 1981, when Reagan made his anti-government speech, the federal government spent $678 billion; in 2006, it spent $2,655 billion. Inflation-adjusted spending increased in every year but two over the past 26 years.[21]

One of the ways in which government supports the economy is in the areas of research and development (R&D). Much of the technology-based economy has rested on the Internet, which government-funded research created. Advances in medicine and biology, just two examples, have depended upon government-funding. Between the 1950s and mid-1990s, federal government-funding accounted for 50-70 percent of the country's total research and development. Lacking such investments, the U.S. would not have been able to take the lead in key industries like computers, semiconductors, life sciences, the internet and aerospace.[22]

Questions to Consider

1. What do you think should be the role of the government in the economy?
2. How does the government impact your life? Is it a positive or negative impact?

INGREDIENT #5: SUPPLY-SIDE ECONOMICS

In 1981, neoliberals rejected the long-standing demand-side, Keynesian economic approach. Instead, they supported the fifth ingredient in the neoliberal stew: **supply-side economics**. This theory stresses the importance of tax cuts in encouraging economic growth. They believe that businesses and individuals will use their tax savings to create new and expand old businesses, which will increase prosperity and lower unemployment. This policy focuses on the total supply of goods and services rather than Keynesian policy, which says there must be demand for goods and services for economic growth.

Supply-siders say that government should make sure that free enterprise and competition flourish. They think the best government can do for the economy is to boost the supply-side – that is, favor wealth holders who will invest in new businesses. This logic has led to huge tax cuts for the wealthy and for business. For example, in 2010, neoliberals were against funding for unemployment insurance and government spending to stimulate the economy in a recession. They say that the government should not increase the amount of money going into the economy through the demand side, which is what these two programs would do. Instead, they supported tax cuts for the wealthy, which they believed would stimulate the supply-side of the economy through business creation. Keynesians, on the other hand, believed that if there is a downturn in the economy, the government should spend more to help create demand.

Critics say a key problem with the supply-side theory is that there is already an over-supply of goods and services compared to the demand, especially since the 2008 recession. Demand is not even throughout the world, since many of the world's poor do not have enough money to purchase goods and services. Therefore, demand is concentrated in the core countries, but many people are heavily in debt for over-consuming in the last three decades. Increasing an already over-abundant supply of goods and services, critics say, will not bring the U.S. out of recession.[23]

Questions to Consider

1. How has the recession affected people in your community?
2. To end the recession, what policy makes more sense to you, stimulate demand or supply-side?

INGREDIENT #6: LOWER TAXES

A sixth ingredient in the neoliberal stew is the reduction of taxes. Neoliberal policies give the wealthy more disposable income through tax cuts. They say higher incomes for the wealthy and higher business profits (because of lower wages) will lead to more investment and more jobs. The big question is: Has this policy worked? Actually, in the 1950s and 1960s, when tax rates for the wealthy and corporations were much higher than today, there was more of a reason to reinvest profits in a business to shelter it from high taxes. This resulted in more business reinvestment, more economic growth, and more jobs. Today, lower tax rates have put more money in the pockets of the wealthy but, in many cases, they have gone on consumer buying binges instead of investing in businesses. Consumer spending on expensive luxury items like cars, jewelry, yachts, and second homes has increased among the wealthy since the 1980s.

Lower taxes have resulted in a concentration of wealth among the top 10 percent of Americans, and particularly the top 1 percent. In 2008, the U.S. had the highest number of billionaires in the world: 355, or 45 percent of the world's total, worth more than $1 trillion. Yet, median income workers in 2006 paid a much higher combined rate in payroll taxes, income taxes, and sales taxes than they did in 1966.[24]

Though corporate profits are a higher fraction of GDP than ever before, the percentage of federal taxes corporations pay has dropped. Corporate taxes were 40 percent of total federal revenue in 1943; 16.1 percent in the1960s; 9.4 percent in the 1990s; and 7 percent today. Even though the highest corporate tax rate is 35 percent, it is easier than ever for business to avoid higher tax rates. After deductions and loopholes, the U.S. has one of the lowest tax rates on corporate profits in the world. But business groups continue to demand tax "relief" and claim that they need low taxes to be competitive.[25]

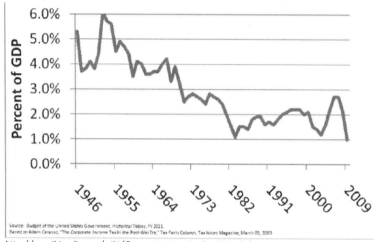

Corporate Income Tax as a Share of GDP, 1946-2009

Source: Budget of the United States Government, Historical Tables, FY 2011.
Based on Adam Carasso, "The Corporate Income Tax in the Post-War Era," Tax Facts Column, Tax Notes Magazine, March 03, 2003

http://en.wikipedia.org/wiki/Corporate_tax_in_the_United_States

Because of lower taxes on capital, ordinary workers and consumers take up the tax-shortage slack. Also, reduced tax revenues mean an increase in the federal deficit, as has happened since the 1980s. Because of large deficits, neoliberals call for cuts to social programs, which mostly hurt the poor.

Warren Buffett, one of the richest people in the world and a shrewd

"Stop Coddling the Super-Rich" by Warren Buffett.

"Our leaders have asked for 'shared sacrifice.' But when they did the asking, they spared me. I checked with my mega-rich friends to learn what pain they were expecting. They, too, were left untouched. While ... most Americans struggle to make ends meet, we mega-rich continue to get our extraordinary tax breaks. Some of us are investment managers who earn billions from our daily labors but are ... getting a bargain 15 percent tax rate. ... Legislators in Washington shower upon us financial blessings. ..It's nice to have friends in high places.

Last year my federal tax bill was $6,938,744. That sounds like a lot of money. But what I paid was only 17.4 percent of my taxable income – and that's actually a lower percentage than was paid by any of the other 20 people in our office. Their tax burdens ranged from 33 percent to 41 percent and averaged 36 percent. If you make money with money, as some of my super-rich friends do, your percentage may be a bit lower than mine. But if you earn money from a job, your percentage will surely exceed mine.

To understand why, you need to examine the sources of government revenue, last year about 80 percent of these revenues came from personal income taxes and payroll taxes. The mega-rich pay income taxes at a rate of 15 percent on most of their earnings but pay practically nothing in payroll taxes. It's a different story for the middle class: typically, they fall into the 15 percent and 25 percent income tax brackets, and then are hit with heavy payroll taxes to boot.

Back in the 1980s and 1990s, tax rates for the rich were far higher, and my percentage rate was in the middle of the pack... And to those who argue that higher rates hurt job creation, I would note that a net of nearly 40 million jobs were added between 1980 and 2000. You know what's happened since then: lower tax rates and far lower job creation.

I know well many of the mega-rich and, by and large, they are very decent people. They love America and appreciate the opportunity this country has given them... Most wouldn't mind being told to pay more in taxes as well, particularly when so many of their fellow citizens are truly suffering.... A billionaire-friendly Congress has coddled my friends and I long enough. It's time for our government to get serious about shared sacrifice."

Questions to Consider

1. What do you think about Warren Buffet's letter in the New York Times? Do you agree or disagree with his position? Why?
2. Why would a billionaire write such an editorial?

investor, caused quite a stir when he talked about the low tax rates the wealthy pay with an editorial in the *New York Times* in August 2011.

INGREDIENT #7: REDUCE THE DEFICIT

Our seventh ingredient, reduce the deficit, has been a hot topic. Many politicians have jumped on the deficit-cutting bandwagon. First of all, what is a deficit? A **deficit** is simply an excess of expenditure over revenue. It can get confusing because we often mix up the term "deficit" with the federal debt. Put simply, when the federal government raises less in taxes and other revenues than it spends, it must borrow the difference. Such annual borrowing is each year's deficit. The U.S. Treasury borrows that money by selling bonds, which are federal IOUs to the people that buy the bonds. Buyers of the bonds are lending money to the government.[27] The annual (yearly) budget can be a deficit or surplus; lately it has been a deficit, a big deficit. But President Clinton balanced the annual budget in 1998, and there was a surplus! The adding up of yearly deficits makes up the national debt. The national debt, or the federal or public debt, is the amount of outstanding debt of the U.S. through its history.

National debt is not necessarily a bad thing if the money is used to invest in a nation's people and their well-being. But most people feel it has ballooned too much in the 2000s. The national debt has increased by over $500 billion each year since 2003, with increases of $1 trillion in 2008, $1.9 trillion in 2009, and $1.7 trillion in 2010. As of September 9, 2011, the gross debt was $14.71 trillion, of which the general public held $10.07 trillion and $4.64 trillion was in government holdings such as the Social Security Trust Fund ($2.2 trillion in 2007).[28] The annual gross domestic product (GDP) as of June

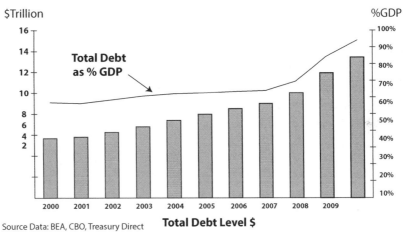

2010 Budget: Total Debt $ and % to GDP 2000-2011

Source Data: BEA, CBO, Treasury Direct

http://en.wikipedia.org/wiki/United_States_public_debt

2011 was $15.003 trillion with gross debt at a ratio of 98 percent of GDP.[29] Now, there are a lot of numbers for you to mull over.

How did the U.S. accumulate so much debt? Let's fast-forward the story of today's deficits in the U.S. to January 2001, as President Clinton was leaving office. If tax collections continued as expected, officials estimated that the government would run a surplus of more than $800 billion a year from 2009 to 2012. Today, the government ran a $1.2 trillion annual deficit in those years. That is roughly a $2 trillion swing coming from four broad categories.[30] To be fair, both political parties and presidents have added to the deficit problem. Let's look at how this happened.

1. The business cycle accounted for 37 percent of the $2 trillion swing. Both the 2001 and 2008 recessions and the 9/11 events resulted in reduced tax revenues, and safety-net programs for those

in need required more revenues. The two events meant the government would collect less in taxes in future years.

2. President George W. Bush's new legislation accounted for about 33 percent of the swing, such as tax cuts and the Medicare prescription drug plan.

3. President Obama extended some of Bush's policies that were about to expire, such as the two wars, tax cuts for households making less than $250,000, and tax cuts for the wealthy. Together with the Wall Street bailout, these figures account for 20 percent of the swing.

4. President Obama's new policies accounted for 7 percent of the swing, such as the stimulus bill signed in February 2009, while 3 percent came from new health care, education, and energy policies.

The solution to the deficit, though, is no mystery. It will involve some combination of tax increases and spending cuts and a re-evaluation of enormous war and military expenditures, as well as skyrocketing medical costs. Taxes will probably go up, and some government programs will become less generous. Reining in the deficits is and will continue to be one of the great political debates of the coming decade.

Questions to Consider

1. Do you think there is a debt problem? What do you think is the most sensible way to solve the deficit (debt) problem?

INGREDIENT #8: MARKETS KNOW BEST

The eighth ingredient in the neoliberal stew is the **Efficient Market Theory.** This theory means that markets are more efficient and accurate in pricing goods and services than the government. Adam Smith reasoned that free markets lead, as if by an "invisible hand," to efficient outcomes; that each individual, in following his or her own self-interest, advances the general interests. Neoliberals reason that, unlike the irrational government, markets are rational and efficient. They believe the market, by its very nature, has the key to unlock human enterprise which will spur economic growth, ultimately benefitting everyone.

The Efficient Market Theory has its critics. Research has long suggested that basic human nature does not mold to the narrow model of economic rationality. The classical economic model, as developed by Smith and others, uses rational human behavior as the basis for mathematical models. Proponents of this model think that rational human behavior is a scientific fact and use these models to make economic policy. But human emotions, according to some observers, are more dominant in guiding human behavior than reason. Along with a rejection of humans as rational robots, some say that markets are not rational either.

Even though markets do work well in certain sectors of the economy, in some sectors the market does not perform well. For example, markets do not perform well in the areas of health care; education from kindergarten through the university; security, such as the military, police forces, fire protection, and prisons; Social Security including disability insurance; some forms of transportation such as mass transit and roads; regulation of the environment; unemployment insurance; public charities; safety net for the poor; public necessities like water and sanitation; research and development; and the post office and mail delivery to all.[31] This means that government has a role to play in the economy. Contrary to neoliberal thought, markets cannot solve all the problems of modern society.

Questions to Consider

1. What would cause the markets to behave irrationally?

INGREDIENT #9: SUPPORT OF CORPORATIONS AND THE FINANCIAL SECTOR

The ninth ingredient in our neoliberal stew is the support of corporations and the financial sector through government policies, such as deregulation and favorable tax policies. A brief history of corporations gives us a context for the growth and power of corporations today.

North America's first corporations in the 17th century were the Massachusetts Bay Company and the Hudson Bay Company. They each had a charter life of 20 years to accomplish their goals. These early corporations were temporary institutions serving the public interest. At the time, the British government needed huge amounts of capital to develop North America. To encourage such a risky enterprise it needed to protect investors from legal and financial responsibility for their undertaking, beyond their initial investment. Thus, the government, for the first time, privileged business investors with limited liability.[32]

HUDSON'S BAY CO.
Hudson Bay Company logo, founded in 1670.

Colonial Americans feared chartered corporations. Colonists fought against monopolistic corporations when they led the Boston Tea Party revolt against the East India Company in 1773. The Declaration of Independence in 1776 freed Americans not only from Britain but also from the control of British corporations. For the next 100 years, Americans remained deeply distrustful of corporate power. Actually, the word "corporation" doesn't exist in the constitution; only states chartered corporations, so local citizens could keep a close eye on them. The founders were clear when they wrote the Bill of Rights: humans had rights, and when humans got together to form any sort of group – including corporations, churches, unions, and fraternal organizations – these human associations had only privileges, which were not guaranteed by the constitution. Thus, by the year 1800, the government kept the 200 or so corporations operating in the U.S. on short leashes.[33]

After the Civil War, the wealthiest of the wealthy, the railroad barons, held great political power. To further their power, these barons schemed to get the courts to give corporations the rights held by individuals. Citing the 14th amendment, they repeatedly attempted to get the court to declare they were persons. They finally got their chance in the famous 1886 Supreme Court case: ***Santa Clara County v. Southern Pacific Railroad***. Even though the Supreme Court strongly objected to the railroad's corporate claim to human rights, the court's reporter, who was in cahoots with the railroad barons, was able to secretly insert into the Court Reporter's headnotes in the case the rule that the railroad corporations were persons in the same category as humans. It held that, under the Constitution, a private corporation was a "natural person," entitled to all the rights and privileges of a human being. This single tricky legal stroke changed the nature of corporations. Thereafter, based on the court reporter's headnotes and ignoring the actual court ruling, later courts have expanded the idea of corporate human rights.[34]

Corporate abuses and consolidation of wealth and power built up in the Gilded Age of the late 1800s. At the height of power and wealth sat John D. Rockefeller, founder of Standard Oil Company. By 1890, he controlled 90 percent of the nation's oil refining capacity; 40 different companies formed Standard Oil. The concentration of wealth and power was so widespread that the Progressive movement in the early 1900s sought to curb their control. They were able to pass numerous reforms such as the Pure Food and Drug Act, Meat Inspection Act, and regulation of the railroads. The government even forced Standard Oil to end its monopoly by breaking it up into smaller companies. More reforms followed, in particular the Clayton Antitrust Act in 1914, which further broke up corporate monopolies.

From the 1920s onward, corporate power has come and gone. The pro-business era of the 1920s was followed by corporate reforms in the 1930s and 1940s. Designed to curb corporate power and corruption, New Deal reforms passed Congress with overwhelming support. A regulating system of checks and balances between three powerful U.S. institutions – labor unions, government, and corporations – marked the post-war years through the end of the 1970s. But by the 1980s corporate dominance had returned.

Favoring the Financial Sector

Many government policies in the last three decades have helped the financial sector make more money. One example of the government favoring the financial sector is its repeated bailouts of financial institutions since the 1980s. Since there have been so many financial bailouts, it is hard put to pick just one for an example. So let's pick one close to home: the 1994 Economic Crisis in Mexico.

American businesses had visions of profiting from Mexico's cheap labor and lax regulations and invested a great deal of money in the Mexican economy. Far more money poured into Mexico than the Mexicans could wisely invest. The rapid inflow of money bid up the value of the peso (currency of Mexico) and financed a brief consumption boom. To attract more money for investment, Mexico offered investors high-yield bonds in dollars rather than the riskier pesos. But as the boom peaked and investors began to cash out, Mexico found it was unable to attract enough new money to pay off its bondholders. It quickly ran short of cash reserves and faced the risk of default. The Clinton administration arranged a $50 billion bailout comprised of various loans and guarantees. With the money Mexico paid off the foreign investors who owned Mexican bonds. The Mexican bailout

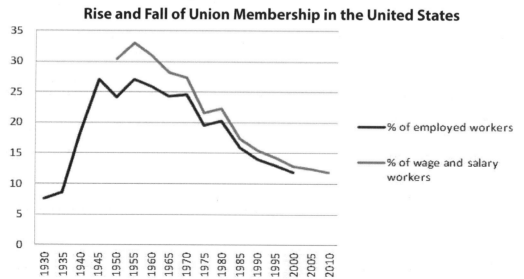

Rise and Fall of Union Membership in the United States

% of employed workers

% of wage and salary workers

http://en.wikipedia.org/wiki/Labor_unions_in_the_United_States

attracted much criticism. The U.S. government came to the rescue by bailing out market excesses, which protected U.S. investors but left Mexico hobbled with even more debt. Critics cried that this was not market capitalism but a form of corporate socialism. The gains were privatized but the risks were socialized.[35]

INGREDIENT #10: LABOR AND NEOLIBERALISM

The tenth ingredient is how labor is folded into the neoliberal stew. **Labor** is productive activity, especially for economic gain. It is also the body of persons engaged in such activity, especially those working for wages. I will use the term labor to include those who are part of the working class, service workers, and members of the middle class.

Labor made real progress in the 20th century. The Great Depression of the 1930s marked a shift from classical, laissez-faire capitalism to a social democratic version that supported policies which more evenly circulated wealth. The post-war "golden era of capitalism" from 1948 to 1973 linked the interests of business, labor, and government into a more balanced relationship than in the past. It was during this time that labor made the most gains in wages and benefits. In 1955, the American Federation of Labor (AFL) and the Congress of Industrial Organization (CIO) merged into the most powerful American union, representing nearly all unionized workers. Industrial labor peaked in the 1950s when 1 in 3 workers was a union member, but that dropped in 2006 to 1 in 10. The heyday of manufacturing unions passed. In 2008, the AFL-CIO had 56 member unions; the largest was American Federation of State, County and Municipal Employees (AFSCME) with one million members.

With the shift to neoliberalism, there are different economic policies regarding labor. Drawing on ideas from the classical era, neoliberals say unemployment exists because labor markets do not follow the principles of supply and demand. In a free market, they claim, unemployment would end with a fall in the wages of labor. When unions or minimum wage laws prevent wages from falling, then unemployment continues. Thus, neoliberals strive to abolish unions and repeal minimum wage laws to have low unemployment rates. Hardship and poverty, they argue, are unfortunate but necessary in the short term if the market is to operate freely and

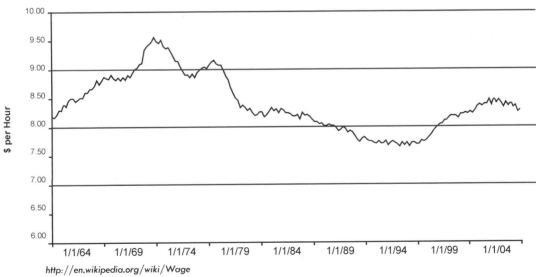

Historical Graph of Real Wages in the US from 1964-2005

http://en.wikipedia.org/wiki/Wage

79

bring about long-term prosperity. They believe that lowering income tax rates would give labor a reason to work since they would earn more take home pay.

There was full employment during the post-war golden years. Unemployment increased during downturns in the economy, but they were generally short-lived. This ended in the late 1970s when the Fed's policies turned to taming inflation. Wages took a hit. The wages of American workers, adjusted for inflation, did not begin rising for 10 years, in 1993, by which time they had fallen 15 percent below 1978 levels. By the late 1980s, the power of the labor movement had been weakening for years.[36] As a result, wages for labor have stagnated or declined since the 1980s.

This labor section affects all of us directly. Since it is so important, I will have a section in chapter 4 to further explain the neoliberal impact on labor.

Questions to Consider

1. What are your thoughts about neoliberals' actions towards labor? Have you or your friends been directly affected by neoliberal labor policies? Have you seen labor changes in the last 30 or so years?

INGREDIENT #11: RUGGED INDIVIDUALISM

The 11th ingredient combined into the neoliberal stew is rugged individualism. Many neoliberals, including Milton Friedman and Alan Greenspan, closely identified with the ideas of the libertarian author quoted below, Ayn Rand (1905-1982). Born and educated in Russia, Rand immigrated to the U.S. in 1926. She gained fame for her best-known work, *Atlas Shrugged*, in 1957. Rand's political views emphasized individual rights (including property rights), neoliberal capitalism, and a limited government. She held that self-interest, greed, and survival of the fittest motivate humans, which is best expressed through the pursuit of financial gains.

Atlas Shrugged[37] by Ayn Rand
"The man at the top of the intellectual pyramid contributes the most to all those below him, but gets nothing except his material payment, receiving no intellectual bonus from others to add to the value of his time. The man at the bottom who, left to himself, would starve in his hopeless ineptitude, contributes nothing to those above him, but receives the bonus of all their brains. Such is the nature of the competition between the strong and the weak of the intellect."

Individualism has been a core American value since the founding of this country. But individualism has also been offset by values of compassion, volunteerism, unselfishness and concern for those less fortunate, especially during the period of social democracy from the 1930s to 1970s. But there was a shift in the winds in the 1980s. Neoliberals have put the individualist mindset at the forefront, as in the late 19th century era of Social Darwinism and survival of the fittest. It was a significant shift in values.

Part of the individualist culture is a widespread worship of business heroes. Successful businessmen (usually men) rise above misfortune and mediocrity to create successful businesses and make a fortune, as well. The hero myth is dangerous in that it continues the idea that anyone can make it big in the business world, with a little luck and pluck. This often hides the fact that making a success in business is very difficult and shifts attention away from the importance of policies.[38]

The emphasis on individualism takes away from the idea of the public good and community. Placing blame on the poorest people in a society who are not able to find solutions to the lack of health care, education and good wages all by themselves is a way to overlook the real issue of policies that favor the wealthy. Instead, neoliberals label the poor as "lazy" or undeserving. It makes rising inequality largely the individual worker's fault rather than a function of how the system is organized and for whose benefit.[39]

Neoliberals have weakened equalizing institutions, such as education from pre-school to the university. Students must now pay more for their own education, with uncertainty as to whether they will be able to find employment after graduation. Many neoliberals claim that one of the reasons for many of the United States' ills is that students do not have appropriate skills and education for today's jobs and, therefore, a more rigorous curriculum that includes repeated testing is the answer. Neoliberals heap blame upon public school teachers for what they claim are their poor teaching practices. Teachers and other educators are the scapegoats for the real agenda of privatizing public schools.

Highlighting human competitive behavior deemphasizes human cooperation. Perhaps it is time to re-examine the ideas we have taken for granted and think about the world we want to leave the next generation. A 21st century society needs a new vision of and for humanity. Human nature may provide the building blocks for an economy built upon values of sharing and cooperation. I have found in my research of world history that the competitive, individualistic behaviors that are part of our society today are, by far, not the values that humanity has held over our thousands of years of human history.

Questions to Consider

1. What are the benefits of rugged individualism? Drawbacks?
2. How is each one expressed in the businesses and organizations in your community?

INGREDIENT #12: SPREADING NEOLIBERALISM

The 12th and last of the dozen ingredients blended into the neoliberal stew is spreading the neoliberal version of capitalism around the world. The fall of communism in the early 1990s made it look like capitalism had triumphed. It recharged a faith in American-style capitalism and the free market economy. There have always been different flavors of capitalism, but in the 1990s and early 2000s Americans thought that their system of capitalism was best for themselves and everyone else as well. However, the Great Recession following the crisis of 2008 seems to dispel this notion.

CONCLUDING INSIGHTS: THE NEOLIBERAL STEW

We have studied the successes and failures of this neoliberal version of capitalism. Some critics say the flaws in neoliberalism outweigh the benefits. Instead, some critics point to the successes of managed capitalism. However, the neoliberal agenda has gained widespread acceptance. I believe the overriding question at this critical turning point in world history is: How do we organize capitalism, and for whose benefit? Various models of capitalism are possible, with very different outcomes. Nothing is inevitable.

Questions to Consider

1. From the short description of neoliberalism presented in this chapter, do you think it has flaws in its theory and actual workings? What are they? Do you think the successes outweigh the flaws?

In the next chapter, we turn to the impact that the neoliberal agenda has had on the U.S. since 1980.

CHAPTER FOUR

The Impact of Neoliberalism in the United States: Ten Consequences

"Markets and money must again become the servants and not the masters of our vision and values."

--- *Jakob von Uexkull*

This chapter continues to examine neoliberalism but shifts its focus to the effects of neoliberal policies over the last 30 years, particularly in the United States. I have organized the consequences of neoliberal policies into 10 impacts. As you will notice in the list of 10 impacts of the neoliberal agenda, all of them are negative. As far as the direction that the U.S. economy has taken in the last 30 years, I have seen a greater negative impact for the majority of American people than positive. An essential question to keep in mind when reading this chapter is "Have neoliberal policies had a positive effect on the majority of Americans and the environment over the last 30 years, or have its policies had the opposite effect?" I think the best approach when learning about the global economy is to ask questions, lots of questions.

The Impact of Neoliberalism in the US: Ten Consequences

1. Reduction of self-reliance and the local economy.
2. Unbridled economic growth
3. Rampant consumerism
4. Increased commodification
5. Concentration of corporate power
6. Rise of external costs
7. Build-up of debt
8. Weakening of labor
9. Widening social inequality
10. Ascension of dollar democracy

IMPACT #1: A REDUCTION OF SELF-RELIANCE AND THE LOCAL ECONOMY

The first consequence of neoliberalism is the undermining of small businesses and farms and local self-reliant economies and communities. A British economist of the 1970s, E.F. Schumacher, coined the phrase "small is beautiful," as an alternative to the more popular phrase "big is better." Neoliberals promote the reduction in small, local, self-reliant economies in favor of large, economies dominated by large corporations. **Self-reliance** is trust in one's own capabilities, judgment, or resources – independence rather than dependence. The phrase self-reliant does not mean that a community is completely self-sufficient – that would be difficult in today's modern world – but it does mean that small local businesses and farms can provide many locally produced goods and services for a large number of people, making a community more self-reliant.

You might be thinking, "How do local economies undermine neoliberalism?" Owners of local businesses circulate money within the local economy benefitting the community, rather than dollars siphoned to core area elites and large corporations such as Wal-Mart. Although wages paid to Wal-Mart workers and sales and property taxes stay in the local community, the profits from the stores make their way into the bank accountants of the Walton family, the wealthiest family in the world. Think of the bonanza if just some of the profits stayed in the community where the store is located.

Many of us are so accustomed to shopping in malls, chain stores, and on-line retailers that we probably have no clue what a local business or self-reliance is all about. I remember local businesses. I would like to tell a story about the local community in which I lived for a number of years.

Self-Reliance and a Local Community: My Experience

From about 1976-1983, my family lived in Dewey, a small town in central Illinois near Champaign-Urbana. Since I wanted to care for my two young children at home, I did not have a wage-earning job at the time. Most of my shopping was with small businesses. I shopped for groceries at a small, family-owned grocery store located in Fisher, Illinois. All the family members worked at the store, even the aging grandfather. If need be, they would offer you credit – you just had to pay them back by the end of the month. No interest was charged. For more variety, I occasionally traveled about

15 miles to a larger grocery store in Champaign. Although it seemed large at the time, it was only a fraction of the size of the Wal-Mart Super Stores today. On occasion I would purchase soda drinks that were sold in returnable bottles that I took back to the grocery store and were rebottled and used again. My husband worked at a co-operative grain elevator, and we purchased a half side of beef from the local farmer that we had processed and packaged at the local butcher shop. We froze the meat in our freezer and had more than enough for the year; in fact, I took the surplus to the soup kitchen in Champaign.

We planted a huge garden. It was easy to grow delicious and nutritious vegetables in the rich central Illinois soil. I canned or froze most of the produce from the garden for the coming winter, almost always having local produce at every meal. It was no problem to find the vegetables I did not grow, since locally produced fruits and vegetables were plentiful. I canned applesauce, peaches, pears, tomatoes, pickles, beets (my young daughter's favorite), beans, and other vegetables. I froze as many vegetables as our freezer would hold. I went to the local U-Pick field and picked a year's supply of strawberries and raspberries that I froze or made into jam. We wasted very little food.

There were few cheap, imported clothes made in China during this time, and since I was an average seamstress I made many of our own clothes. I mostly stuck to fairly simple things such as knit t-shirts for the kids but also ventured into clothes for myself and some shirts for my husband. For other clothing needs I loved to shop at two wonderful women's clothing stores that were located in nearby down-town Rantoul. Local women owned the stores and they offered stylish, high-quality clothes made in America.

Most of my shopping was at local businesses. There was a "Five and Dime" store that had just about everything in it; my son particularly loved to look at all the toys, located conveniently on the lower shelves. There were also men's stores, shoe stores that also repaired shoes, a drug store and pharmacy, and about anything else you could possibly want. There was no McDonald's. We would occasionally go to

Downtown Rantoul, Illinois

a locally owned pizza parlor that had family specials that stuffed us all.

We were quite self-reliant housing-wise as well. As a young family, we were eager to move out of our cramped mobile home to a house with enough room for our expanding family. Since we did not have enough money saved up to buy a house, and I was not employed at the time, we decided to build one ourselves. Since my father was a housing contractor and my husband was quite handy, we took on the challenge with gusto, or perhaps stupidity was more accurate. There was certainly a learning curve, but with the help of family and friends and some knowledgeable sub-contractors, we finished it in six months and moved in before winter. We did all the framing, roofing, electrical, plumbing, insulation, painting, trim work, and even poured the footings that support the foundation walls, a task I will always remember. Footings are concrete poured into 2-foot-wide trenches dug below the frost line, about 3 feet down in our case. I don't think I have ever been so exhausted in my life, wading through semi-solid concrete in rubber boots frantically trying to level it before it hardened. It's a wonder I wasn't cemented into the concrete for all eternity. Although building your own house seems a difficult task today, it wasn't that uncommon in farming communities. Farmers have always prided themselves in being self-reliant and ready to tackle problems that arise. In fact, we liked building the house so much we decided to build two more over the next few years and remodeled five more. Thankfully, I decided that pouring the concrete footings was a job I didn't want to tackle again.

Does this sound like your life today? I imagine not. But it is far different from my life today as well. The point I would like to make in this short trip down memory lane is that small businesses were very much part of the landscape a generation or two ago. Rural communities and small towns prized self-reliance. We moved from that small community in the mid-1980s to a larger city, and when I returned a few years later I noticed that many things had changed. The Rantoul downtown was losing its small businesses; the clothing store I loved so much had shuttered its windows and many other businesses had been boarded up. They said they couldn't compete with the big box stores that were cropping up on the farmland just north of Champaign. Neoliberalism had arrived and displaced the small towns and local business owners with franchise stores owned by investors in larger cities, such as Chicago to the north. The prosperity of small town businesses and small farmers was beginning to disappear in the 1980s and this trend continues today.

Questions to Consider

1. Are you or is anyone you know self-reliant today? If so, in what ways?
2. Do you shop at any small, local businesses? What do they sell? Why do you shop there?

IMPACT #2: UNBRIDLED ECONOMIC GROWTH

Hamsters: Big Hamsters

Let's talk hamsters, big hamsters. Some of you may have a hamster for a pet. Hamsters don't weigh very much. But let's imagine for a moment that from birth to puberty a hamster doubled its weight each week. Instead of leveling off in maturity as animals do, the hamster continued this trend. How much do you think the hamster would weigh on its first birthday? We would be facing a nine billion metric ton hamster! If it kept eating at the same ratio of food to body weight, its daily food intake would be greater than the total, annual amount of corn (maize) produced worldwide! Hardly a sustainable pet.[1]

Nature knows when things should stop growing. I love to watch my spring flowers grow. My children grew up to be responsible adults. There are lots of different ways in which we use the word grow. Growth means to spring up and develop to maturity. In other words, growth gives way to a steady-state balance in nature in which the rate of inputs is equal to the rate of outputs. For example, a bath would be in balance if water flowing into the tub from the tap then escaped down the drain at the same rate. The total amount of water in the bath does not change, despite being in a constant state of flux.[2]

Growth cannot continue forever. There are limitations. Impact #2, **economic growth**, is where wealth increases over time as the economy adds new market value to goods and services. Growth and capitalism are two sides of the same coin. Capitalism is different from other economic systems because of its built-in tendency to expand and create new wealth. Through history, the invention of new technology went on at an even-handed pace, often needing decades or even centuries to develop. But under capitalism technology has sped up. The capitalist economy is a machine whose output is economic growth.[3]

The Western economy faithfully follows economic growth. Watch any newscast or read any news report about the economy, and I wager that they will mention the word growth. Economists constantly watch growth's movements, measure it to the decimal place, praise or criticize it, and judge it as weak or healthy. Every global, national, corporate, local, and academic institution wants to grow. I hope to grow my organization – the Center for Global Awareness – and sell lots of educational books. In our daily lives we assume that growth is one of those good things. Promoting economic growth may be the most widely shared and powerful cause in the world today. Some say it is the new world religion.

Through history humans have sought more comforts and surplus food to make their lives easier and more secure. As populations have grown, so have their economies. Yet, the specific policy of economic growth has a short history. Since 1945, it has come to be a central feature of U.S. economic policy. In 1949, a government report stated that growth would be a new key principle for the economy, rather than economic stability. Hopping on the economic growth band-wagon were big business and organized labor, which both saw in growth a way to further their interests. Economic growth meant that Americans would produce and consume more goods and services. Workers in factories and businesses would have jobs and thus spend their wages on more consumer goods. Americans were eager to shed the hardship of the depression years and start a new way of life based on a seemingly endless supply of comforts. Economic growth and consumer spending went hand and hand.[4]

Another advantage to the policy of economic growth was that economists could scientifically measure it. They came up with the **Gross Domestic Product** (GDP) – an official measure of a country's overall economic output. It is the market value of all final goods and services made within a country in a year. Since Americans have an unshakable faith in numbers, they widely considered GDP to be a good measurement of a country's living standards. A high GDP is often a stand-in for measuring the standard of living. This measurement assumes that when the GDP is up, the country's living standard also improves. A recession negatively describes the absence of growth. Prolonged recessions are depressions. A scientific number joined to rising living standards was important to Americans and later the world.

Unlimited growth made sense decades ago when the human population of the world was relatively low and natural resources for human consumption appeared to be endless. But the world has changed in the last 60 years. We now live in a world full of humans and all the things associated with our lives. In this world, the available labor supply is enormous, while the natural resources to support human life are limited. There is a dawning recognition that the growth model industrialized countries eagerly adopted is no longer working for the world we know today. It is geared towards a time in the past. All this is happening at the expense of our natural world, which is battered by the demand to produce more for human

Vessels combat the fire on the Deepwater Horizon while the United States Coast Guard searches for missing crew. The clean-up of the BP oil spill added to GDP.

87

consumption and absorb our wastes.

The fact is that a growing economy tells us nothing about the quality of our economic activity. For example, when the British Petroleum's (BP) oil spill spewed crude oil into the Gulf of Mexico beginning in April 2010, it actually added to the GDP! The number of dollars spent on cleaning up after disasters, such as the BP oil spill or Hurricane Katrina in 2005, all add to an increase in GDP. Growth in GDP doesn't say if the activity is good or bad. Spending on prisons, pollution and disasters pushes up GDP just as surely as spending on schools, hospitals and parks.

Recession is not necessary bad. Oddly enough, history shows that in times of recession, for example, life expectancy can rise in rich countries even as income decreases. This is probably due to a number of factors: people become healthier by consuming less and exercising more, or by using cheaper, more active forms of transport such as walking and cycling. In 2008, my son's employer laid him off from his construction-related job in Phoenix, Arizona. Because of a decline in income, he and his wife ate out less, had more time for exercise, and began to cook healthier foods at home. As a result he lost 15 pounds, and she lost 10 pounds!

Mainstream economics is frozen in its one-eyed fixation with growth. But growth has a surprising drawback. The industrial world has come to expect growth of around 3 percent a year. At this rate, the economy will double in just over 23 years. The 10 per cent growth rate of some rapidly growing economies, such as China and India, will double the size of those economies in less than 7 years. This astonishing rate of growth is unsustainable.[5]

The challenge for those who take a holistic view of environmental crises, global poverty and inequality is how to face up to the persistent belief that humanity's prosperity is dependent on the growth of GDP. This type of economic growth is unsustainable, unjust and unnecessary.

Questions to Consider

1. Why do you think your nation wants to continually grow its economy? What are the dangers to this way of thinking? What are the benefits?

IMPACT #3: RAMPANT CONSUMERISM

Impact #3 is rampant consumerism. To grow, capitalism needs constant new sources of wealth. Since the 1980s, consumer growth has spurred the U.S. economy. Today 90 percent of the American work force is directly and indirectly in the business of producing consumer goods and services.

Amusement park at the center of the Mall of America in Bloomington, Minnesota, the largest shopping mall in the United States.

Private consumption expenditures make up about 70 percent of GDP. First used in the 1960s, the term **consumerism** means the desire to purchase goods or services in ever greater amounts. It is an approach to life or state of mind that promotes the material conditions of life over the spiritual and social aspects. A consumer society acquires goods and services not only to satisfy needs, but also to secure identity and meaning. Advertising, social pressures, and emotional associations shape consumption patterns.[6]

Neoliberals have been successful in exporting consumerism around the world.

Many think of it as the new religion of the world, worshipping at the altar of the shopping mall or the on-line retailer and performing a ritual of purchasing dazzling items. On a summer 2011 trip to China with fellow educators, I was dismayed to see the number of late model cars in the cities of Beijing and Shanghai. I was dismayed because the smog hung so thick in the cities that it stung my eyes and hindered my far-off vision. I found out that consumerism had taken hold. The most desired purchase was a late model car, preferably one with high status, such as the racy Audi sports car displayed at the airport in Xian, China. Who says the U.S. doesn't export our culture? We have exported consumerism, and the rest of the world loves it.

Capitalism has been successful at producing goods and services for about 20 percent of the world's wealthiest people. In fact, it has produced too many goods and services. Have you ever been to a store that has racks and racks of clothes waiting for purchase and wondered who is going to buy all these items? Producers have had to become creative in seeking ways to get consumers to buy more – more than they need. Enter the advertising industry. The single goal of this industry is to get customers to buy more and more things. The traditional values that have shaped America since the founding of the country include thrift, hard work, long-term planning, rational behavior, stability, and respect for rules and laws. But advertisers have found that a person with these values does not impulsively consume. The industry figured out that it needed to change traditional individual behaviors and values, and it launched a bold campaign to do so. The industry sought to change the rational behaviors of mature adults into behaviors that are impulsive, irrational, self-centered, and reckless. Billions of dollars later, its efforts have proven to be worthy of its investment.[7]

The advertising industry also sought to change children's and teens' behaviors. Since children have not fully developed rational, mature behaviors, their impulsiveness is perfect for consuming. But advertisers needed to refocus children into desiring more profitable adult products. Their aim was to get children as young as toddlers to identify with their brands. They have found that this early brand identification would be set in for the rest of their consuming lifetime. Teens are prime advertising targets. With their impulsivity and need for peer status, they must have the latest products, which were typically reserved for adults in the past. They impulsively buy high end goods, technological gadgets, or a closet-busting wardrobe of the latest fashions.

Adults holding to a consumerist mindset are pawns to the advertising industry. Their sense of belonging and identity has shifted from national or ethnic roots to embrace brands of consumer products. These branded identities linked to 'lifestyles' replace their traditional ethnic, cultural, and national identity. The brands selected by an individual or family show a particular income, class, and place. Although it appears that we freely choose these identities, actually commercial culture influences every part of our lives. Advertisers happily promote this brand identification among consumers because it cuts across national and ethnic lines to mold a true globalization of identity.

The impact of advertising on consumers actually narrows choices and variety. Although there are many consumer choices, the actual choices are second order choices. A first order choice might be to have a real choice in public transportation, such as buses or trains, since we realize that automobiles contribute to climate change, and they are expensive. The second order choice would be to select a particular automobile, since that is the only transportation choice available in many areas. Another first order choice would be to pick from a variety of high quality, nutritious foods offered at a reasonable price in a convenient location. Instead, we have a whole range of artery-clogging, pound-packing, second choice fast foods readily available for our immediate consumption. We need to be able to make both first and second order choices, if we are to have a truly democratic consumer society.

Perhaps this would all be fine if the consumption of goods and services made us happier and healthier and resulted in loving relationships and a sense of well-being, something that advertisers promise. But we are not happier, and we are certainly not healthier. In fact, studies have shown that rampant consumption actually leaves us more depressed and unsatisfied. Of course, this is exactly what advertisers have planned all along, since these emotions make us consume more goods in an endless cycle of trying to reach satisfaction. Fortunately though, we do have the choice to reject or participate in the consumerist society.

Questions to Consider

1. Are you or is someone you know an avid consumer? What motivates that consumption?

IMPACT #4: INCREASED COMMODIFICATION

A Cup of Coffee

Have you ever gone to a Starbucks and purchased a coffee product that cost you $5 (US) or more? If you are a person earning minimum wage, you could easily spend an hour's pay on your coffee. My cousin's 10-year-old granddaughter recently purchased a grandee latte at Starbucks with all the works, and it set her back her whole week's allowance! During the mid-1960s, I remember my father, a World War II veteran, going to a nearby diner's lunch counter and getting a cup of coffee for 10 cents, and it was refillable! In fact, the diner advertised that it had "Bottomless Coffee Cups." But he didn't have a choice of a latte or cappuccino; it was just regular coffee served in a ceramic cup and saucer. What happened? How did coffee become so expensive? Coffee has been commodified.

Starbucks Coffee in Singapore

Commodification is a big word for impact #4. It comes from the word commodity, which in economics means an exchangeable unit of economic wealth, like a primary product or raw material. I like to use the word because it shows a part of capitalism that has expanded with neoliberalism. **Commodification** is turning something with little or no economic value into a product or service that has a particular value or a higher monetary value. In the example above, coffee is a commodity. Although coffee was a commodity in the 1960s, its value has increased today because of added marketing value. In the case of Starbucks, through clever advertising and enhancing the taste, Starbucks turned a low value commodity into a high value one that has led to a greater profit margin. Commodification is everywhere.

Commodification changes things, concepts, activities, services, events, ideas, products, relationships, labor, identities, and even people into products that are for sale. It even includes relationships, which were formerly not commercial, into relationships that have an exchange value. For example, companies such as E-harmony have turned the dating experience into a commodity which connects single people together for a fee. Since capitalism needs to constantly grow, commodification is one way to create new products and services that add economic value. Corporations and entrepreneurs are continually searching for goods, ideas, services and even individuals that they can turn into commodities.

Commodification is not necessarily bad but it has grown since the 1980s; nothing escapes its reach. To the right is a list of just a few of the many arenas of commodification since the 1980s.

Commodification Since the 1980s

domestic (maid) service, funerals, elder care, day care, child's play, children's birthday parties, weddings, family meals, medical services, beauty, dating, culture, art, performances, family reunions, high school prom, exercise, music, handyman repairs

Some of these are services that the family or neighbors used to provide for free or very little money, but are now commodities. I am sure you can think of more.

Commodification has hit weddings. Several decades ago most weddings were low budget affairs, with the reception held in a church basement, with cake and punch, mints if you were lucky. Today many weddings are extravagant affairs that even necessitate a costly wedding planner. Costs skyrocket upward into thousands of dollars. Or some couples choose a pre-packaged wedding in Las Vegas, Nevada, or on a Caribbean Island. My son and daughter-in-law chose to skip the hassle of a big wedding and instead, they and another couple wed at a resort in Jamaica. They had a lot of fun, and it was relatively easy. But I missed attending their wedding. My daughter and her husband, on the other hand, decided to have a medium- sized wedding, but to save money they did much of the planning and work themselves. It was a lot of work, but it did have a personal touch that made it truly their own. They were able to do it by making their family and friends work! A "crew" of us put together the wedding programs, arranged the flowers, shined the glasses, hauled supplies, cleaned up, and even set up tables. It was fun, though.

The majority of women just a generation or two ago – especially those with young children – were not in the full-time paid work force. Their labor was mainly at home taking care of family and home and perhaps taking in some part-time work here and there. In other words, their labor was not commodified.

The following story of my mother tells of women's typical non-commodified labor prior to the late 1970s.

A Mother in the Post-War Years

My mother was a stay-at-home mom in the 1950s and 1960s, although she also did part-time accounting and other clerical tasks for my father's home construction business. She did all the cooking, washing, ironing, cleaning, gardening, shopping, caring for my sister and me, and helping with the care and transportation of elderly relatives. She was also involved in the school, the Parent Teacher's Association (PTA), Brownies, 4-H, League of Women Voters, and other activities. She was always busy and took pride in her activities. One of the most time consuming tasks that my mother performed was making family meals and shopping for food. We rarely ate out at restaurants, nor did we have take-out meals; our meals were nutritious and home-cooked – three times a day.

We find today that a full-time working woman is unable to carry out all these time-consuming tasks as my mother did generations ago. Since the 1970s, women have increasingly been entering the paid work force, which means commodification has stepped in to fill the void of women's unpaid labor services with comparable services that private business now performs for a market price. One is the family meal. Food is a commodity unless you grow your own, but the labor at home to transform the food into meals is unpaid. The food industry has found a way to commodify the labor of making meals. The food industry calls take-out meals or prepared meals at grocery stores "home-replacement meals." They state that people want the experience of the home-cooked dinner: the family gathered at its own table, the familiar smells and tastes, and the resemblance to a home cooked meal.

Another task that women (it was usually women) performed at home was the care of children and elderly parents or relatives. I felt I was lucky to be able to partially care for my children at home before they reached school age, although many times I needed day-care services, and other family members helped out when I was teaching. Although parents still perform most childcare, there is a demand for day care for children either at home through the employment of nannies, through informal arrangements with relatives, neighbors or friends, or through for-profit day care corporations.

Bottled water is an example of the commodification of a previously free resource. An increasing share of the bottled water sold in the U.S is coming from municipal water supplies. Categorized as "purified" by the bottled water industry, bottling companies purchase municipal tap water, put it through a filtration process, bottle it and then sell it back to consumers for hundreds to thousands of times the cost. Between 2000 and 2009, the share of purified tap water bottled sold in retail stores has increased by almost 50 percent. The bottled water trend in reality is a marketing gimmick that has fooled consumers into believing that water in little plastic bottles and priced 200 times higher than tap water is somehow healthier. Bottled water, however, generates over 20 billion plastic bottles added to landfills annually.[8]

I am now part of the commodification craze. Even though we are a non-profit, the Center for Global Awareness sells educational books and resources about world history, global issues, and cross cultural topics. I have commodified my ideas and put them into books that we sell in the marketplace. None of us can escape commodification!

Questions to Consider

1. What forms of commodification do you encounter in your daily life? Are they beneficial or detrimental to your life?
2. In what ways have the services that women performed in the past been commodified? Do you think this is good or bad?

IMPACT #5: CONCENTRATION OF CORPORATE POWER

The fifth impact of neoliberalism is the concentration of corporate power. If capitalism is a growth machine, corporations are doing the growing. Corporations can vary in size and complexity from small companies run by a few people to huge organizations that are larger than many nations.

I once was the president of a corporation! To be truthful, it wasn't a multinational corporation but rather a small sub-S corporation called the Willow Basket that consisted of my partner (my sister-in-law) and me, and about three part-time employees. We sold an assortment of gifts and home decorating products in a downtown location in Normal, Illinois. Since my partner and I both had young children at the time, we shared the work, and generally it was fun and profitable. However, I yearned to go back into the education field and after eight years sold the business. But our small, family-owned corporation was a far cry from the giant corporations that reach their tentacles around the world today.

I am making a distinction between huge corporations and small to medium sized corporations that are the cornerstone of the American economy and way of life. In 2000, of the 100 largest economies in the world, 53 were global corporations; only 44 were countries. In 2010, Wal-Mart was the largest publicly-traded corporation in the world with revenues of $408.2 billion and profits of $14.3 billion. The second largest were Royal Dutch Shell and Exxon Mobil.[9] Today many state-owned enterprises (SOE) or partially state-owned enterprises dwarf them in size. For example, Saudi Aramco, the state-owned oil company of Saudi Arabia, had an estimated market value of $781 billion to $7 trillion (US$).[10]

Sam Walton's original Walton's Five and Dime store in Bentonville, Arkansas, now serving as the Walmart Visitor Center.

Corporate CEOs have profited from a shift to neo-liberal policies. The total compensation for the average CEO of one of the 500 largest companies in 2006 was $14.8 million, which declined slightly to $10.8 million in 2010. In contrast, the pay for the average worker in 2010 was $33,121, up just 3.3 percent over the year before.[11] In 1970, the ratio of compensation for a corporate CEO in the U.S. to that of an average worker was 45:1. It jumped in 2000 to 300:1, declined slightly in 2005 to 262:1, and rose a little to 263:1 in 2009. Despite the recession, it jumped to the highest ratio on record in 2010: 325:1![12]

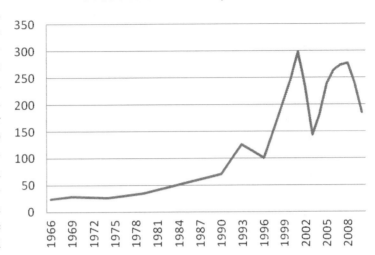

Ratio of Average Compensation of CEOs and Production Workers, 1965-2009

Source: Economic Policy Institute. 2011. Based on data from Wall Street Journal/Mercer, Hay Group 2010.

Corporate Consolidation, Mergers, and Acquisitions

In the post-war years, an oversupply of goods and services contributed to the crisis of the 1970s.

Safeway Supermarkets: A Corporate Takeover[13]

In 1986, Safeway Supermarkets owned 2,365 stores and employed 172,000 workers. Its employee motto was "Safeway Offers Security." The company offered good job benefits and decent union wages. In 1985, the company reported record profits of $231 million. All changed in July 1986 after a hostile takeover bid by a group of corporate raiders. Alarmed, Safeway's management called in a leveraged buyout specialist to help ward off the corporate raiders. They came up with a plan that that included $130 million of investors' money, then borrowed more than $4.3 billion to buy up all the company's stock. In return, the buyout specialist received $60 million in consulting fees for the transaction. When added to fees received by investment bankers, lawyers, and accountants, more than $200 million went towards the buyout.

At this point the new private owners needed to come up with more than $500 million a year to pay off the interest and debt on the buyout. Taxpayers unwillingly kicked in their share; the company stopped paying $122 million a year in taxes and even received a U.S. refund check for past taxes of $11 million. But that only paid for part of the debt. The rest had to come from selling stores, firing workers, and cutting wages. The new corporate owners eventually sold more than 1,200 stores, putting 63,000 people out of work. In the Dallas Safeway, for example, the owners fired 60 percent of the former workers. Those who were able to work for the bought-out stores saw their hourly wages drop from $12 to $6.50. Although the Dallas stores made a small profit, liquidating them and selling off their inventory and equipment made far more money. Employees lost all their health benefits within two weeks and received a maximum severance pay of eight weeks. However, the chairman kept his million-dollar-a-year-job.

A 1990 business magazine article said it was *The Buyout that Saved Safeway*. It noted that profit margins were higher, largely because the company got rid of surly unions and uncompetitive stores. Somehow the author thought that undermining American workers and a tax subsidy exceeding $500 million was good for the economy. No mention was made of the welfare, unemployment, and health benefits which the firings have cost all Americans, nor the loss of those hundreds of millions in taxes which tens of thousands of former Safeway workers no longer pay. Had the government insisted that existing labor contracts needed to be enforced and limited the tax deductions that corporations could take for their interest expense on debt, the corporate takeovers of the 1980s would never have happened.

Corporations faced fierce competition from each other, which usually resulted in a decline in their profit margins and market share. Corporations do not like competition because it cuts into profits. To prevent corporations from forming monopolies that restrict competition, the U.S. has passed anti-trust laws, such as the 1913 Clayton Antitrust Law. However, enforcement of these laws is up to the courts. Since the 1980s, the courts have favored large corporations that have tried to eliminate or reduce competition. One of the strategies to reach this goal is consolidation, mergers, or acquisitions.

The 1980s was a time of "**hostile takeovers**" by "**corporate raiders**." These raiders bought up a company's stock when it was undervalued, which meant the company's assets were worth more than their stock. The raiders would sell off the assets of the raided company to make a profit, but as a result, the companies raided went out of business. Some companies, in an effort to ward off the dreaded raiders, carried out what were called "**leveraged buyouts**," in which the soon-to-be raided companies would "go private" by buying up their own stock with borrowed funds to avoid the takeover of their corporation by another. This was very unproductive; takeovers added nothing of value to the economy. Financial specialists who put together the deals were usually the only ones to make money on the activity. The leveraged buyout of Safeway Supermarkets exemplifies the 1980s corporate takeover culture.

Questions to Consider

1. What do you think of the corporate takeover of Safeway?

IMPACT #6: RISE OF EXTERNALIZED COSTS

A sixth impact of neoliberal policies is the increase in **external costs** or **externalities** since 1980. These are the costs not paid by the producer but which others must pay. The price of the goods and services we consume most often does not take into account external costs.

Price

Many corporate products have inaccurate prices because they fail to account for external costs that corporations should be responsible for. Instead, they shift the costs to the general public which picks up the tab. Prices would more exactly reflect

Categories of Externalized Costs[14]

1. Social Costs...paying less than a living wage, safety issues like poor working conditions.
2. Health Care Costs...government pays for the uninsured, increased private insurance premiums, increased Medicare and Medicaid costs.
3. Environmental Costs...toxic waste clean-up, air and water polltion, oil spills and others.
4. Military Costs...used to defend the nation, protect scarce resources, access natural resources.
5. Security Costs...for fire protection, police, border patrols, airline security, homeland security.
6. Subsidies...corporate welfare, direct loans, loan guarantees, trade protection, exemptions.
7. Tax Deductions...tax loopholes, excessive executive salary, bonuses, perks, and deductions.
8. Infrastructure Development...payments for infrastructure that business disproportionately uses.

their true value if corporations included externalized costs. The inaccurate pricing of scarce resources, such as clean air and water, leads to their abuse. A classic example is the factory that spews smoke over a nearby neighborhood. The factory forces a real cost onto society in the form of dirty air, but this cost is external to the company. Or, if you are debating between a car that has good miles per gallon and one that does not, the price of the gas-guzzler does not figure in the cost of pollution.

A Big Mac at McDonald's

The carbon footprint of a Big Mac shows externalities and mispricing in action. I bet most of you have had a Big Mac at some point in your lives but never knew its external costs. One estimate says the energy cost of the 550 million Big Macs sold in the U.S. every year is $297 million, producing a greenhouse gas footprint of 2.66 billion pounds of CO_2 equivalent. Add to that the environmental impact of water use and ruined soil, together with the hidden health costs of treating diet-related illness such as diabetes and heart disease. If you add in all of these external costs to the price of a Big Mac, what do you think would be the cost? One estimate figures it would be about $200. It would be big time sticker shock if you pulled up to the drive-through window, and the McDonald's clerk said $400 for two Big Macs.[15]

McDonald's Big Mac, introduced in 1968.

The market externalizes health care costs, as seen in the McDonald's example. Those who consume excessive sugar-laden or artery-blocking foods do not pay the real costs for these foods. Instead, present-day unhealthy eating habits result in higher health care costs down the road. These costs, such as a heart surgery, fall to private insurance companies, Medicare, or Medicaid. Critics say a "sugar tax" would help to stop external costs, but the soft drink companies and others have lobbied against such a law.

The classic case for externalizing health care costs to the general public is the cigarette companies. The price paid for a pack of cigarettes does not reflect the added health care costs to health insurance companies and public health programs that treat the chronic smoker. A study found that if the market added health-related costs to a pack of cigarettes the actual costs of smoking would be nearly $40 per pack. That included roughly $33 for reduced life expectancy and tobacco-related disabilities; $5.44 for the costs of secondhand smoke, and $1.44 for pooled-risk programs like Medicare, Medicaid, group life insurance and sick leave. Although the cost of cigarettes has increased over the years, it is far from reaching the $40 a pack price tag that reflects its real costs.[16]

Arguably, the all-time best poster child for externalizing costs to taxpayers is the world's largest retailer: Wal-Mart. The company offers the lowest overall prices in the retail industry. Wal-Mart has reduced costs through very efficient manufacturing and distribution networks and utilizing cheap Chinese labor to make most of their products. But if we look at their low prices as a system we can see that the price of an item does not include externalized costs, such as health insurance for all employees. If the company paid its external costs instead of the taxpayer, Wal-Mart's prices would be much higher. As it is, Wal-Mart's inaccurate low prices give them an unfair advantage in the marketplace. If Wal-Mart prices were more accurate, many locally-owned businesses would be able to compete against them and other "big box" stores. Imagine the economic boost to local economies if the profits funneled to the Walton family – the richest family in the world – were instead circulated in local communities.

Subsidies

Subsidies are one of the most common forms of external costs. Although there are many different forms of subsidies, we will look at subsidies that go to corporations. In order to reduce their costs and increase their profits, corporations try to find government subsidies, tax breaks, and loopholes. A **subsidy** is a form of financial assistance paid to a business or a particular economic sector. Supposedly, the government gives most subsidies to producers or distributors in an industry to prevent

95

the decline of that industry. For example, the U.S. heavily subsidizes farm products such as corn, soybeans, wheat, and cotton, which drives down the cost of these commodities for consumers. But when exported to countries that grow these crops, these farmers cannot compete with the subsidized low prices [17]

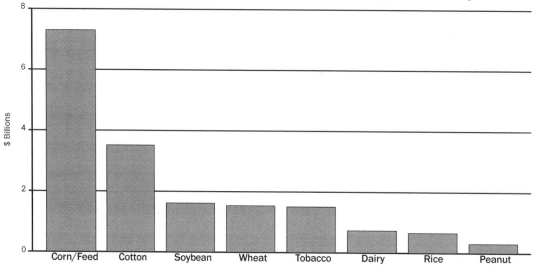

Farm Subsidies in 2005, from a Congressional Budget Office Report

Subsidies misrepresent markets. For example, Mexican farmers have grown corn for centuries. Yet with the passage of NAFTA in 1994, they must now compete with subsidized corn grown in the U.S. and imported into Mexico. The price of Mexican corn is much higher than U.S. corn. This means that many Mexican farmers have had to give up their livelihoods. Forced to feed their families and desperate for work, many of the ex-farmers have migrated to the U.S. or to the teeming cities of Mexico for jobs.

Wal-Mart leads the pack in attracting subsidies. A study found that 90 percent of Wal-Mart distribution centers received tax breaks and other subsidies, valued at an average of $7.4 million per distribution center. Wal-Mart sought and received subsidies averaging about $2.8 million at 1,100 of their locations, about one-third of its U.S. stores.[18] Local officials argue these big stores warrant subsidies because of the jobs and tax revenue they generate. But in most cases the big boxes do more harm than good. When big box stores move to town, other businesses shrink or close completely with hundreds of jobs lost, many of which provide higher wages and better benefits than Wal-Mart or other big box chains.

Questions to Consider

1. What are some examples of externalities that you encounter in your daily life? Subsidies?

IMPACT #7: BUILD-UP OF DEBT

Have you ever been or are you currently in debt? For many of you the answer may be yes! Debt is more a fact of life today for young people than when I grew up. Some of my peers had student loans, but they usually paid them off in a couple of years. They had no credit card debt because no one I knew had a credit card! In fact, I remember getting rejected when I applied for my first credit card – and I was a teacher at the time and didn't have any debt! Today the words debt and deficits are on the lips of everyone – from homeowners, to credit card holders, to students, to retirees, to government. Big time debt. In this section we will examine three kinds of debt: consumer debt, student loan debt, and the national debt.

1. Consumer Debt

In the post-war years, American families borrowed for consumer purchases, but usually it was not too much and kept pace with the growth in their incomes. But the rise in incomes in the post-war years gave way to stagnant incomes for most Americans. Yet from the 1980s onward, despite flat incomes, families have kept on spending. How did families manage this trick? First, women streamed into the paid work force. By the late 1990s, more than 60 percent of mothers with young children worked outside the home, while in 1966, only 24 percent did. Second, everyone put in more hours at work. By the mid-2000s, the typical male worker clocked in roughly 100 more hours each year than two decades before, and the typical female worker about 200 more hours. Third, when American families couldn't squeeze out any more income from work, they went deeper into debt. Their home served as their personal ATM. Through refinancing their homes, Americans took out $2.3 trillion. Eventually, the debt bubble burst – and with it, the last way to cope with falling incomes.[19]

Consumer debt is simply debts that are owed as a result of purchasing consumable goods that do not appreciate in value. For example, a house is not consumer debt because its value can increase with time. A designer purse or a computer game is a consumer item because once out of the store, it loses its value. Consumer spending drives 70 percent of the economy. Total U.S. consumer debt, as of May 2011, was $2.43 trillion. About 50.2 million households carry credit debt, which averages out to about $15,799 per household. There were 176.8 million credit cardholders in 2008.[20] This means some people owe a lot more money than they are bringing in. But, paradoxically,

One of the former Visa logos, used from 1970 to 2006. Visa is the largest credit card company.

in order for the economy to recover from the recession, consumers need to consume more, which means running up more consumer debt.

2. Student Loan Debt

Do you have student loan debt? The younger generation appears to have mortgaged its future earnings in the form of student loan debt. In 2012, total student loan debt in the U.S. reached over $1 trillion. In 2008, 62 percent of students from public universities obtained student loans, 72 percent from nonprofit private universities, and a whopping 96 percent from for-profit schools. Neoliberals seek to decrease funds for public education, which indirectly pushes more students into private institutions. Enrollments at for-profit colleges have increased in the last ten years by 225 percent. From 1994 to 2008, average debt levels for graduating seniors more than doubled to $23,200. Loans now saddle more than 10 percent of those completing their bachelor's degree with over $40,000 in debt.[21]

Of the $1 trillion in outstanding federal and private student-loan debt, students are actively repaying only about 40 percent of that debt. The rest is in default or in deferment (when a student requests temporary postponement of payment because of economic hardship). When the loans go into default, taxpayers are required to pick up the tab, since the federal government backs just about all loans extended before July, 2010. Two out of every five students enrolled at for-profit schools are in default on their educational loans 15 years later. There is no screening to receive these loans.

A credit score is not required for federal loans. Neither is information regarding income, assets, or employment.[22]

The two largest holders of student loans are SLM Corp (SLM) and Student Loan Corp (STU). SLM – Sallie Mae – started in 1972, and the government privatized it in 2004. Sallie Mae jumped onto the securitization bandwagon by repackaging a large portion of its loans and selling them as bonds to investors. Financial firms packaged many of the student loans into the same securities that helped trigger the financial crisis. Bankruptcy laws release credit card and even gambling debts, but non-repayment of a student loan is almost impossible. While those with a college degree tend to make higher incomes, during the last 8 to 10 years the median income of highly educated Americans has been declining. Also, a college education has been producing diminishing returns, especially at non-select colleges.[23]

> **Questions to Consider**
> 1. Do you, your friends, your children, or others you know have student debt? Do you or they think it was worthwhile to incure the debt? Are you or they having difficulty paying it back?

3. National Debt

In 1980, the national debt stood at $1 trillion. Over the prior 204 years, the nation paid for the Revolutionary War, the Civil War, World War I, the Great Depression, World War II, the Korean war, the Vietnam war, and the better part of the Cold War, and through all that, still only borrowed $1 trillion. Over the next 12 years of relative peace and prosperity, the national debt quadrupled to $4 trillion. In the 1990s, as taxes on the wealthy increased and government spending declined, the national debt stabilized. In 2000, President Clinton produced a $140 billion surplus, the first budget surplus since 1969. The deficit-producing policies of neoliberalism returned in the 2000s. The government lowered taxes on the wealthy to the tune of $1.6 trillion, in which 50 percent of the gains went to the top 1 percent of income earners. Two wars and a $600 billion prescription drug plan for seniors exploded spending. In 2000, the national debt stood at $5.6 trillion; at the end of 2011 the national debt was almost $15 trillion. Bring in less income while spending more money and the result is debt. Mountains of it.[24]

IMPACT #8: WEAKENING OF LABOR

As of this writing, one of the most important debates in our political arena is about jobs, which leads us to the eighth impact of neoliberalism: labor. Unemployment since 2009 has hovered around 8 to 10 percent. The days of fewer than 5 percent unemployment rates during the 1990s and the 2000s are gone. You probably know someone close to you who is unemployed. Two of my cousins have been unemployed in Rockford, Illinois, my former home-town, for over two years now. One of the vibrant manufacturing centers during the 1950s and 1960s, Rockford has experienced the shift of well-paying, manufacturing jobs to low-wage countries like China. The current recession has taken its toll on this former factory town.

I will be discussing two aspects of labor in this book. One is the impact of neoliberal policies on the workforce, primarily in the U.S. The second part of the labor topic is discussed in the economic globalization chapters.

Since neoliberals believe that unions and minimum wages restrict the supply and demand of labor, weakening the impact of unions and minimum wage laws are part of their overall strategy. One of the first acts of this strategy was a stand-off between President Ronald Reagan and the air-traffic controllers union.

After the air-traffic controllers' strike in 1981, unions declined, and the number of strikes

PATCO vs. Reagan

Most unions opposed Ronald Reagan, the Republican candidate for president in 1980. But the Professional Air Traffic Controllers Organization (PATCO) union had supported him. In August 1981, the union rejected the federal government's pay raise offer and sent its 16,000 members out on strike to shut down the nation's commercial airlines. They demanded a reduction in the workweek from 40 hours to 32 hours, a doubling of wages, a $10,000 bonus and early retirement. Federal law said the strike was illegal. The strikers had 48 hours to return to work; if not, they would be fired and banned from ever working in a federal job. One-fourth of the strikers came back to work, but 13,000 did not. The strike collapsed, PATCO vanished, and the union movement as a whole suffered a major setback, causing a decline in union membership in the private sector.[25]

Questions to Consider

1. Do you think Reagan was justified in his showdown with the PATCO union?

dropped. The year 1953 marked the height of union strength when 32.5 percent of the U.S. labor force was unionized. In 1979, there were 21.2 million manufacturing jobs in the U.S. manufacturing sector. In 1983, the union membership rate was 20.1 percent of the workforce, and there were 17.7 million union workers. By 1992, there were only 16.7 million such jobs. Total union membership in 2010 was 11.9 percent of the workforce, down from 12.3 percent a year earlier. In 2012, the unionized percentage of private-sector workers was 6.9 percent. [26] This is due in part to increasing automation and the outsourcing of manufacturing jobs to low-wage countries.

One of the effects of the drop in union membership is that workers' wages have not kept up with rising productivity levels. In principle, wages are supposed to rise with productivity. **Labor productivity** is the amount a worker produces in a unit of time, usually per hour. But whether wages actually rise with productivity depends on the bargaining power of workers and agreement by employers. In the early 1950s, there was an understanding between employers and labor, which said that worker compensation would grow at the rate that labor productivity increased. This understanding between labor and businesses continued until the crisis of the 1970s, when wages were higher than worker productivity. This period when wages were higher than hourly productivity

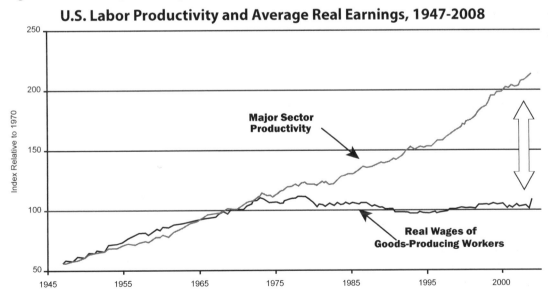

U.S. Labor Productivity and Average Real Earnings, 1947-2008

http://en.wikipedia.org/wiki/Workforce_productivity

99

contributed to inflation. This basic agreement made sure that workers would share in the fruits of future economic growth; however, since the crisis of the 1970s, this agreement has been broken.

If the agreement between labor and business had held, a study has estimated that $1.91 trillion over the past 40 years should have gone to non-supervisory and production workers in the form of higher wages and benefits because of higher productivity. If workers had received the value of their annual productivity increases, as they had in the past, they would have earned an average of $35.98 per hour in compensation in 2009 instead of the $23.14 they actually got. The difference is $12.84. On an annual basis each worker lost an average of $22,701. From 1972 through 2009, productivity benefits have shifted from non-supervisory workers to managers and owners. This upward redistribution of $1.91 trillion has largely remained hidden. It has taken various forms – bonuses, outsized salaries, stock options, padded consulting fees, lavish offices, expensive conferences, large staffs, private corporate dining rooms, and generous retirement benefits.[27]

The total increase in the wages paid to all 124 million non-supervisory workers was less than $200 million in six years – a raise of $1.60 per worker – not per hour but a grand total of $1.60 in higher wages per worker over nearly six years! In contrast, during the 1990s, the reported pay of senior corporate executives increased almost fivefold. If worker's median pay had grown at the same rate as CEO's pay, their pay would be over $200,000 a year.[28]

Today three Americans in four pay more in regressive Social Security taxes than they do in progressive income taxes. **Regressive tax rates** decrease as the amount subject to taxation increases, which means those who have a higher income pay less of their total income on taxed items. **Progressive tax rates** increase as the taxable base amount increases, which means those who have a higher income pay more of their total income in taxes. Employees and employers each pay a Social Security tax rate of 6.2 percent, but in 2012, the rules capped an employee's pay at a yearly income of $110,100. A worker paid a minimum wage pays 6.2 percent of earnings in Social Security taxes and 1.45 percent in Medicare, while a person earning $2 million pays about an equivalent of 1/3 of 1 percent.[29] Hence, it is a regressive tax.

Neoliberals and the business community generally disagree with federal minimum wage laws, but these laws determine the wages paid to those at the low end of the service sector. The minimum wage in 2007 was $5.15, an hourly rate that had remained the same since 1997. But figuring in inflation, the actual value of the $5.15 minimum wage has gone down since 1997 to only $4.15 in 2006. Congress passed a law in 2007 to raise the minimum wage to $5.85 an hour; it increased to $6.55 an hour in 2008 and $7.25 an hour in 2009, where it remains in 2015. When adjusted for inflation it is at a 50 year low.[30]

Unemployment compensation now covers relatively fewer workers and replaces a lower percentage of wages than at any time since the Great Depression in the 1930s. In 2011, there were nearly 14 million unemployed workers, and that was not counting those who have given up looking or those who are looking for full-time work but employed part-time. Meanwhile, there are a little more than 3 million job openings. The economy must produce 150,000 jobs each month just to absorb population growth. Among the 18-25 year old group, the unemployment rate is around 20 percent, and in some locations and among some socio-demographic groups, twice that rate.[31]

Questions to Consider

1. Are you currently looking for a job? If so, what is your experience in your job search?
2. If you have a job, have you received a raise in the last four years? If not, how has this affected your standard of living?

IMPACT #9: WIDENING SOCIAL INEQUALITY

The bottom line is that people who work for a living are getting a smaller and smaller slice of the nation's economic pie. The #9 impact of neoliberalism is the growing gap between rich and poor in the U.S. and worldwide. We will concentrate on the U.S. in this section and look into global inequality in chapter 6.

The neoliberal solution to poverty is to grow the economy. As President Reagan announced, "A rising tide will lift all boats." But a rising tide has not lifted all boats; some critics claim the rising tide has only lifted the yachts. If the government spread the benefits of economic growth more equally throughout society, everyone should have been almost 20 percent better off in 2008 than they were in 1998.[32] This has obviously not happened. The assumption that continuing growth would close the social gap has not happened; in fact, it has gotten worse. Growth will not reduce social inequality.

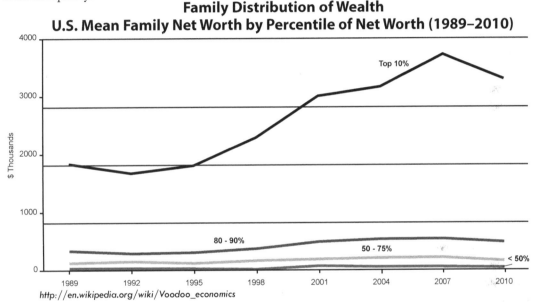

Family Distribution of Wealth
U.S. Mean Family Net Worth by Percentile of Net Worth (1989–2010)

http://en.wikipedia.org/wiki/Voodoo_economics

The postwar years ushered in such programs as an expansion of public higher education, which reduced economic inequality and helped to expand the circle of prosperity. Income tax rates of 70 percent to 90 percent on the highest incomes paid for most of these social programs. Real wages for workers in manufacturing rose 67 percent and real wages overall rose 81 percent. Income of the richest 1percent also rose 38 percent. This period marked the expansion of the American middle class. As this group shared more of the economic gains, they were able to buy more of the goods and services the economy produced. Growth was widely shared, and income inequality continued to drop. [33]

Income Inequality by Percentages

When looking at inequality, it helps to look at the levels of income and wealth distribution. Where to start? Let's start at the top.

1. The Top 1%

Where have all the economic gains gone in the last 30 years? To the very top. The lives of those in the top 1 percent have improved considerably. In 1979, they had 9.3 percent of all income in the U.S.; by 1985, their portion had climbed to 12 percent; by 2000, the share was 17.8 percent; and in 2011, it stood at 24 percent. In terms of wealth rather than income, the top 1 percent had 33.4 percent of the total net worth in 2001, while in 2011, that climbed to 40 percent. These figures are the highest since 1928, just before the Great Depression.[34] The richest 1 percent of households earned as much each year as the bottom 60 percent put together; they possessed as much wealth as the bottom 90 percent.[35] The top .01 percent has made even greater gains. Between 2001 and 2007, the 400 richest individuals in the U.S. saw their wealth increase from $1 trillion to $1.6 trillion – an increase of $600 billion.[36]

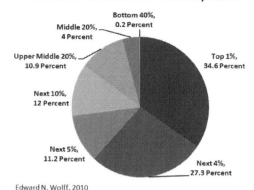

U.S. Distribution of Wealth, 2007

Edward N. Wolff, 2010

The distribution of net wealth in the United States, 2007. The net wealth of many people in the lowest 20% is negative because of debt.
http://en.wikipedia.org/wiki/Voodoo_economics

2. The Top 2-20%

A tiny 1 percent elite continues to float above everyone else. Below it, sits the professional middle class – an upper level of college graduates. Families earning about $113,000 annually in 2009 would be in the top 80 percent in income. College graduates make up only about 30 percent of the population, and throughout the 2000s, their incomes barely budged. A college degree may be losing some of its economic luster. As more Americans have gone to college, the quality of college education has become more inconsistent, and the value of a degree from a nonselective school has gone down. The future for an average college graduate is not bright, while that of a student from a selective college is good. A college degree is not the kind of protection against job or wage loss that it was in the past.[37]

3. The Middle Class: 20-85%

An important economic trend in the United States over the past couple of generations has been the sorting of Americans into winners and losers and the slow hollowing-out of the middle class. The incomes of the bottom 90 percent of Americans have been stagnant for almost three decades. Between 2000 and 2010, median income for working households fell from $61,574 to $55,276.[38]

The true center of American society has always been its nonprofessionals – high-school graduates – who make up 58 percent of the adult population. And as manufacturing jobs and semi-skilled office positions disappear, much of this group is drifting downward. For young adults without family wealth to help them, trying to join the upper economic tier is like running after a departing bus. Were it not for the fact that the average family was working at least 500 more hours a year in 2000 than in the 1970s, mainly because of women's entry into the labor force, incomes for the middle class would have fallen even farther.[39]

The bottom 30 percent of Americans – 100 million people – have an average net worth of $10,000 or less. And, more than 50 million Americans have negative net worth – they owe more than they own.[40]

4. Poverty: 15% and Below

Increasing poverty is one result of rising inequality. The combined impact of high unemployment and declining wages has resulted in a national poverty rate in 2010 of 15.1 percent. This was up from 14.3 percent in 2009. State-wide, poverty rates range from 8.3 percent in New

Hampshire to 22.4 percent in Mississippi. Since 2010, poverty has expanded by an additional 2.6 million people, bringing the total number of Americans in poverty to 46.2 million. The poverty rate for children was 22.0 percent in 2010, representing 16.4 million kids living in poverty. In 2010, more than one-third (35.5 percent) of all people living in poverty were children.[41]

Fifty million people or 17.4 million families couldn't buy sufficient food in 2009. About one million children from more than a third of these households missed meals regularly. A total of 1.6 million people used emergency shelters or transitional housing during 2007 – 2008, suggesting that 1 in every 50 Americans used shelters at some point. About 170,000 families lived in homeless shelters.[42]

Percent and Number of People in the U.S. Below the Poverty Threshold

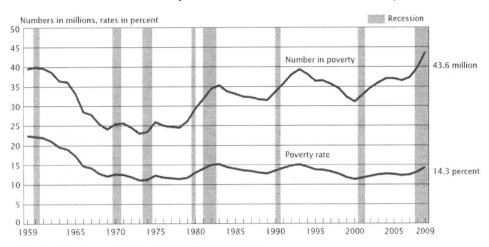

Note: The data points are placed at the midpoints of the respective years.
Source: U.S. Census Bureau, Current Population Survey, 1960 to 2010 Annual Social and Economic Supplements.

Insights: Inequality and Neoliberalism

The neoliberal policies of the last 30 years and the double whammy of economic globalization have hurt the bottom 80 percent of the U.S. population. Economic history has shown that the more laissez-faire an economy, the more unequal it tends to be. If you are in the top 20 percent of the income scale, you are likely to gain something from neoliberalism, and the higher you are up the ladder, the more you gain. On the other hand, the bottom 80 percent all lose, and the lower you are on the ladder, the more you lose.[43]

Many neoliberals do not believe their policies have contributed to greater social inequality. They counter that those whose wages have stagnated should improve their skills by getting further education. Yet, the weakening of all the equalizing institutions mentioned above contributes far more to the new inequality than changes in demand for skills. Blaming the economic plight on the individual is a handy escape hatch for politicians, economists, and commentators to avoid discussing the more politically loaded factors, such as how the system is organized and for whose benefit.

Moreover, focusing on education conveniently blames the government and public school teachers for the problems. Neoliberals have a ready solution to education shortfalls: school vouchers and privatization of education.[44]

Questions to Consider

1. Do you think the emphasis on social inequality should be a major concern for Americans today?

IMPACT #10: ASCENSION OF DOLLAR DEMOCRACY

Impact #10, the ascension of dollar democracy, reflects how neoliberal policies have influenced the U.S. political system. Both the Republican and Democrat parties support neoliberal policies, although it would be fair to say the Republicans have embraced them more enthusiastically. Neo-liberals channel money into the political system to support candidates who favor their policies. This vicious cycle has compromised our democracy and increased inequality. This cannot go on indefinitely, since the interests of the wealthy elite are not necessarily in the best interest of the whole nation.

Elite democracy and participatory democracy are two parts of the political process. **Elite democracy** is where elites use their influence for their own self-interest. They donate huge sums to political campaigns to buy the loyalty of consenting politicians. Politics in the U.S. has evolved into a system in which politicians need large sums of money to mount expensive campaigns for offices ranging from city council to president. Donations pour into the advertising media where candidates say their message is good for the public but really it serves the interests of the elites providing large campaign donations. The politicians then promote the elites' self-serving agenda, such as privatization of community-owned assets, economic growth without regard for the environment, and military power to exert dominance throughout the world.

In contrast to elite democracy, **participatory democracy** attempts to check the abuses of elite democracy and corporate power with careful oversight of the whole process. Increasingly, participatory democracy involves citizen groups who are playing a "watchdog" role over giant corporations in an effort to curb their financial excesses and harmful corporate policies.

CONCLUDING INSIGHTS:
THE TEN IMPACTS OF NEOLIBERLAISM

I have included in this chapter the 10 impacts of neoliberalism that I think are the most significant and destructive. You may ask, "Didn't anything good come out of neoliberal policies?" What about the internet, the technological achievements, and the amazing drugs we have now to save people's lives? I would agree that these examples are noteworthy. But government funding created the internet at one of the state-supported research universities, the University of Illinois. Also, the government funds much of the research for new life-saving medical drugs at research institutions. Neoliberals, generally, do not support government sponsored research and development.

Neoliberal policies have shaped government policy since the 1980s, but managed capitalism has not disappeared altogether. There are still public schools, government funding for research, public parks, and regulations. But neoliberal policies have been whittling away at managed capitalism for decades. Even though neoliberals have made major headway in putting their agenda into action, it has not been all smooth sailing – there has been resistance on many fronts.

The U.S. at the time of this writing is in gridlock. Neoliberals are locked in a heated war to preserve as much of their agenda as possible, such as low tax rates for the elite, and to push the privatization of Social Security. Will neoliberalism succeed? The cards are stacked in their favor.

Questions to Consider

1. Do you think these 10 impacts of neoliberalism on American society accurately portray the situation?
2. How do you think a neoliberal might explain each of these 10 impacts?

CHAPTER FIVE

The Economic Globalization Puzzle: Ten Pieces

"We have a tug-of-war, really, between a domestic economy and a global economy."

--- Bill Gross, founder and investor PIMCO Bond Investments

AN INTRODUCTION TO ECONOMIC GLOBALIZATION

Is Economic Globalization Good or Bad? It Depends on Your Point of View.

Think of economic globalization as a train, a fast moving train. If you are lucky and can catch the train and take a good seat, then economic globalization seems like a great idea. But if you are on the tracks trying to catch the train, and it is not stopping to pick you up, then economic globalization is not all it's cracked up to be. If you are a student who is about to graduate with a high school degree and cannot find a good job because most have been outsourced to a lower-wage country then you might not cheer for globalization. But if you are the company that outsourced that job to a lower-wage country you might cheer for economic globalization because your wage costs have gone down. If you have a business that imports washing machines made in China for a good price that you can turn around and sell to U.S. consumers for a sizable profit, then you might cheer economic globalization. But if you are a worker in the U.S. factory that made the washing machines that the owners closed down because the jobs went to China, then you won't cheer for economic globalization. If you are a farmer in a periphery country that relies on free irrigation water to grow your crops, and then a multinational corporation (MNC) buys up the water rights, which means that you now have to pay for water, then you would curse economic globalization. But if you are an investor in the multinational water company, and you are making good returns on your investment, then you might praise economic globalization. In other words, your opinion of economic globalization depends on your point of view. Ask different people from different walks of life, and you are bound to get different answers.

Promoters of economic globalization often portray it as inevitable, the result of economic forces that are beyond human control. They persuade nations that if they are not on board the economic globalization train, then they will be left behind at the station. Therefore, you must jump on board the globalization express for the fast ride to economic prosperity. We have seen economic globalization played out during the 1896-1914 classical era of capitalism. Yet, the economic integration of the world during that period of history pales in comparison to today. As we have seen, there were three responses to the 1970s economic crisis: neoliberalism, economic globalization, and financialization. We have already discussed neoliberalism in the last two chapters; I will examine economic globalization in this chapter and the next.

Economic globalization operates according to capitalist principles, but there are different versions of capitalism. It draws in different national economies. The U.S. promotes neoliberalism as the favored economic system but, for example, Europe is a more mixed economy and China, Russia, Brazil, and India favor a more state-capitalist model. National economies follow their own version of capitalism, which may range from participating very little in the capitalist economy to full emersion of their national economy into the world economy. For example, Cuba is a socialist country yet exports sugar on the world market and hosts tourists from Europe. Venezuela has prided itself on renouncing the U.S. and its policies of neoliberalism but gladly sells its oil to the U.S.

One of the gates to the Grand Bazaar in Tehran, Iran. Although its economic influence has diminished somewhat in recent years, it remains the largest market of its kind in the world.

Many nations differ in how they think capitalism should operate. Some nations with long histories of market activity and trade wish to keep their traditional market economy. For example, in Iran the bazaaris or merchants that sell goods at the souk or marketplace have followed this tradition for hundreds of years. If Iran would "open up" to economic globalization and neoliberalism, the bazaaris and souks would give way to big-box chain stores that would offer more "choices" of consumer items but would drive the bazaaris out of business. For the time being, Iranian politicians have favored supporting the bazaaris.

Certain factors are necessary for economic globalization to operate. I have organized these factors into 10 puzzle pieces that when pieced together make up an economic globalization puzzle. All of the puzzle pieces are needed for the full picture of economic globalization to emerge. Using a systems approach, let's look at each of these separate pieces of the whole picture.

The thinking has been that economic globalization would be good for core countries. It might be hard a first, but all would look rosy in the future. Although many manufacturing and low-skilled jobs would be lost, the government would retrain these workers as high-skilled service workers and reap the benefits of economic globalization. This has not been the case. In fact, economic globalization has hurt the core countries, except for the top 10 percent. Some middle and periphery nations, such as China, have manipulated economic globalization to seize an economic advantage for themselves. Even though some middle and periphery countries are profiting, there are vast economic differences among its citizens. On the other hand, many of the core countries are reeling with high unemployment rates and too much

Ten Pieces of the Economic Globalization Puzzle

1. Reduce the local
2. Economic growth
3. Promoting network
4. Rules
5. Free trade
6. Privatization and commodification
7. Corporate and state enterprise concentration
8. Specialization
9. Squeeze labor
10. Military hegemony

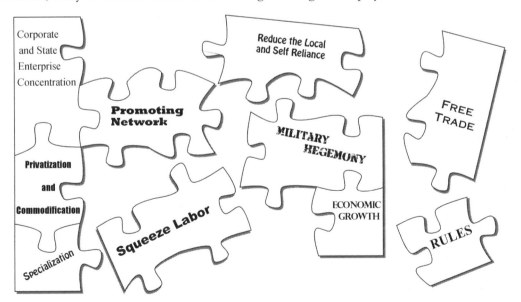

The Economic Globalization Puzzle

debt. This is not how economic globalization supporters in the core countries pictured the outcome.

You may be surprised to find that many of the puzzle pieces are similar to the dozen ingredients in the neoliberal stew. That is because the core nations, especially the U.S., that are championing economic globalization have neoliberalism as their preferred national economy. They wish to spread their neoliberal version of capitalism to as many parts of the world as possible. Although they have been successful in many countries, many nations have defied the U.S. and have state capitalism or managed capitalism. The world is not neatly packaged into just neoliberalism, which makes studying this subject more challenging but interesting. Join with me now in piecing together the 10 parts to the economic globalization puzzle.

Questions to Consider

1. Have you benefitted or not benefitted from economic globalization? Explain.

PUZZLE PIECE #1: A REDUCTION OF LOCAL COMMUNITIES AND SELF-RELIANCE

In the first piece of the economic globalization puzzle, businesses push to reduce individual, local, community, and national self-reliance and replace it with integration into and dependence upon the global economy. Reducing self-reliance means replacing small, local businesses with large mega-stores owned by those outside the community and replacing small, local, farms with corporate-owned, industrial-scale agriculture. Large corporations do not profit from self-reliant communities.

Corporations' first commercial target was to integrate local, self-sufficient agriculture into the world economy. Until recently, most of the world's people were farmers; today only one in eight is a farmer.[1] Economic globalization pushes self-reliant farmers to abandon their land and community and engage in some way in the capitalist economy. Colonizers pressured farmers remaining on their land to give up subsistence agriculture and work as laborers on large monocrop plantations geared to export. The plantations specialized in particular cash crops that the owners sold on the world market. Currently in China there has been a policy shift from supporting agriculture in the countryside to favoring industry in the cities. Thus, poverty has increased in rural areas resulting in farmers or their family members leaving for the cities to find work in construction or factories.

A historical example shows how the shift from self-reliance to integration into the global economy took place in Africa during the heyday of imperialism 1870-1914. Most Africans neither joined nor fought Europeans colonizers; they tried to continue living as they had been for centuries. But this was difficult to do; colonial rule upset their traditional way of life. Colonial officials handled commerce, legal disputes, and land ownership very differently from the way they had been in the past. Their traditional rulers lost all authority, except where Europeans used them as local administrators. Changes in landholding were especially troublesome, since most Africans were farmers or herders, and their land was important to them. In places such as Egypt and West Africa, the colonial rulers left farmers in place but encouraged them to grow cash crops and then collected taxes on the crops. Elsewhere, the new rulers declared any land that farmers did not cultivate to be "waste" or "vacant" land and gave it to private companies or to European planters and ranchers. Thus, many Africans ended up squatters, sharecroppers, or ranch hands on land they had held for generations. In South Africa, colonizers forced many people off their lands and onto "reserves," like Native Americans in the U.S.

Colonial rulers were also interested in African labor. But they did not want to pay wages high enough to find workers voluntarily. Instead, they set various taxes, such as the "hut tax" or the "head tax," which Africans had to pay. To find the money to pay the tax, Africans had little choice but to accept whatever wage-paying work the Europeans offered, no matter how poorly paid. Colonizers recruited lowly-paid Africans to work on plantations, railroads, and other modern enterprises. In South African mines, the owners paid African miners on average one-tenth as much as European miners.

Despite the low wages, many Africans left their rural villages for cities and mining camps. Many migrated great distances and stayed away for years at a time. Most migrant workers were men who left their wives and children behind in villages or on reserves. This caused great hardship for African women, who had to grow food for their families during the men's absences. Colonial rulers also replaced traditional African communal property rights with the modern concept of private property. They gave the property rights to men as head of the household. They tricked many men into selling their private property to pay taxes or get a little extra money.

President of an agricultural cooperative in Guinea, Africa in an onion field. Practicing subsistence agriculture as in the past.

With integration into the global economy, there was an effort by the colonizers to shift farm production from local consumption to specialized crops for export. Since the marketplace paid small farmers the world price for their specialized cash crops, in effect the small African farmer was competing with other farmers around the world. Many small farmers could not make a living doing this and either sold their farm land to large landowners and moved to cities or became a hired hand on their former land.

This story of Africa in the late 19th century has been repeated untold times through modern history. Even after former colonies became independent nations, many continued with the same type of economy as before. Today, the economies of the world's periphery nations remain in a weakened state.

Economic globalization presents difficult challenges to nations. It has transferred economic power away from national governments and into the hands of global corporations or state enterprises. National economies no longer operate within their national borders alone. Nations participating in the global economy must follow the rules of global institutions that override national laws, such as the World Bank and WTO. Economic globalization also undercuts managed capitalism and a nation's efforts to provide good jobs.

Questions to Consider

1. Why are large corporations and state enterprises targeting local, self-reliant and independent national economies with managed capitalism for integration into the world economy? Are they successful?

PUZZLE PIECE #2: ECONOMIC GROWTH

One impact of neoliberalism, as we have seen, has been a fixation with economic growth. Economic globalization supporters see growth as a way to measure "progress" and "lift" the poor out of poverty and into the middle class. They assume that growth will provide more people with a comfortable standard of living. However, I consider three important outcomes of growth: growth and inequality, growth and the environment, and growth and well-being. I will cover all of these topics in chapter 6.

PUZZLE PIECE #3: THE PROMOTING NETWORK

The third piece of the economic globalization puzzle is the promoting network, which has three parts: consumerism and advertising, media, and education. The message of the promoting network is that economic globalization is good for everyone.

1. Consumerism and Advertising

The world's consumers must continue to buy things, and new consumer products need to be added every year for our economy, as it is organized, to continue to grow. The world is consuming goods and services at an unsustainable pace with serious consequences for the well-being of people and the planet. Around 1.7 billion people worldwide – more than a quarter of humanity – are adopting Western diets, transportation, and lifestyles. In China alone, 240 million people have joined the consumer ranks.[2]

Consumerism requires certain behaviors and values. Advertising agencies, whose job it is to push people to consume certain products, create and support consumer behaviors. Critics say that consumer-focused values promote instant gratification, constant unhappiness, individualism, and selfishness. Consumers need constant stimulation, are restless, experience mood ups and downs, and place importance on outward appearance. They are always looking for something new and throwing away what is old. If the consumer isn't pleased, the product is thrown away. These values and behaviors even carry over into relationships and politics.

Most of us, including myself, want to enjoy a comfortable living standard and have modern conveniences that make our lives easier and more enjoyable. But there is a wobbly line between what boosts our well-being and what is too much. I am not here to tell you where that line is, even if I could. In fact, that line has wobbled throughout my life. As I mentioned before, for many years I was very satisfied living a simple life. Then in 1983, I started my own gift and decorating business. Twice a year my partner and I went to gift shows to buy merchandise for the next season. Suddenly all the merchandise at the gift shows glittered like gold, and my personal consumption increased. I not only bought consumer items for others to consume, I consumed the merchandise myself! Truly, it was a consumers' delight. At first I was happy decorating my house and making it stylish and comfortable for my family. I also enjoyed showcasing our purchases at our small retail shop. But then I found that the glitter of consumption began to wear off after a few years. I experienced the constant dissatisfaction that often accompanies the overly-active consumer – no consumer items made me happy anymore. I had already decorated my house and my closets were full. What next? I wanted a simpler life, and I wanted to pursue what I considered more meaningful work. We sold our business and I decided to return to the education field after a 12 year absence. I enrolled at Illinois State University to pursue my graduate degrees and taught there as well. My story of consumerism is one often repeated. It reminds us that we, including myself, need to be aware of the emotional pull of consumerism and how it can affect our lives.

2. The Media

The media spouts consumerism. At the heart of the media lies a blurry line between information, entertainment, and promotion of products. The media has shifted its content into opportunities to sell ideas, values, and products. In many markets, major MNCs own media stations and influence their content. This concentration reduces diversity and depth of content for the public, while increasing the corporate message. Ownership interests affect what is and is not covered. Stories can end up being slanted or omitted so as not to upset advertisers or owners. For example, one cannot expect Disney to report on sweatshop labor if it is accused of being involved in such things itself. As we all know, an informed population is key to a lively democracy, but now corporate media threatens it.

World's Largest Media Conglomerates (*Fortune 500*, 2010)

Company	Revenues in $ million	Profits in $ million
Walt Disney	$38,063	$3,963
News Corp	$32,778	$2,539
Time Warner	$26,888	$2,578
CBS	$14,059	$ 724
Viacom	$13,497	$1,548

3. Education

Education is the third factor in the promoting network. Since many of you may be students or educators, you may find this a bit odd that I am saying that education today promotes economic globalization. I would like to make two points in making my case: 1. Education is increasingly focusing on training for specialized jobs in a highly competitive globalized society and 2. Corporations are having a greater influence in shaping curriculum, and education is becoming increasingly a profit-making sector.

First, you may say that it is the mission of educators to train students to find a job in a highly competitive global economy. I don't disagree, but I might add that the laser-like focus on specialized training has left a yawning gap in students' understanding of the world in which they live. Instead, educators train students to be robots in a globalized economy, competing for the scraps thrown to them by the corporate world. The message of competition, individualism, and consumption is everywhere; every billboard or 30 second commercial drums in this message. This constant drumbeat needs to be countered by educators teaching critical and creative thinking and promoting global awareness.

Second, corporations are having a greater influence on our educational system. For example, in 2007, global energy giant British Petroleum (BP) selected two universities to lead a $500 million research effort to develop new sources of energy.[3] It is the same BP that spilt oil into the Gulf of Mexico in 2010. Also, governments around the world are eroding the right to free, public education. Privatization of education is increasing. For example, textbooks are using corporate logos in their materials, and corporations provide free materials for students. Corporate sponsors consider students to be "customers" who come to schools looking to purchase a commodity and expect the grades to reflect their financial investment.

Questions to Consider

1. What do you think is the most significant promoting network for economic globalization? Why?

PUZZLE PIECE #4: MAKING THE RULES

Our national economy needs rules to run smoothly. But today our economic boundaries have expanded beyond the national economy to include the world. You may be surprised to learn that often the rules that guide a national economy are at odds with the rules that direct a global economy. But the big question is – "Who makes these rules?" All kinds of different groups want to make the economic rules to benefit them. But I believe the global economy should operate fairly, justly and sustainably and bring prosperity and well-being to as many people as possible. When evaluating the global economy, I look for ways in which it accomplishes these ideals. If it fails, I am critical of it. So who makes the rules for the global economy and what are these rules? These are the very two questions that we will address next.

The rules for the global economy have a birth date, July 1944, and a birth place, Bretton Woods resort. The 730 delegates attending the Bretton Woods conference were from all 44 Allied nations who gathered together to create a new economic order toward the end of World War II. The U.S. had the strongest economy at the time and, thus, directed the writing of the rules. The delegates wanted a new global economic system with new institutions and rules to further economic development. The new institutions were the World Bank, the International Monetary Fund (IMF), and soon after (1948), the General Agreement on Tariff and Trade (GATT), which would turn into the World Trade Organization (WTO) in 1995. The purpose of the World Bank is to loan money when needed to middle and periphery countries. The IMF regulates monetary flows around the world to insure stability. And from 1948 on, the rules of GATT regulated global trade, but it was mainly limited to manufactured goods.

Since the U.S. was the world's leading creditor at the time, its delegation made sure that the more money a country put in, the more votes it had. Thus, the U.S. had enough votes to block any decision it didn't like. They also decided that national debts would be redeemable for gold, and that gold could be changed into dollars. Both the IMF and the World Bank are located in Washington D.C.

The World Bank

The **World Bank** makes loans to middle and periphery countries for programs that reduce poverty. Private banks shy away from these investments because they are risky. For example, in the post-war years the World Bank loaned money to Europe for reconstruction. After first focusing on Western Europe, the World Bank shifted its lending to middle and periphery countries. It helped them develop their natural resources, get clean water, escape poverty and enter the modern economy.

World Bank headquarters in Washington D.C., USA

World Bank projects – dams, harbors, highways and airports – helped borrowing countries become part of the global economy.

From 1968 to 1980, the World Bank made more loans for social services and infrastructure than previously. In 1968, World Bank policy shifted from only infrastructure loans to building schools and hospitals, improving literacy and modernizing agriculture. In addition to private banks, the World Bank added the global bond market, which issued bonds, as a new source for loans. But this increase in lending to periphery nations was adding to their debt. From 1976 to 1980, their world debt rose at an annual rate of 20 percent.[4] This debt was difficult to repay because of rising interest rates and an economic slowdown. From 1980-1989, periphery nations had to borrow more to repay their increasing debts.

The World Bank's lending appeared to be admirable; however, their actual lending practices were another matter. The focus has mostly been to loan money to build expensive infrastructure – railroads, highways, electric power plants, airports, bridges, ports, dams, and communication networks. But the World Bank largely ignored smaller-scale, less-expensive, and locally-appropriate alternatives. Since many of these big infrastructure projects required large contractors and equipment, those getting the loans needed the materials and technical expertise of large corporate contractors from core countries. Keep in mind that investors in the core countries largely finance the World Bank by selling bonds to investors in the core countries. Thus, the World Bank must collect interest and principle from the taxpayers of the countries who are receiving the loans. The result is the World Bank tends to finance bigger, more expensive projects which support large corporations in the core countries and big investors. This means more debt for the periphery. For every $1 going to the World Bank, U.S. exporters win back more than $2 in bank-financed contracts.[5]

The International Monetary Fund (IMF)

The **International Monetary Fund** is very powerful – yet few know how it really works. The IMF is a "manager" of the international credit system. Bretton Woods established the IMF to regulate an international monetary system based on exchangeable currencies (currencies were pegged to the US dollar). The IMF encouraged economic growth rather than deflation. Unlike today, in the past there were no speculative markets in international currencies because there were fixed exchange rates.[6]

In the 1980s, the IMF changed from the Bretton Woods with acceptance of different economic systems to promoting neoliberalism as the version for all nations to follow. This model included low taxes, financial speculation, few social services, and opening financial markets to outside investment. This new IMF formula, known as the **Washington Consensus**, was named for the three institutions that shaped its policies, all located in downtown Washington D.C.: IMF, World Bank, and the U.S. Treasury Department. In the 1980s or 1990s, the nations that borrowed too much and got into financial difficulties had to agree to an IMF program of opening their markets to outside investment, as well as budget austerity, in order to qualify for a loan to repay their debt. The IMF decided how much debtor countries could spend on education, health care, and environmental protection, which most often is a reduced amount from their previous budgets. If countries followed these IMF rules then the debtor nation could take on more debt. This IMF policy did not help long-term development and resulted in extreme debt for the debtor nations. In fact, the middle and periphery nations that thrived in the 1980s and 1990s were those of East Asia, with managed markets that had rejected the Washington Consensus rules.[7]

If the indebted nations are unable to pay back the loans (must be paid back in US$), the IMF oversees their financial punishment. The indebted nations must open their markets, inviting foreign corporations to "invest" in their economies. They must also sell their natural resources at world market prices to anyone who wishes to purchase them. The IMF expects the debtors to cut government funded social programs, such as medical care and education. With this money, debtor nations must repay loans to the World Bank, IMF, bondholders, or private banks. The consequences for indebted countries' citizens have most often been bleak. **Fiscal austerity** – raising taxes and reducing government spending – taps down demand, leading to higher unemployment. Tight monetary policy and high interest rates stop long-term investment in its tracks. Privatization of public utilities, transportation, and banks puts more money in the hands of the wealthy. The IMF claims that in the long run these policies will help everyone.[8]

At the beginning of this section I asked, "Who makes the rules for the global economy?" On this global playing field, MNCs have found a way to make the rules of the World Bank, the IMF and the World Trade Organization (WTO) to benefit them. Rules made by these institutions are stronger than national laws. Thus, these three global institutions have replaced the oversight of corporations by national governments. Let's turn to the third global rule-making institution: the World Trade Organization (WTO).

PUZZLE PIECE #5: FREE TRADE AND THE WORLD TRADE ORGANIZATION (WTO)

The heart of economic globalization is #5 in our puzzle – free trade. Free traders demand that national governments get rid of regulations, laws, or tariffs that slow down trade across national borders. The goal of free trade is admirable – global integration through trade in order to have a high standard of living for all of the world's people. Who can argue with that? However, in this section we will explore more than just the rosy surface of the global free trade debate.

Man Controlling Trade in Washington D.C.

When we think of free trade we usually think of goods imported and exported across national borders so that consumers can enjoy inexpensive clothes made in China, savor specialty cheese from France, pump cheap gasoline into our cars from Saudi Arabia, and take pleasure in movies from Hollywood. Free trade also involves trade in such services as insurance, accounting, legal assistance, and sales. It includes patents that protect inventors of medicines, music, books, and even seeds. Today free trade also applies to capital – currency, stocks, bonds, and U.S. treasury bills. Technology has made it possible to shift large sums of money across borders anywhere in the world at the strike of a computer key.

The third institution to manage the world economy was set up in 1995 to govern the global rules of free trade: the World Trade Organization (WTO). Before the WTO was the 1948 General Agreement on Tariffs and Trade (GATT). It reduced tariff rates among core countries, but it was limited to manufactured goods. Before Bretton Woods there was trade among nations, but countries made bilateral trade deals, which were one-on-one, country-to-country agreements. After Bretton Woods there was an effort, led by business interests, to expand world trade. Corporations pushed for access to more unregulated and non-union labor, more consumer markets, and ways to get cheaper natural resources. In addition to manufactured goods, corporations also wanted trade rules for investments, services, copyright laws, and patents. They started working to form a powerful institution to enforce trade rules.[9]

The WTO was born on January 1, 1995. It first was an agreement among 125 countries, which has since expanded to 153 countries. Headquartered in Geneva, Switzerland, 625 people currently staff its operations. The WTO's stated aims are to promote free trade and stimulate economic

114

growth.[10] It regulates 97 percent of world trade between participating countries. It also has a way to force participants to follow its rules. Decision making is generally done by consensus, and the larger the market size of a nation, the more bargaining power it has. Therefore, the U.S. and EU have a powerful voice in the WTO.

Article III of the WTO does not allow countries to ban goods for trade based on "process and production methods." This means a country does not even have the right to ban the import of products produced in an environmentally harmful way. This favors commercial interests, which was seen in one of the first cases brought before the WTO to test its rulings. In September 1997, a WTO panel ruled that the EU was illegally buying higher priced bananas produced by its former colonies in the Caribbean. The U.S., which does not produce any bananas, brought a lawsuit against the EU on behalf of the U.S.-based Chiquita Corporation. Chiquita grew lower-priced bananas in Latin America on huge plantations using low-wage farm workers. In the Caribbean, banana producers tended to be small-scale farmers who owned and worked their own land (an average of

Cavendish bananas are the most common banana type sold in the world market.

three acres), usually having higher production costs. The U.S. and the EU hurled threats at each other, nearly setting off a trade war. The EU eventually gave in and said that it would go along with the WTO rules and would not favor Caribbean producers. The small-scale farmers would thus have to compete against large-scale corporate plantations.[11]

The WTO: Is It Beneficial?

If the WTO had been around in 1933, we might not have one of the largest corporations in the world today. In 1933, an Asian clothing manufacturing company decided to branch out into the manufacture of automobiles. It had everything going against it – it had no natural resources to make automobiles nor experience with the product, plus other nations (particularly the U.S. and Great Britain) were already making most of the cars in world. But the company caught the attention of its country's leadership, and the government decided to help it along. Government subsidies helped the company make its first car. Decades of high import tariffs protected it from foreign competition as it grew into a serious company. Domestic laws required that the company use parts made in the country, which supported domestic companies – from tires to machine tools and electronics – that created jobs. In 1939, the government did not allow either GM or Ford to sell automobiles within the country. The government even bailed out the struggling textile manufacturer as it moved forward in its business.

Originally known as the Toyoda Automatic Loom Company, today the company is called Toyota and it is the world's largest automobile manufacturer.[12] The example of the Toyota Corporation shows that free trade does not benefit a country that is developing its infant industries. Of course, now Toyota doesn't like any tariffs or trade policies that restrict the sale of its automobiles.

Insights: The WTO and Free Trade

As we have seen, the world's dominant economic power with the most competitive industries wants free trade. The core countries like free trade when it benefits them. With free trade, local industries cannot compete with larger corporations, and the marketplace either wipes them out or larger corporations buy them. Wages collapse. The middle class becomes the working poor. This has happened in Argentina, Chile, Mexico, and is happening now in a core country, the U.S. In the process, the largest corporations and wealthiest individuals in the world become larger, stronger, and wealthier.

Free trade is a key ingredient of neoliberal capitalism. But as we have seen, if neoliberalism is not the best version of capitalism domestically, it is not the best brand of capitalism internationally. The rosy story of free trade is at odds with the way economic globalization actually works. In practice, free trade causes the U.S. government to sacrifice its national interest for the self-interest of economic elites. There is almost no discussion of how to line up the goals of free trade and still keep a high living standard in the U.S. and other core countries. The interests of corporations and the interests of the citizens do not match.

One way in which national economies grow is that government policies help decide which industries are worth growing and which are not. It was important in my home-town of Rockford,

Illinois, in the 1960s to have a strong machine-tool industry that created well-paying jobs, and it was in the nation's interest, as well. Machine tools are necessary for virtually every other form of heavy manufacturing. Once the government identifies key industries, it encourages and protects their domestic growth through subsidies, legal protections (such as patent laws), import tariffs, regulation to ensure quality, and building suitable infrastructure.[13]

A die for automotive bushings at Rockford Toolcraft, Inc. Rockford, Illinois a tool and die manufacturer.

But MNCs have touted the false slogan of "free trade will benefit us all."

I believe that as the loss of its national industries under free trade policies continues to batter the U.S., and as China becomes a more dominant economic power, the U.S. government will ease its push for free trade to a policy more beneficial to its economic situation.

Questions to Consider

1. Could the policies of free trade promoted by politicians and the mass media actually hurt the majority of Americans? How could this happen? What do you think?

PUZZLE PIECE #6: PRIVATIZATION AND COMMODIFICATION
Schmeiser v. Monsanto

For over 60 years, Percy Schmeiser and his wife, Louise, worked their fifth-generation family farm in Bruno, Saskatchewan, Canada. Schmeiser considered retiring around 1995, but Louise wondered what he would do with his spare time, so he decided to keep farming for a while longer. What to do with his spare time was decided for him in 1998, when the agri-business corporation Monsanto sued Schmeiser for patent violation. Monsanto charged that it had found GMO (genetically modified organisms) canola seed in Schmeiser's field, and that he had to pay a $15 an acre fee for using its patented GMO seed.

Monsanto, headquartered outside St. Louis, Missouri, is the world's leading producer of genetically engineered (GE) seeds. It alters GE seeds genetically to boost productivity. In Monsanto's case the seeds can be used with their herbicide (weed killer) marketed as Roundup, of which Monsanto is also the world's leading producer. Monsanto is determined to defend its very profitable GE seed business.[14]

Schmeiser never had anything to do with Monsanto. But Schmeiser and around 400 farmers have received threats of legal action from Monsanto. Few of these cases ever get to court because most farmers simply give in because they don't have the money to outlast Monsanto's deep pockets. The company hears their cases in Monsanto-friendly courts in Missouri. This can add thousands of dollars to a farmer's legal bills. Several of the cases that have gone to court are enough to scare farmers into surrendering to Monsanto's demands. The courts fined Mississippi farmer Homan McFarling $780,000 for growing Roundup Ready soybeans without paying Monsanto's licensing fee. The courts fined Tennessee farmer Ken Ralph $1.7 million and sentenced him to eight months in jail for a variety of offenses against Monsanto.[15]

Percy Schmeiser a farmer from Bruno, Saskatchewan Canada had his field of canola seed contaminated with Monsanto's Round-Up Ready Canola.

In the Schmeiser case, the judge and appellate court ruled in Monsanto's favor. The court decision prohibits Schmeiser from using his seed again and requires him to pay Monsanto about $10,000 for its user fees and up to $75,000 in profits from his 1998 crop. The Schmeisers appealed their case to the Canadian Supreme Court, which said Monsanto's patent is valid, but the court did not force Schmeiser to pay Monsanto anything as he did not profit from the GE canola in his fields. The family felt somewhat relieved after the verdict. In the fight against Monsanto they received support from around the world. But there has been a financial toll. Their legal fees alone were more than $400,000. The Schemeisers realized that it was nearly impossible for an individual to stand up to a large corporation such as Monsanto.[16]

Privatization

Number six in the economic globalization puzzle is the increasing privatization and commodification that is occurring on a worldwide scale. When Western economic consultants and World Bank advisors meet with officials from periphery countries about how to compete in the world economy, one of the first steps these advisors tell them to do is to privatize their commonly held land. Their advice is to shift land from collective ownership into individually-owned parcels of land. The owner of the individual parcel will hold a legal deed that shows ownership. The owner can buy and sell the land in the market place. The individual owner of the land also has an asset which s/he can use as collateral to borrow money from a bank.

Privatization is familiar to Westerners, since the law of property ownership has been in place for centuries. For example, I own my own house, and I have a deed to prove my ownership. But to some people who live in communities, such as villages or tribes, individual ownership is unfamiliar. For many, their group owned the land collectively for generations. An individual may farm a small plot of that land and call it his/her own, but s/he does not legally own it. If the group goes ahead

117

with privatization of the land, each individual may use the land as collateral to borrow money. But if an individual cannot repay the loan, s/he risks losing the land that the bank has used as collateral for the loan. The land that has been part of the community for generations is passed on to a bank or money lender for repayment of the debt. The family land is lost forever.

The World Bank, IMF, and WTO seek to privatize public services. This means selling public assets to private (usually foreign) corporations that are run for profit rather than as a public service. A list of about 160 threatened public services includes education, health care, elder and child care, sewage, garbage pick-up, parks, energy, water, banking, telecommunications, construction, insurance, transportation, shipping, postal services, and tourism. In most countries, privatization is already well underway. The following is a brief description of two privatization efforts.

1. The Privatization of Gazprom in Russia

After the break-up of the Soviet Union in 1991, the new Russian government privatized in part its natural gas and oil industries. A cut-throat scramble to pick up Russia's vast natural resources at bargain-basement prices took place among hopeful Russian entrepreneurs. Although private interests latched on to much of the natural gas industry, currently the Russian government holds a controlling stake in what was the world's third largest corporation in 2009: Gazprom. It is the largest producer of natural gas in the world and Russia's largest company. Gazprom's activities accounted for 10 percent of Russia's gross domestic product in 2008. To show the close connection between government and corporations in state-capitalist Russia, Demitry Medvedev, elected president of Russia in 2008, was Gazprom's former Chairman.

2. The Privatization of Telemex in Mexico

The world's richest person in 2009-2010 was the Mexican billionaire Carlos "Slim" Helu. He was worth $53.5 billion, just edging out the American Microsoft founder Bill Gates who held assets worth $53 billion.[17] Slim owns many enterprises but amassed a fortune with the purchase of 50 percent of the stock in Telemex in 1990. Telemex was Mexico's state-owned telephone company, which the IMF pressured the government to sell off to comply with its push for privatization in the 1980s. Service to customers has had mixed results but has helped to concentrate wealth among a very few well-connected business people.[18]

Privatization of Water

The privatization of water involves putting public water systems into private hands. Increasing demand and shrinking supply has attracted the interest of global corporations who want to sell water for a profit. Some national governments have invited private companies to take over the management, operation, and sometimes even the ownership of public water systems. The World Bank says the privatization of water is a potential trillion-dollar industry. Investors dub water as the "blue gold" of the 21st century.[19]

Leading the charge for privatization are three big transnational corporations based in Europe: Vivendi, Suez, and RWE. All three dominate the global water businesses and planned to take over the public water systems in periphery countries. Instead, a series of protests in periphery countries have stopped their plans.[20]

Since the protests in Cochabamba, the big water companies are now changing their strategy and investing in more secure markets in North America and Europe. In the U.S., 85 percent of all water services are still in public hands, but that's a tempting target for water corporations. They have bought up the leading U.S. water companies – U.S. Filter, United Water, and American Water Works – intent on privatizing water in the U.S. and beyond.[23]

The Cochabamba Water Wars

Cochabamba demonstrators demand removal of consortium and end of privatization of water works in 2000.

One of the best known battles over privatization of water took place in Cochabamba, the third largest city in the Latin American country of Bolivia. The privatization of their municipal water supply sparked protests in 2000 called the "Cochabamba Water Wars." The Bolivian government experienced problems in the 1980s and turned to the World Bank for loans. In order to get the funds, the World Bank demanded that Bolivia privatize its railways, telephone system, national airlines, and oil industry. In 2000, the World Bank also told Bolivia to privatize its water industry. The Bolivian government agreed to the terms of the company, *Aguas del Tunari*, and signed a $2.5 billion, 40-year agreement. The government guaranteed the company a minimum 15 percent annual return on its investment.[21] Upon taking control, the company raised water rates an average of 35 percent to about $20 a month. This was a lot since customers only earned about $100 a month, and $20 was more than they spent on food. Protests erupted among the poor. Middle-class homeowners and business owners joined in the protests when their own water bills shot up. The protests grew larger and more intense. The government declared martial law and called out troops. As the protests turned violent, authorities killed one teenage boy and wounded more than 100 people. But the protesters carried on, and after five years the company finally left the country.[22] The people of Bolivia did not choose to privatize their public water systems; the World Bank forced them to as a condition for aid in the mid-1990s.

Questions to Consider

1. Who owns the water in your locality? If your water is not privatized, are there any plans to do so?

PUZZLE PIECE #7: CONCENTRATION OF POWER: MULTINATIONAL CORPORATIONS AND STATE ENTERPRISES

A **multinational corporation (MNC)** is an enterprise that manages production or delivers services in more than one country. Since the 1980s, several hundred global corporations and banks have driven economic globalization. Corporations are moving power and influence away from national, state, and local governments and communities to themselves. Corporations are not necessarily bad. There are many responsible corporations that are excellent employers and care about the planet and people. But, generally speaking, the power of huge MNCs has become excessive: their ownership has become more concentrated, they influence governmental policy, and the systems of checks and balances on their power at the national level are gone. Even fewer checks on their power exist on a global level.[24]

MNCs span every sector of the global economy. In 2007, there were 63,000 MNCs, increasing from 60,000 in 2000; in 1990, there were roughly half that number. Some estimates figure that just 500 of the largest MNCs account for at least 25 percent of world production and 70 percent of world trade, while their sales are equal to almost 50 percent of world GDP. In 2002, the top 200 corporations had combined sales equal to 28 percent of world GDP. But these 200 corporations only employed 0.82 percent of the global work force. In the U.S., 98 percent of all companies account for only 25 percent of business activity; the remaining two percent account for nearly 75 percent of the remaining activity. The top 500 corporations, which represent only one-tenth of one percent of all U.S. companies, control over two-thirds of the business resources in the U.S. and collect over 70 percent of all U.S. profits.[25]

Corporate growth is around four times as high as global economic growth. *Forbes*, a business magazine, did a Global 2000 study to highlight the growth of the 2,000 largest public companies on the planet (there are also private corporations worth billions). In the 2008 total, the Global 2000 companies accounted for $30 trillion in revenues, $2.4 trillion in profits, $119 trillion in assets and $39 trillion in market value. Around the world, just 72 million people, a very low number, work for these companies.[26]

Corporations actively direct cultural habits and consumer demand. The attraction of television and the increasing number of hours people, especially children, watch are disturbing to critics. In the U.S., watching TV is the third most time-consuming pastime after sleeping and working. And in the U.S., the 100 largest corporations pay for 75 percent of commercial and 50 percent of public television time.[27]

Corporations use their political and economic power to shape governmental policies. For example, interest groups lobby for lower tax rates and tax loopholes that benefit their corporate clients. Although the U.S. corporate tax rate is 35 percent, among the highest of core countries, the number of corporations who pay this rate is very low. A study found that two out of three U.S. corporations paid no federal income taxes from 1998 to 2005. It also found that 95 percent of corporations paid less than 5 percent of their income in taxes. The corporate share of taxes paid fell from 33 percent in the 1940s to 15 percent in the 1990s. On the other hand, the individual's share of taxes has risen from 44 to 73 percent.[28]

> **Questions to Consider**
> 1. If we want more jobs in the global economy, is turning to MNCs the answer? Explain.
> 2. Can you think of ways to curb the influence and power of global corporations?

PUZZLE PIECE #8: SPECIALIZATION

The eighth piece of the economic globalization puzzle is specialization, a term that has many different meanings. We will use it here to mean when companies, nations, and workers decide what goods and services to produce. With specialization individuals and organizations focus on the limited range of production tasks and skills they perform best. The key is efficiency. With specialization workers give up performing other tasks at which they are not as skilled, leaving those jobs to others who are better suited for them. An example of specialization is an assembly line, where individual workers perform specific tasks in the production process. Countries also specialize in products they produce best. For example, the American Midwest specializes in growing corn, and Central America grows bananas. The Congo in central Africa specializes in minerals, in which it is abundant. China specializes in low-wage manufacturing because it has an abundant supply of labor. The list goes on.

Wealthy Nation	Poor Nation
Commodity importing	Commodity exporting
Industrial exporting	Industrial importing

Specialization is similar to comparative advantage, which says that countries should specialize in the goods they produce most efficiently, rather than try to be self-sufficient. Adam Smith wrote about specialization and the division of labor. He described how each worker in a pin factory performed a single specialized task: One worker measured wire, another cut it, one pointed it, others made the head and so on. With specialization, workers made thousands more pins than if each worker made each pin separately. Thus, specialization increases output. Specialization can be profitable for companies, but it also can be repetitive and boring for the workers. Just ask any assembly line worker who performs a single task throughout the day sapping their creativity and spirit.[29] I know, I was one of them!

A Summer Job in a Potato Factory

I remember my assembly line summer job in a potato chip factory in Rockford, Illinois. I was an unskilled, but specialized worker. The potato chips traveled on a three-foot-wide, ceiling-level conveyer belt along one end of the factory. Along that belt were sloping metal chutes in which the potato chips slid down at exact times, every few seconds or so. I stood at the end of the metal chute holding a packaging bag, labeled with a particular potato chip brand. I placed the bag over the end of the chute, and into it the potato chips dropped.

Although more automated, this is a potato chip factory similar to the one I worked in.

Once the bag was full, I would send it through a sealing-machine, and then the sealed package of potato chips fell onto another conveyor belt bound for the packing room. I was bored after 10 minutes on the job! But I had to stay alert, because if I didn't pay attention and missed packaging the surging potato chips from the chute, I would end up with a pile of unbagged, salty potato chips at my feet. As you can imagine, it was hard to concentrate on such a dull task for hours on end. After every two-hour shift I had to step out of the mound of potato chips encircling my legs. Sometimes "sweepers" would come by and clean up the pile that collected around the "chute workers" ankles.

Since management knew that the workers got bored quickly, they switched us to different but equally boring jobs. My favorite job was packing the potato chip bags into cardboard cartons bound for supermarkets and discount stores. My least favorite task was when I had to pick out bad potatoes from a sea of potatoes coming down an ever-rolling, noisy conveyor belt. They came fast and furiously. Since there were just a few of us on this task, I worried that many bad potatoes slipped by my ever-watchful gaze and nimble fingers and ended up sliced into bad potato chips on someone's plate, but management didn't seem to be as worried as I was. Although the work was boring, my co-workers were nice and the pay was pretty good, especially with lots of overtime. I worked the whole summer. Since university tuition was very inexpensive during this time, the wages from my summer job were just enough to get me through a year of tuition, books, and living expenses.

Specialization is a vital part of economic globalization. To show the change over time, from generalization to specialization, I will tell another story about my experience with a non-specialized farm family of the 1960s. Since I grew up in the Midwest, the region will serve as an example of how specialization has destroyed economic livelihoods of the past.

Specialization has affected farmers. Many Americans have a romantic view of farming. I probably, do as well. I remember as a youngster, my family had good friends who lived nearby and farmed a couple hundred acres. I often visited their family and stayed with them on many occasions. They had dairy cattle – about 50 – and milked them precisely at 6 in the morning and 6 at night, seven days a week. It was physically demanding work, since they carried pails of milk to the gleaming steel pasteurizer in their barn, cleaned the barn, hauled in feed for the dairy cows, and handled hundreds of other daily chores. It was especially uncomfortable in the cold winters of northern Illinois, when the farmers herded the cattle from their daytime pastures to their nighttime barn. They had a number of chickens, and when visiting, I helped collect the eggs from the chicken coop. They sheared a small herd of sheep every spring, and they bundled and sold the wool. They had a few pigs for their own consumption and a large garden in the summer. The farmers grew corn and hay for animal feed, which they bailed and stored in the hay maw above the barn. They also had a couple of horses that we rode around the farm or out into the countryside. The men were always working outside, and the women were always working in the kitchen or in the garden.

121

To the six people living and working on the farm, it may not have been an ideal life, but I thought it was. As a youngster, being in the fresh air and around animals was my idea of heaven. But I did not have to do it every day, 365 days a year. The farm came to an end when the father suddenly died of a heart attack around the age of 45. The four children decided not to be farmers. They sold the farm, and when I visit Rockford, I am amazed that the farm on the hill overlooking a peaceful valley is now a shopping center circled by a busy four lane highway with cars whizzing by.

Dairy barn is similar to my friend's farm in the 1960s.

Food and Specialization in the Midwest

Farms are not like they were in the 1960s. Few of them exist anymore. Generalist farms, such as the one I visited as a youngster, have given way to specialist farms. Today's farmers are specialists. One specialist farmer, Melvin Stucke, operates an egg farm in western Ohio. He specializes in eggs – lots of eggs. Two huge henhouses, each longer than a football field, house 180,000 chickens. Each henhouse measures 450 feet long, and six narrow aisles divide it. Four stacks of cages line each aisle – each cage is 16x20 inches. The owners cram six 3-pound hens into just one cage, an animal rights nightmare. Each hen lays on average of 5-6 eggs a week. The cages are slightly tilted so that the eggs can roll down a conveyor belt running the length of the henhouse to the packers. Each day the chickens lay 165,000 eggs, which workers pack into 460 giant cases. The cases are then shipped to an enormous cracking plant, where the eggs are cracked and poured into huge vats of liquid eggs bound for fast food restaurants. Once the hens are too old for laying eggs, they end up as the main ingredient in dog food.[30]

How many times did I mention giant, fast, or mega? Everything I mentioned was gigantic. This is in keeping with specialization. Stucke is a typical mega-farmer. In an era of globalized agriculture,

Chickens in battery cages, part of factory or industrial farming.

farmers must specialize in one branch of farming, such as egg production, hogs, dairy cattle, corn or soybeans, cotton, or plantation crops. This is not only in the U.S. but worldwide. Each farm has thousands of acres and deals with such giant global agricultural corporations as ADM, Bunge, and Cargill. During the 1980s, many farmers, unable to make the transition to specialization, ended up selling their family farms to larger farmers or corporations. Some of the large agribusinesses even own the farms and hire the former landowners as employees.

Some farmers still own their own land, but, as in the case of many chicken producers, they contract with large chicken processors such as Tyson, to whom they sell their products. Although the farmers may still own their own land, they really work for corporations.[31]

Farming has changed from my idealized vision in the 1960s. Farms have become factories. Economic globalization is changing farming according to the same pattern that changed manufacturing. It pits farmers who till high-priced land and expect a good standard of living against large farmers in Brazil, for example, who farm less expensive land and hire low-wage laborers who have no expectations of a standard of living like an American farmer.[32] Many experts predict that both farms and corporations will get bigger, and highly-advertised brands will be more dominant.

Questions to Consider

1. List areas of specialization that you see around you today. Is this area of specialization new?

PUZZLE PIECE #9: SQUEEZE LABOR

Let's start this section on labor – #9 of the puzzle pieces – with the Stolper-Samuelson theorem. Although this theorem dates back to 1941, I think it is useful for those of you trying to find jobs or expect to have high salaries if you do land a job. The theorem basically says that the effect of trade between a core and a periphery nation is that the wages for the unskilled labor force in the core nation will be lower because they are competing globally with the unskilled workers in a periphery nation.[33]

This theorem is being played out today. For example, when the global economy added two billion low-wage workers from China, India, Eastern Europe and the former Soviet Union, wages fell across the board. When a core, capital-abundant country (such as the US) trades with a labor-abundant country (such as China), wages in the rich country fall, and corporate profits go up. The economic logic is simple. Free trade means an increase in the core country's labor supply, since the products made by periphery country workers can now be imported. Demand for workers in the core country falls as corporations shift labor-intensive production to the periphery country. The net result is an increase in the labor supply and a decrease in labor demand in the core country; thus wages fall.[34] Economists find that the globalization of the American economy has helped to freeze or lower middle-class incomes, further widening the gap between the very rich and the middle class. While America's rich are enjoying the sweet fruits of economic globalization, America's middle class and lower class are swallowing its bitter pill.

Outsourcing is contracting out a business function to an outside provider, usually to a low-wage country. One of the reasons for the rapid decline in manufacturing jobs in core countries is the outsourcing of jobs to low-

Chinese workers perform final testing before sending drives off to customers on its 2.5-inch notebook lines. With free trade, products made in China with low-wage labor are exported tariff free to Western countries.

wage periphery countries, such as China, India, and others. For example, many Mexican farmers left their villages to seek jobs in Mexico's maquilladores, which were factory cities built along the U.S. border in the 1980s and 1990s. One of these cities, Juarez, employed thousands of Mexican workers in factories that made everything from television sets to auto parts for the U.S. market. But many of these factories have now closed, as manufacturers left to seek even lower-wage workers elsewhere. This market shift has now left Juarez with high unemployment and a staggering crime rate.

Outsourcing is not just happening to manufacturing workers. The same is happening for professional and higher-paid workers in core countries with similar effects. A study found that corporate owners could send offshore between 13 and 50 percent of the jobs of software, banking, insurance, and engineering workers. Thus, in core countries most new jobs are in domestic services and low-paying retail work.[35]

PUZZLE PIECE #10: MILITARY HEGEMONY

You may be wondering what this big word that is hard to pronounce has to do with the #10 piece of the economic globalization puzzle. My answer: a lot. First of all, hegemony is the political, economic, ideological or cultural power a dominant group exerts over other groups. The dominant group gains control through consensus, not force. Hegemony is about creating a world order on terms that will guarantee a smooth-running world system that benefits the hegemonic power.[36]

Core nations use hegemony to make sure they have access to cheap natural resources and to ensure they have markets for their goods. A problem in capitalist economies is stagnation, which was one of the reasons for the economic globalization push in the late 1970s. It occurs when there is over-production of goods and services and not enough demand to absorb the over-capacity. There was over-capacity in the 1970s as there is today. The export-oriented economies, such as China, Japan, and the "Asian tigers," have the capacity to churn out many goods. Most of the goods are bound for the U.S., whose consumers have reached a point where they can't buy all the goods because of too much debt, especially since the recession. This scenario is not new to capitalist economies, as it has happened in the past as well.

A Brief History of Colonialism, Imperialism, Development, and Hegemony

1. Colonialism describes the first phase of capitalist expansion (1500-1750). Around 1500, Europe imported more goods from Asia, particularly China, than they exported. More wealth was leaving Europe then coming in. European countries responded by sending explorers to find new trade routes. They chanced upon the Western hemisphere that they used as their private source for cheap raw materials, produced by cheap labor. Around 1700, European rulers brought the Western hemisphere, India, and some coastal cities in Asia and Africa under their control. Europe took commodity wealth such as sugar, furs, silver, gold, tea, spices, and tobacco from their colonies, which helped to fuel the later industrial revolution.

2. Imperialism (1870-1914). During its heyday, there was a 300 percent increase in Europe's possession of colonies. For the first 75 years of the 19th century, colonial powers took over an average of 240,000 square miles each year, compared to an average of 83,000 square miles a year during the earlier period of colonialism. The cast of imperialist characters was the early colonial powers – Spain, Portugal, Britain, France, and Netherlands – plus a few new ones: Germany, Belgium, Russia, U.S., Italy and later Japan. With industrialization, intense competition among the imperialist nations heated up for markets and resources. Profit margins narrowed and labor costs rose. Economic

stagnation followed, and imperialism followed economic stagnation. In response to stagnation, imperialist nations searched for new markets, investments, and consumers. Capitalist economies must grow and expand or die. Since there was stagnation in the core countries, there was a drive to pull more areas into the capitalist web. The pace of growth depended on new products, inventions, and populations for nations to conquer or convert.

3. Economic Development (1945-1990) is geared towards increasing the standard of living of a nation's population through economic growth and inclusion within a global economy. Developers say that it benefits the developing countries, and in some cases it does. Development requires a transition from a simple to a modern economy. This means a shift from a local, self-sufficient economy to a specialized and dependent economy. The U.S. and Soviet Union rushed to convert new nations emerging from colonialism to capitalism or communism. They either traded or took resources from their new allies. Therefore, the two superpowers picked allied countries which had natural resources they needed. For example, for a while the U.S. was particularly close to Iran, since it had abundant and cheap oil. In return, Iran was an eager purchaser of America's expensive, advanced weaponry.

Critics see modern development as a continuation of colonialism and imperialism, except under a friendlier cover. The process replaced locally controlled systems of agriculture, governance, health care, education, and self-help with systems that outsiders more centrally controlled. Developers assumed that all societies should evolve from simple to complex: simple meant primitive and a low standard of living, and complex meant capitalist and a high standard of living. If followed, the steps to modernization would result in a high standard of living and a modern society.[37]

Americans had such faith in the superiority of its capitalist economic system (most still do) that it blindingly thought that others would join in with a ground-swell of appreciation. This did happen in many instances. Some former colonial leaders liked modernization and gladly accepted development assistance checks. But many periphery countries thought that the pledge from U.S. leaders to help them modernize was really a way for them to get their natural resources cheaply.[38]

4. Hegemony 1990-Present. After the fall of communism in the 1990s, the U.S. was the world's leading power. There were no rivals. Many Americans boasted that the collapse of communism was the final judgment on the superiority of American-style capitalism. The U.S. took the fall of communism as a sign to expand its reaches into new lands. It announced human rights as key in its foreign policy goals. While spouting democratic ideals, it was actually promoting neoliberalism and economic globalization.

Despite U.S. aggression and meddling in many parts of the world, many global citizens still admire America's democratic ideals and open society. Today, 118 nations – containing over 55 percent of the world's population – govern with some form of democratic organization, an accomplishment that the U.S. had a hand in attaining.

Hegemonic Military Power in the United States

You would expect that the world's largest economy would have the world's largest military. After all, skilled diplomacy alone is not enough to keep all the hegemonic power's national interests in line. Indeed, the U.S. has the world's largest military, the biggest by a long shot. Of the world's total military spending, the U.S. spends almost half of the total. Adding up all defense spending in the public sector in 2009, the U.S. government plowed over $1 trillion into its military (this figure includes defense related costs from all departments). Figures from just the Department of Defense (DOD) were $663 billion. This figure alone was more than second place China, which clocked in

Camp Bondsteel in Kosovo. As an example of privatization, the corporation Kellogg, Brown, and Root (KBR) is the prime contractor for the operation of the camp.

at $99 billion. The UK came in 3rd with $69 billion, only slightly more than 4th place France with $67 billion. Russia rounded out the top 5 with $61 billion. India was in 10th place with $36.6 billion.[39]

The United States' hegemonic power is seen in the sheer number and location of its military bases. They are today's version of colonies. In 2008, there were 761 military bases encircling the planet. These bases in 151 different countries stationed 510,927 service personnel: troops, spies, contractors, dependents, and others. Some say the actual number of bases would top 1,000, but no one knows the exact number for sure. Even though these numbers are high, during the Cold War in 1967, the number was 1,014 military bases.[40]

Questions to Consider

1. Do you think our military is outsized and needs to be reduced? How would you reduce it?

CONCLUDING INSIGHTS: ECONOMIC GLOBALIZATION

I started this chapter with the statement that our individual opinion about economic globalization depends upon our particular circumstances. Hopefully this chapter has helped you form a more complete picture of economic globalization than whether it just benefits you or not. One of the criticisms that I have with the way we make decisions as a nation is that the deciding factor is, "Does this help me?" We cocoon our ideas and actions into a myopic vision of our individual needs, while the fate of global humanity lies in peril. Turning to a way of thinking that is more inclusive and more global in scope can help inform the monumental decisions we need to make as a society.

Let's turn to the next chapter and look at the consequences that economic globalization has had on humanity and the environment.

CHAPTER SIX

The Impact
of Economic Globalization

"Socialism collapsed because it did not allow the market to tell the economic truth.
Capitalism may collapse because it does not allow the market to tell the ecological truth."

— *Oystein Dahle, former Vice-President, Exxon, for Norway and the North Sea*

EVALUATING THE IMPACT OF ECONOMIC GLOBALIZATION

Economic globalization has changed the world, in both core and periphery countries. But a question to ask is, "Has economic globalization been beneficial or detrimental?" Of course, as I point out in Chapter 5, it depends upon your point of view. If you are a highly educated stock broker in Tokyo, you might think that economic globalization is a great thing. If you are a middle-aged male assembly line worker in a U.S. factory with a high school diploma, you might not like the outsourcing of your job. If you are a well-educated, middle-class man who lived in a rural Chinese village and now manages a Western-owned factory in a Chinese city, you are happy that economic globalization has helped you have a higher standard of living.

I will use certain measures to evaluate whether economic globalization is beneficial or detrimental. I have picked measures that I think are the most important issues of our day: the environment, social inequality, and human well-being. There are many other issues that are important as well. You could make the case that education, jobs, economic growth, national debt, human rights, consumer choices, medical care, an entrepreneurial spirit, financial opportunities, military might, food safety, terrorism, religious freedom, individual rights, or ethics should be the measures. As an educator I debated about including education in my top three, but I am still sticking with my three measures.

Landing in the top spot for evaluating economic globalization is the health of the earth. When thinking about the next generations, this clearly has to be at the top of the list. Even if you don't believe that human activities cause climate change (global warming), there are many other dire environmental problems that human activity affects: scarcity of fresh water, air and water pollution, top soil erosion, ocean acidity, desertification, species extinctions, and the list goes on. We tend to fixate on one issue, such as climate change, and not see the big picture of environmental decline. The fierce debate about climate change is a distraction from all the urgent environmental issues that we are ignoring.

Earning the second spot in the measures for evaluating economic globalization is the growing social and economic inequality found throughout the world. Economic globalization has made the gap between rich and poor worse. Critics cry that closing the socioeconomic gap means redistributing wealth so that everyone has the same. But there is a clear difference between closing the socioeconomic gap, which I favor, and the unsound idea that everyone should have the same income, which I do not favor. There are ways to close the inequality gap other than taking wealth from the rich and handing it to the poor.

The third measure asks the question: Does economic globalization provide an acceptable standard of well-being for most people? Now that is a tall order! It would be impossible for all the people on earth to have a standard of living equal to a middle class American, complete with two cars, a house, and all the consumer comforts. But I ask if economic globalization provides an acceptable standard of well-being, not a standard of living. There is a big difference. It might be surprising to find what really makes people happy, instead of what advertisers tell us will make us happy.

In addition to the three measures for evaluating economic globalization, we will look at how economic globalization has affected a periphery country, the Democratic Republic of the Congo in central Africa, and a middle or periphery country, Bhutan, located high in the Himalaya Mountains northeast of India. But let's first turn to the environmental impact of economic globalization.

Questions to Consider

1. What do you think are the top three most important measures for evaluating economic globalization? Top five? What is your top pick?

THE ENVIRONMENT

A critical factor in the debate about economic globalization is the impact on the environment. We know that the resources of the earth are necessary for us to survive, yet we treat the earth as if it is able to always churn out these "free" resources without any fuss. The earth doesn't work that way. The earth is beginning to make a fuss, and we should listen to its distress signals.

We have a very fragile relationship with the earth. One of nature's species – ours – is going beyond sustainable limits, threatening future generations. This grim prospect reminds me of a story about goats.

During the days of sailing ships, sailors would leave goats on islands to make sure that on their return trips they would have fresh meat to eat. But with no natural predators, the goats bred faster than the sailors could eat them. Lacking natural limits, the goats in the end ate all the island's vegetation so that even native species could no longer grow. Eventually, the swelling population of goats starved to death. The lessons of this tale are valid today. Our "island," the earth, has suffered because of our goat-like instincts to consume everything in sight without thought for the future. With no self-imposed limits we might suffer the same fate. The more aware we become of our impact on the planet, the greater is the likelihood that we will create environmental solutions and stop abusing the earth.

We next turn to the effects of economic globalization on the environment. Although economic globalization may not be directly the cause of all these problems, it has at least indirectly made these environmental problems worse. A systems approach is helpful when looking at these issues.

The Earth's Free Ecosystem Services

1. Purification of air and water.
2. Water absorption and storage, helps lessen droughts and floods.
3. Decomposition, detoxification, and holding of wastes.
4. Regeneration of soil nutrients; buildup of soil structure.
5. Pollination, seed and nutrient spreading.
6. Pest control.
7. Moderation of wind and temperature extremes.
8. A variety of agricultural, medicinal, and industrial products.
9. Biodiversity that performs all of the above tasks.
10. Aesthetic, spiritual, and intellectual uplift.

1. Desertification

Advancing deserts and expanding sea levels are squeezing our global community. These forces are changing the physical geography of our planet. Expanding deserts – **desertification** – are mainly the result of deforested land and also overstocked and overgrazed grasslands. This is a global problem, but it is especially bad in China. From 1950 to 1975, over 600 square miles of land gave way to the desert each year, but by 2000 over 1,400 square miles were yielding to the desert's steady expansion. Forest rings around the city of Beijing are the Chinese government's attempt to keep the prowling deserts at bay. Chinese officials report that within the last 50 years, residents deserted over 24,000 villages in northern and western China

The encroaching desert, anti-sand shields in north Sahara, Tunisia.

as drifting sand silently buried their settlements.[1]

The Sahara Desert in North Africa is pushing its people northward toward the Mediterranean Sea. The demands of growing numbers of people and animals, along with the effects of climate change, are rapidly switching arable land to desert. In Mexico, the United States' southern neighbor, about 70 percent of its land is at risk of desertification. Ruined cropland forces some 700,000 to 900,000 Mexicans off the land each year. Most flee from the arid and semi-arid regions of Mexico, where desertification yearly causes the desertion of another 400 square miles of farmland. Desperate former farmers direct their search for jobs to nearby cities or immigrate, either legally or illegally, to the U.S.[2]

2. Deforestation

A wide belt of forests of great diversity and importance to our earth's ecosystem stretches out from the equator. But large-scale forest clearance is changing the tropical rainforests. Loggers are reducing these ancient forests at the rate of about 100 acres per minute as humans harvest timber and clear the natural landscape to make room for farms and pasture. More than half the loss of the world's natural forest has happened since 1950. If the clearing rate continues, the unprotected forests will be gone in 95 years. The tropical forests suffer most of the loss. Although they cover only about 7 percent of the earth's dry land, they hold half of all species. Many species can only be found in small areas; their specialization makes them especially in danger of extinction.[3] Forests are valuable to the planet.

Small ranchers and farmers are switching forests to agricultural or grazing land in order to earn a living. And landless people scramble for firewood or a patch of land on which to grow food. When farmers clear an area for agriculture, they burn the remaining trees and vegetation to create a rich deposit of ash for crops. But after a few harvests, they use up the soil's nutrients. The farmer leaves the site and moves to another location to start the destructive cycle once again.

Forests take in great stores of carbon dioxide, helping to balance the stock of it in the atmosphere and ease the greenhouse effect. In the Amazon alone, trees hold more carbon than 10 years' worth of human-produced greenhouse gases. And when people start fires in the forest, carbon stored in the wood streams into the atmosphere, making the greenhouse effect and climate change worse. Once the farmer clears the forest, the soil can become a source of carbon emissions instead of carbon storage.

Deforestation for oil palm plantation. The last batch of sawwood from the peat forest in Sumatra, Indonesia.

People have been deforesting the earth for thousands of years, but recently they do this to meet global consumption demands, not just to meet local and national needs. Multinational timber companies also contribute to the loss of tropical forests. In Indonesia the cutting down of tropical forests to plant commercial palm tree plantations to produce bio-fuels for export is a major cause of deforestation.[4] The national government encourages road-building and forest clearing. To pay back foreign debt, IMF rules force indebted periphery countries to sell off their natural resources on the world market. For example, one old-growth tree can be worth $10,000 or more. These valuable lumber products are in high demand in core countries, where most of their forests have already been cut.

3. Fresh Water

Most people still think of water as abundant and renewable. It isn't. The amount of fresh water available to us is limited, and the world is quickly running out of it. Only 2 percent of the earth's water is fresh water fit for human use, and two-thirds of this amount is trapped in ice caps, glaciers, and underground reserves too deep or remote to tap. Only 0.01 percent (one-hundredth of one percent) of the planet's water is reachable for human use. If the entire world's water supply was contained in 26 gallons (100 liters), then what is available to humans would be one-half teaspoon.[5]

Per capita water use is rising twice as fast as the world's population. Wasteful sanitation systems, particularly those in core nations, have encouraged people to use far more water than they need. Yet even with this increase in personal water use, households and municipalities account for only 10 percent of water use. Industry claims 20-25 percent of world fresh water supplies. Many of the world's fastest growing industries are water intensive. For example, the computer industry alone uses almost 400 billion gallons of water each year. But irrigation is the real water hog, claiming 65 percent to 70 percent of all the water used by humans. It takes some 500 gallons a day to produce the food each one of us consumes. Water-intensive farming often uses wasteful practices. Generally, the government subsidizes water use and farmers don't have to pay the real costs of their water use. This discourages farmers from using more conservation practices and to install more water-saving drip irrigation systems.[6]

Greater water use accompanies rising standards of living. For example, diets of the wealthy contain less grain and more meat. It takes about 1,000 tons of water to produce a ton of grain and 3,000 tons of water to produce a ton of rice. If grain is fed to animals for human consumption, the amount of water in our diets increases. It takes 16 pounds of grain to produce one pound of beef – and no less than 2,500 gallons of water! As you can imagine, water use is becoming unsustainable with an increase in more Western style heavy meat diets by wealthier Chinese, Indians and others.

Irrigation of land in Punjab, Pakistan.

Irrigation for food production depends on aquifers that farmers are depleting. China produces over 70 percent of its food with irrigation. Water tables on the fertile North China Plain dropped more than 12 feet in a recent three-year period. Now the number of cities in China with water shortages represents about half the country's urban areas. India, with a population of over 1.3 billion, uses irrigation to produce 50 percent of its food, and the rate of groundwater use is twice that of the recharge rate, a deficit higher than any other country.[7] The U.S. produces 20 percent of its food with

131

irrigation and sees falling water tables, as well. The enormous Ogallala Aquifer providing ground water throughout most of the Great Plains and in the American Southwest, is dropping. Droughts in the American Southwest have put greater demand on the region's rivers, including the Colorado and Rio Grande, which provide water for much of the Southwest. They are unable to keep up with growing demand.

Climate change and pollution are making it difficult for periphery countries to provide food for themselves. Africa has 9 percent of the planet's water resources but uses only 3.8 percent because of distribution problems. Many of its water sources are also dwindling. Lake Victoria, for example, Africa's largest freshwater reserve, fell two meters below normal in 2005.[8] In central Asia, Iran, a country of 80 million people, is facing water shortages. The water table fell by 2.8 meters a year in the late 1990s. Iran must now import more wheat than Japan, the world's leading importer in the recent past.[9]

In the past, water shortages have been local, but today water scarcity crosses national borders. Countries facing water shortages redirect water to their cities and then import grain to offset the loss in agricultural production. Since a ton of grain equals 1,000 tons of water, importing grain is an efficient way to import water. But this depends on other countries, mainly the U.S., to continue to export plentiful grain at cheap prices and to use up their diminishing reserves of fresh water. Also, the use of grain for ethanol production drives up grain prices and adds to already strained food budgets for the poor.

4. Climate Change

Climate change takes place when the climate is altered during two different periods of time, with changes in average weather conditions. Nature causes changes, but humans also cause climates to change by releasing greenhouse gases into the atmosphere. The popular term **global warming** describes general shifts in climate, but it refers specifically to any change in the global average surface temperature. The world will not warm at the same rate, however, some areas warm more than others, such as the North and South poles. Some areas will even become cooler, so I will use the more accurate term, climate change.

The earth's climate has gone through countless cycles of warming and cooling in its long history. Over the past 10,000 years the amount of greenhouse gases in the atmosphere has been fairly stable. But around 1800, the amount of greenhouse gases began to increase as a result of industrialization, rising population, and changing land use. Now excessive greenhouse gases are life threatening. A major human contribution to greenhouse gases over the last 200 years is the release of carbon dioxide from the burning of fossil fuels. For example, current coal

Hurricane Sandy, late October 2012. Damage to Casino Pier in Seaside Heights, New Jersey, U.S.

132

consumption has jumped to 100 times more than it was in 1800, and current oil consumption has gone up more than 200-fold in the 20th century. Deforestation also contributes to climate change, since fewer plants and trees are around to absorb carbon dioxide. Methane is a greenhouse gas. The larger number of rice paddy fields needed to feed Asia's growing population release volumes of methane gas from wet and decaying vegetation. The large number of domesticated animals raised for meat consumption release methane from animal waste into the atmosphere.

The scientific community agrees that our world is getting warmer, and humans are contributing to the warming. Scientists predict that hotter temperatures and rising sea levels will continue for centuries, no matter how much we now do to control pollution. This evidence makes it impossible to say natural forces are to blame. Disbelievers are finally beginning to change their position. Glaciers have been retreating and sea levels have risen. The last few decades have been the warmest on record. According to meteorologists, the 10 warmest years in thousands of years have all happened in the past 15 years.[10]

The U.S. has five percent of the world's population but accounts for nearly 25 percent of global greenhouse emissions. It is crucial that the U.S. participates and actively provides leadership in efforts to address climate change and protect the livability of our planet for future generations.

5. Sea Levels

Melting polar ice caps are raising sea levels. The atmosphere's protective ozone shield is thinning at a rate of about one percent per year through holes above the North and South poles. During the 20th century, sea levels rose by 6 inches but during the 21st century estimates show that seas may rise by 4 to 35 inches. Since 2001, record-breaking high temperatures have stepped up the melting of ice. If the Greenland ice sheet, a mile thick in some places, melted entirely, sea levels would climb by 23 feet or 7 meters. A one-meter rise in sea level would displace 30 million Bangladeshis. London, Bangkok, Shanghai, New York, and Washington D. C., along with hundreds of other cities, would be at least partially underwater.[11]

6. Soil Depletion

Soil depletion has occurred as a result of erosion and desertification. One estimate says that topsoil is being lost 16 to 300 times faster than it can be replaced. Over the past 1,000 years, humans have turned about 2 billion hectares of productive farmland into wasteland. That is more than the total area farmed today. About 100 million hectares of irrigated land have been lost to salinization, where there is too much salt in the soil. Per capita grain production peaked in about 1985, and it has been falling slowly ever since. Between 1950 and 2000, world grain production more than tripled. From 1950 to 1975, grain output increased by an average of 3.3 percent per year, faster than the 1.0 percent per year rate of population growth. Yet during the past few decades, the rate of grain production increase has slowed until it has fallen below the population growth rate. Still there is enough food, at least in theory, to feed everyone. The total grain produced in the world around the year 2000 could keep eight billion people alive at a subsistence level, if it were evenly distributed – not fed to animals and not lost to pests.[12] Yet, in 2008, food riots in poor countries, such as Haiti, Egypt, and Bangladesh point to the difficulty of providing food for everyone. Ethanol production for transportation uses valuable grain supplies. But grain production cannot supply enough ethanol to meet the needs of motorists and enough food for the world's poor at the same time.

The recent methods of commercial agriculture that produced abundance for several of the past decades are unsustainable. Thus, efforts to conserve worn out soil using methods that have been successful for centuries are underway. Agricultural methods such as terracing, composting, cover-cropping, polyculture (as opposed to monoculture), crop rotation, and contour plowing do not use chemical fertilizers and pesticides, and yet, these types of farming actually produce crop yields equal to conventional methods. They can also improve soil fertility. These methods have been successful in a small Mexican village called Vincente Guerrero in the state of Tlaxaca that I visited in the summer of 2007. Drought, soil depletion, NAFTA policies, and migration hit the area's farming community hard. Yet this small village is staging a comeback. Farmers are producing organic and local food. By using these farming methods and lots of hard work, the soils are slowly recovering. These efforts signal hope that farmers can reverse soil depletion and small agricultural villages can be sustainable.

7. Carrying Capacity

Earth's resources are being consumed faster than they can be replaced by her most greedy species, us! We have overshot our earth's **carrying capacity,** which means we are taking more from the earth than it can replace through natural processes. **Overshoot** means to go too far, to go beyond limits accidentally or on purpose, and without thought about the consequences. Our **ecological footprint** is calculated by adding the amount of land needed to supply resources, such as grain, food, water, and wood, and absorb wastes such as carbon dioxide and pollutants. Our footprint has become as large as Bigfoot's! Since the late 1980s, humans have been using more of the planet's resources each year than are renewed. The ecological footprint of our global society has overshot the earth's capacity to provide.[13] Some experts say that we are 20 percent above the earth's carrying capacity. Some say that it will be 100 percent by 2050. In other words, by 2050 humans will demand twice the resources than the planet can provide.[14] While this imbalance can go on for a while, continued overshooting will use up the planet's resources.

How many people can the earth sustain? It depends. The earth has the carrying capacity for 4 to 5 billion people, according to some estimates, yet in 2012 over 7 billion people lived on the planet. The fear is that even if population growth slowed, greenhouse gases will go up as more people adopt Western lifestyles and consumption habits. For example, India and China are affecting climate change. China is opening one coal-fired power plant a week to meet its population's demand for electricity.

If all the people on earth consumed at the level of the U.S. and EU, the planet could support only 1.8 billion people. For example, to feed Americans who consume a heavy meat diet, each farm animal needs to consume 1,760 pounds of grain annually. Grain consumption in the U.S. is far greater than in India, where each person eats about 440 pounds of grain a year. If everyone else in the world ate this same amount, the world's grain production could support about 10 billion people.[15] The average American eats 20 times as much as the average African. Some estimates say that the U.S. has the resources to support less than half of its current population of over 320 million. While the average American ecological footprint is about 22 acres, the average citizen of India has a footprint 1/16th that size. Although not very appealing to Americans, if 7+ billion people were to share the world's resources equally, Americans would have to reduce consumption by 80 percent for each of us to have a sustainable ecological footprint of about 4.4 acres.[16] This would mean a drastic cutback in energy use, meat consumption, transportation, and housing.

Our use of the world's resources has reached such a level that only a planet 25 percent larger can sustain us. In the early stages of overshoot, which is where we are now, the signals from the earth are not yet strong enough to force an end to growth and the overuse of resources. Systems thinkers call it a **delay in feedback**. In other words, we are not yet in a situation where the stresses on the earth have sent strong enough signals to force us to shrink our ecological footprint. Overshoot is possible because we can draw down on accumulated resource stocks. For example, you can spend more money each month than you earn if you have saved enough. You can remove timber from a forest above its annual growth rate as long as you start with a stock of wood that has grown over many decades. The larger the initial stock, the higher and longer the overshoot. If a society takes its signals from the available resources rather than from their rates of replacement, it will overshoot.[17]

Easter Island (1600-1799) experienced severe erosion due to deforestation and unsustainable agriculture. Topsoil loss led to ecological collapse, causing mass starvation and civilizational disintegration.

Any population or economy that has feedback delays and slow responses to the signals of overshoot and yet keeps on growing is out of control. If a society constantly tries to speed up its growth, eventually it will overshoot. No matter how fabulous its technologies, no matter how efficient its economy, no matter how wise its leaders, it can't ignore the consequences forever. Overshoot does not necessarily lead to collapse but it does require fast action to avoid collapse. It is necessary to reduce both population and unsustainable living standards for humanity to lower its ecological footprint.

8. Human Population

Human population has surpassed the 7 billion mark and is climbing rapidly. Every year the world adds approximately 80 million people to its total number. In fact, population time clocks tick away the number of people added to our planet every few seconds![18] The overall growth rate hit a peak of about 2 percent in the late 1960s, and the good news is it has recently fallen to 1.3 percent.

A 2007 United Nations forecast says that world population will rise to 9.2 billion by 2050, while some estimates say it would reach nearly 12 billion. The increase in population will take place mostly in middle and periphery nations. The core regions expect population numbers to remain unchanged at 1.2 billion. An increase in ageing populations will continue into the future. Between 2005 and 2050, half the increase in the world's population will be in the number of people 60 and over, whereas the populations under 15 will decline slightly. Core nations expect their population 60 and over to nearly double, while the population under 60 will probably decrease.[19]

World food production increased in the 1950-1960s. The use of life-threatening chemical fertilizers and pesticides made this possible. At first these inputs increased production rates about 2.5 times, but increasing population levels consumed the surplus. Recently worldwide agricultural production has stabilized and declined in many areas. This shows the long-term consequences of chemical use on soil fertility and productivity, as well as desertification, and dropping water tables.[20]

The population of the U.S. is over 320 million. It is supposed to reach 400 million by 2043 and will climb to 420 million by mid-century. The U.S. population grows by almost 1.8 million people each year or 0.6 percent; each day adds about 8,000 more people. Another person joins the nation every 11 seconds. This contrasts with Europe and Japan, where populations are either stable or declining slightly.

There are several reasons for population growth in the last two centuries, especially the last half of the 20th century. One reason has been the shift to carbon-based fuels in which the burning of coal, gas, and oil has produced energy to fuel the large scale machinery that mass produces agricultural products to feed a mushrooming population. Another reason is that clean water, sewage treatment, antibiotics, and medical breakthroughs have resulted in lower death rates and increased life-expectancy. Paradoxically, the creative forces that have made it possible for many of us to live longer and healthier lives has the destructive flip side of increasing our capacity to multiply our numbers and consume more resources, placing our planet in peril.

9. Natural Populations

Another environmental challenge facing us today is the ongoing loss of biodiversity through species loss. Although extinction is a natural process – the basis of evolution is the appearance of some species and the disappearance of others – this extinction is different: humans are almost wholly responsible. Fifty percent of the plants and animals on earth – cattle, hogs, chickens, corn, soybeans, wheat – are for human use. Since these species consume scarce resources, this puts stress on the species not contributing to human consumption, as well as the world's ecosystem as a whole.

The Siberian tiger is a subspecies of tiger that is critically endangered; three subspecies of tiger are already extinct.

This extinction of species – the sixth extinction – follows upon the five previous known extinctions in the Ordovician, Devonian, Permian, Triassic and Cretaceous periods. The rapid loss of species is between 100 and 1,000 times higher than the expected natural extinction rate. But some say this may be too low; current extinction rates could be as high as 1,000 to 11,000 times the expected extinction rates. Habitat loss threatens 86 percent of all birds, 86 percent of all mammals, and 88 percent of all amphibians.[21]

Why should we care? Although the morality and ethics of contributing to the destruction of our fellow species are important, there are also practical reasons to try to halt this destruction. Living organisms keep the planet habitable. Plants and bacteria carry out photosynthesis, which produces oxygen, while trees absorb carbon dioxide, which helps combat global warming and produces food for humans. The monetary value of goods and services carried out by natural ecosystems is about 33 trillion dollars per year. But the monetary value means little to us if we create a world that is uninhabitable for us and other species.[22]

Insights: The Environment

My argument is that economic growth has been the chief force driving our global community past its ecological limits. Sooner or later we will hit the earth's limits. It takes the earth almost 18 months to produce the services that humanity uses in one year. For example, for the whole world to consume and produce waste at the level of an average person in the United Kingdom (UK), we would need at least 3.4 planets like the earth. Once the ecological footprint has grown beyond the sustainable level, as it already has, it must eventually come down – either in an orderly way or through the work of nature. There is no question about whether an enlarging ecological footprint will stop at some point; the only questions are when and by what means. Population growth will decline because of a reduction in the food supply, and conflict over scarce resources will take place.[23]

After reading and reflecting upon the state of our environment, many of you may feel a sense of depression and hopelessness. I felt the same way when I was researching and writing about this topic. But depression and hopelessness are the easy way out. Even though we are overshooting our earth's carrying capacity, it is not too late to make changes. Our human capacity for thinking long-term, globally, and holistically does not have a proven track record, yet it is not beyond our capabilities. We can change, and it is my belief that we must do so. Adjusting our thinking to view the long-term consequences of our actions is vital. In my humble opinion, we need to reconsider growth as the key principle of our society. Instead, living within the limits of our earth holds the key to our future well-being and survival.

This overview of environmental issues is a way each one of us can become more aware of how the issues interact together and affect us all. Much of the environmental destruction is due to human activities, but on the bright side we can make changes to soften this destruction. Many organizations provide ways to become actively involved in positive environmental action. Through individual and collective actions, we can turn around these disturbing trends or risk being overwhelmed by them. Hopefully, we will feel empowered to act in positive ways to prevent further environmental decline and usher in positive changes.

Questions to Consider

1. What can you do to help stop environmental destruction? Explain.

THE GROWING SOCIOECONOMIC GAP BETWEEN RICH AND POOR

When I visited London, UK in summer 2000, I traveled on its very efficient subway system throughout the city. As the doors of the subway cars opened, a computerized female voice warned passengers to "mind the gap." The gap was the narrow space between the subway car and the landing platform, which would have been near impossible for anyone's foot to lodge into. But someone with a cane or a person wearing high-heeled shoes could have possibly wedged a cane or heel into the gap and suffered a fall. Therefore, I heeded "her" warnings, and it would ring in my mind every time the doors opened. I think this is a warning that we as a global society should heed as well: "mind the gap." By the gap I mean the socioeconomic gap that is widening, not only among Americans but across the world as well.

In my second criterion for evaluating the impact of economic globalization, I ask the question: Does this economic approach bring greater prosperity to a majority of the world's people than other economic systems? We constantly hear in the media that millions of poor villagers in China have been "lifted out" of poverty to become middle class consumers in the cities. But to me, nagging questions about economic globalization remain. Can everyone find a job in a globalized world? What kinds of jobs? What happens to the world's farmers? Should farmers leave their villages for the cities to find work? Should industrial agriculture grow our food? Should consumerism be the foundation of economic growth? There are many questions to ask about economic globalization and the growing gap between rich and poor.

What do I mean by a **socioeconomic gap**? The **social gap** is a situation in which individuals in a society do not have equal access to the social programs provided by the government for its citizens. These include voting rights, freedom of speech and assembly, legal rights, security, quality education, health care, job training, and so on. The **economic gap** is the uneven distribution of economic resources to society. Governmental rules determine the distribution. Today, the rules favor the rich over the poor.

What Causes Inequality?

Inequality is the differences between rich and poor. But what causes inequality? A common response is that greed, power, dishonesty, and money create inequality, which is true, but that is only part of the story. In core nations, the political left usually says that inequality is a moral responsibility or a social justice issue which worsens social unity and weakens the fabric of society. The political right in core nations makes the case that there is equality of opportunity, and individuals should be responsible for their own situation. Both viewpoints have some merit; individual responsibility is very important, but government policy shaped by those with wealth, power and influence builds inequalities into the system.

With economic globalization, social classes that were once situated within nations are now globally situated. The American economy has been in the midst of a sea change, shifting from industry to services, and integrating itself more tightly into a single, global market for goods, labor, and capital. China, India, and other middle countries are now global economic competitors with an abundant labor force and lower wages. This shift has been underway since the 1980s, but the pace has quickened, and even more so since the 2008 financial crisis.[24]

Favela (slum) in Sao Paulo, Brazil.

The hollowing out of the American middle class is taking place at the same time there is a growing middle class in Brazil, Russia, India, China (BRIC), and other countries. Like the economy, social classes are now global in scope. Thus, the wages for the new global middle class are increasing, based on supply and demand globally and not nationally. Thus, the gap between the global rich and poor is due in part to economic globalization sweeping the world.

Three Socioeconomic Classes

Our study of socioeconomic inequality continues with an examination of the following social classes in the world: the elite, the middle class, and the poor.

1. The World's Elite

You might think the world's most expensive home belongs to the Bill Gates' family; after all he has topped the list of the richest people in the world for many years and lives in the richest country: the United States. No need to worry, Gates does have a very large home. His family home is a large earth-sheltered mansion built into the side of a hill overlooking Lake Washington near Seattle,

Washington. It is 66,000 square feet in size (the average American home is 2,349 square feet) and is noted for its up-to-date design and technology. In 2009, its value was $147.5 million. Yet, the Gates family home pales in comparison to the world's most expensive home which is in India – with a never-before-seen $1 billion price tag. Mukesh Ambani, India's richest man and the fourth-richest man in the world, owns the 27-floor, 570-foot-tall home located in Mumbai, India, one of the most unequal cities in the world. The home has a health club with gym, a dance studio, at least one swimming pool, a 50-seat movie theater, a ballroom, three helipads and an underground parking lot that holds 160 vehicles.[25]

Antilia is a 27-floor personal home in South Mumbai, India belonging to businessman Mukesh Ambani. A full-time staff of 600 maintains the residence.

Gates and Ambani are among the elites of the world, both billionaires and symbolic of the growing gap between rich and poor. While Gates is better known as founder and CEO of Microsoft, Ambani, born in 1957, is a rising Indian entrepreneur, and for a time in 2010, the richest man in the world. He owns 48 percent of Reliance Industries, the largest private sector enterprise in India. Founded in 1966, Ambani took over the company from his father, who entrusted leadership to his two sons – Mukesh and his brother Anil. The two brothers had business disagreements and split up the company. Both are billionaires.

In a world where the 400 highest income earners from the U.S. earn as much money every year as the total population of 20 African countries, inequality seems out of bounds.[26] At the very top of the global wealth pyramid, there are over 1,000 billionaires, of which 245 are in Asia Pacific, 230 are in Europe and 500 are in North America. Moving down the wealth pyramid, there are 80,000 ultra-wealthy individuals with worth over $50 million each. Added into this wealthy summit are another 24 million adults with worth between $1 million and $50 million. Below this, more than 330 million individuals have average wealth per adult of $100,000 to $1 million. The world's richest 1 percent – adults who have at least $588,000 to call their own – holds 43 percent of the world's wealth. No other nation holds as much total wealth as the United States. With only 5.2 percent of the world's population, the U.S. boasts 23 percent of the world's adults worth at least $100,000 and an even greater proportion, 41 percent, of the world's millionaires. The U.S. also has the largest inequality gap between rich and poor compared to all the other industrialized nations.[27]

Switzerland and Norway have emerged as the richest nations in the world in terms of average wealth per adult, which stands at $372,692 and $326,530 respectively. Australia is in third place with average wealth per adult of $320,909 and Singapore has $255,488. Figures for Australia and Singapore have both doubled in the last decade.[28]

2. The World's Middle Class

A global trend today is the surfacing of one billion individuals sitting in the middle segment of the wealth pyramid. This is the global middle class. The middle class has average wealth per adult of $10,000 to $100,000 and owns one-sixth of global wealth. Almost 60 percent or 587 million individuals in the middle segment are located in Asia Pacific, the fastest-growing economies of the world. The middle class of this region is expected to replace U.S. middle class households as the global growth locomotive.[29]

The world's middle class is a tale of two groups: one is the old middle class of the core nations, and the other is a newly emerging middle class of the middle and periphery countries. The old middle class is seeing the erosion of its way of life, and the new middle class is creating its own standards. Economic globalization links both groups. The period of 1948-1973 was a time when the American and European middle classes made real headway. It was mostly a result of governmental policies that supported the growth and prosperity of an expanding middle class. As I mentioned in chapter 1, the government largely determines what groups reap the most economic spoils. During the post-war years, American and European governmental policy was firmly in the middle class camp.

The American Middle Class Way of Life

job security, retirement pensions, disposable income, home ownership, two cars, free highway transportation, free, quality public education in grades k-12, low-cost higher education, the chance for upward mobility, leisure time, low-cost medical care, low-cost material comforts, cultural stimulations, honest institutions, personal security, safe and low-cost food, low taxes, array of social services

A double-edged attack by two policies that favor the wealthy – neoliberalism and economic globalization – have changed the core nations' middle class way of life since the 1980s. As we have seen, the wealthy designed the rules of neoliberalism and economic globalization to benefit them. Policies that favor the middle class – higher incomes tax rates on the wealthy, ample funding for education, low-interest loans for education, research and development that encourages job creation, a significant inheritance tax rate, and private pensions for retirement – have all been worn away since the 1980s.

Middle class in Beijing, China. Photo Denise Ames

Why is the middle class expanding in Asia Pacific countries and shrinking in core nations? Mostly, many countries simply stopped making things and started buying them from the Asia Pacific countries. Since 2000, the U.S. has lost 5.7 million manufacturing jobs; Brazil has lost 2 million since 1998, and South Africa has lost nearly 1 million. In the past, Argentina assembled televisions; now it purchases most of them from abroad. Mozambique in Africa packaged its cashew crop 15 years ago; today the country ships its raw nuts overseas for others to bottle. Zambians made their own clothes in the 1980s; now they sort through bundles of clothes shipped from the U.S. and Europe. San Francisco in the U.S. used to manufacture the ships that delivered American-made goods to the world; now the ships docked in its ports are mostly from East Asia, unloading foreign-made goods for U.S. consumers.[30] These changes have taken their toll on the middle class outside of Asia Pacific.

3. The World's Poor

The world's poor make up at least 80 percent of humanity. They live on less than $10 a day, which does not include people living on less than $10 a day from core nations.[31] The IMF finds the earnings of 10 percent of the richest global citizens is 117 times higher than the poorest 10 percent, this is an increase since 1980 when it was around 79 times greater.[32]

At the other end of the global economic spectrum are parked three billion people – more than two thirds of the world's adults – whose wealth averages less than $10,000 per person. About 1.1 billion of them have a net worth of less than $1,000 and of that number 307 million are in India. Half the people on earth who are 20 and older hold under $4,000 in net worth (subtract debts from assets). They hold less than 2 percent of global wealth.[33] There are now 1.3 billion people who live on less than $1 per day.[34]

The gap between rich and poor, both within and between countries, is a worldwide crisis. Supporters of economic globalization firmly say that it is the only path leading to poverty reduction, while the causes of inequality are because countries have failed to integrate fast enough into the world economy. They claim more, rather than less, globalization is the solution to global poverty. And many sincerely believe that the way to end poverty is to grow the economy. They say the number of middle class Chinese and Indians are proof that growth ends poverty. Wealth from growth will trickle down to the poor.

Inequality Facts

- Over 3 billion people live on less than $2.50 a day.
- At least 80% of humanity lives on less than $10 a day.
- 22,000 children die each day due to poverty.
- Around 27-28% of all children in periphery countries are underweight or stunted.
- Nearly a billion people entered the 21st century unable to read a book or sign their names.
- Every year there are 350–500 million cases of malaria, with 1 million fatalities.
- Of the 2.2 billion children in the world, 1 billion live in poverty – every second child.
- 12% of the world's core population uses 85% of its water.
- 1 billion people in 2009 were hungry.
- At least 1.4 billion people live in extreme poverty.
- One out of every five people does not have access to clean drinking water.
- Over a billion people – the majority of them women – lack a basic education.
- In 2008, the richest 2% of adults owned more than half of the world's assets.

Growth will not abolish poverty. In fact, growth increases the gap between the rich and the poor. The 14-fold boost in economic output since 1930 has made some people very wealthy, but it has not ended poverty. Another 14-fold increase (even if that were possible within our earthly limits) would not end poverty.[36] Decades of economic growth have not made a dent in global poverty. In fact, in the 1980s, 2.2 percent of global growth went to the poor, compared to only 0.6 percent in the 1990s. Unsurprisingly, the world is increasingly unequal, with the richest 10 percent having gained 3,000 times more wealth than the poorest 10 percent over the years.[37]

The following interesting fact questions the claim that growth will reduce world poverty. Between 1990 and 2001, for every single dollar of poverty reduction, it took $166 of global production and consumption. Ever smaller amounts of poverty reduction amongst the poorest people of the world have required ever larger amounts of consumption by the richest people.[38] In other words, the world's richest people cannot reduce world poverty by just consuming more.

Starving girl in Africa.

Insights: The Socioeconomic Gap

My argument is that the neoliberal policies that have shaped economic globalization have largely contributed to the growing socioeconomic gap between the rich and poor and squeezed the middle class in core countries. Ever-expanding growth and consumption is not the answer to reduce social inequality. It does, however, allow us to skirt around the bigger issue relating to the work-and-spend lifestyles of core nations, which we assume to be the best development model for all nations to follow. For decades, it has been unheard of for economists or politicians to question economic growth, but we must rethink growth and ask questions about it (see right).

Questions About Growth

1. Growth of what?
2. Growth for whom?
3. Who pays for growth?
4. At what cost is growth?
5. What is the real need?
6. How much is enough?
7. What are the obligations to share?

Questions to Consider

1. How would you and your friends or colleagues answer the above questions?

WELL-BEING

Human Development Report from the United Nations

Human development is about much more than the rise or fall of national incomes. It is about creating an environment in which people can develop their full potential and lead productive, creative lives in line with their needs and interests. People are the real wealth of nations. Development is, thus, about expanding the choices people have to lead lives that they value. This way of looking at development, often forgotten in the immediate concern with accumulating commodities and financial wealth, is not new. Philosophers, economists and political leaders have long emphasized human well-being as the purpose of development. Yet, these "full rights" are not available in many societies from the richest to the poorest. When political agendas deprive people of these possibilities in any nation, how can it develop? Is this progress?

Has economic globalization contributed to the well-being of the world's citizens? Now that is a question sure to get different answers. First of all, here is a definition of well-being. **Well-being** is

Smiling girl, !Kung, (Bushmen) in southwest Africa. Photo Izla Bardavid

contentment, happiness, or a state of life-satisfaction, the state of being happy, healthy, or prosperous. Well-being is a good or satisfactory condition of existence, a state characterized by health, happiness, and prosperity; welfare.[40] Many years ago, my mother-in-law gave me a nice gift – a round pewter plate with the words "health, wealth, and happiness, and the time to enjoy them." I think that sums it up.

Those studying well-being are critical of economic growth. Studies have found that in core nations, work and consumption fail to deliver life satisfaction. Even with high levels of economic growth in the West over a period of 60 years, most people are no more satisfied with their lives now than they were in the 1950s! At the same time, patterns of work chip away at well-being by undermining family relations and personal time. Once people are able to meet their basic needs and able to live with reasonable comfort, then higher consumption levels do not lead to higher levels of well-being. Instead, people quickly adapt to a higher material standard of living, and soon return to their former level of life satisfaction. But the consumer culture says that higher levels of consumption will lead to a better life. This means that higher expectations leave people "running faster" to consume more in order to be happier.[41]

Life satisfaction figures stay flat once a fairly low level of GDP per capita is reached. For example, in the U.S., people in the 1950s scored higher than today on life satisfaction surveys, even though their standard of living is considered lower than today's.[42] We wonder how they could be happier without cell phones, internet, and Facebook! If we assume that growth will give us better lives, and this is its purpose, it has not lived up to its promises.

Some critics of the current Gross Domestic Product (GDP) method of economic measurement suggest using a **Genuine Progress Indicator** (GPI). The GPI measures the general economic and social well-being of all citizens. For example, if a business harms the environment in some way, such as an oil spill, the costs of the clean-up increase GDP, since the total dollars spent on the clean-up add to the national economy. But the GDP ignores the environmental damage done to the earth. In figuring the GPI, the costs of the oil spill would be subtracted from the national economy, since it damages the environment over the long-term. Interestingly, if using the GPI, the U.S. economy has been sluggish from 1970 to 2004.[43]

Questions to Consider

1. How would you define well-being? Do you have a high level of well-being? Does your family?

TWO NATIONS AND ECONOMIC GLOBALIZATION

Parts of Africa have suffered under economic globalization. One reason why Africa is poor is the profitability of the current economic arrangement, and the Democratic Republic of Congo (DRC) exemplifies this economic situation. After reading this, you will get a better idea of why the region is poor and its future bleak. Yet, each nation has somewhat of a choice in deciding its own future. I don't want to end on a note of despair. In contrast to the Congo, is the small Himalayan nation of Bhutan which is attempting to shape its own destiny. It is fashioning its own future by weaving the benefits of economic globalization into its future while casting off the harmful parts. The two nations are a study in contrasts.

The Tragedy of the Congo

The Democratic Republic of the Congo is a huge country located in Central Africa with an ethnically diverse population of just over 66 million people. It is about one-fourth the size of the U.S. Straddling the equator, the Congo has the second largest rain forest in the world. It is often confused with its similarly-named neighbor the Republic of Congo. Known through modern history as the Belgian Congo, Zaire, and the Congo Free State, it is one of those ill-fated countries that is resource rich, yet its people are poor.

Congo's modern exploitation started with European colonization from the 1870s until the 1920s. The British explorer and missionary, Sir Henry Morton Stanley, explored the region with the backing of King Leopold II of Belgium. Wanting to keep up with the British and French, who made earlier inroads into colonizing Africa, Leopold had designs on colonizing land in central Africa. He got rights to the territory in 1885 and made the land his private property. He ruled until 1908. After 1889, the exploitation of the Congo began with the take-off of the ivory and rubber trades. The booming demand for rubber and its soaring prices sealed the fate of the Congo's people for years to come. Leopold built huge infrastructure projects such as railroads to increase his investment returns. But, these projects did not benefit the Congolese people. Leopold even used the Congo as his personal jewelry box, taking precious gems worth a fortune. Under his rule, the Congo suffered the worst abuses of modern European colonialism.

The colonists ill-treated the local people to produce rubber. Used primarily in the manufacture of bicycle and automobile tires, rubber was plentiful but difficult to harvest cheaply. Since slavery had been outlawed, the colonizers needed a labor system that forced the Congolese people to work to collect rubber. The plan was to impose a general tax on the people. To pay taxes one needs to have money. Most Congolese were self-sufficient villagers who had no need for money. Since they lacked money to pay the taxes, they had to collect rubber to earn money to pay the taxes. The Belgians also forced them to work on roads and harbors. Often the taxes were levied on village chiefs who supplied slaves (although supposedly illegal) to the Belgian state. Once the plan was set in place, rubber harvesting began.

Those in the rubber industry schemed up ways to get even more rubber. The industry hired agents to set collection quotas for villages. The agents rounded up workers and sent them to rubber vine regions, where they collected the latex. Failure to meet the high quota resulted in harsh punishment. The most shocking practice to get more rubber from the workers was to punish them by cutting off their hands and feet. Approximately 10 million died during Leopold's rule, more than in the Holocaust during World War II. Famine, disease, overwork, hunger, and unsanitary living conditions took the lives of millions. The English author, Joseph Conrad, wrote *The Heart of Darkness* in 1902 about conditions in central Africa. Responding to international pressure, finally the Belgian parliament in 1908 ended the abuses under King Leopold II. It took over the area as a colony and named it the Belgian Congo.

Amputees in the Congo as a result of not meeting rubber quotas.

The Belgian Congo declared its independence in 1960. Shortly after the democratically elected prime minister was sworn into office, rebels overthrew the popular Patrice Lumumba in a military coup, and later they executed him. The U.S. and Belgium supported the coup. The Congo has vast mineral wealth, in particular copper and diamonds, and both countries wanted to get a share of it. After five years of uproar, Joseph Mobutu strong-armed his way to power in 1965. Because of his anti-Communist stand, Mobutu had U.S. support for his 31½ year reign. While in office, he regularly tortured or murdered his rivals. He looted the country's vast natural resources and stashed money into his own personal piggybank.

Mobutu almost destroyed his country's economy. While the nation's roads crumbled and people starved, he traveled between his palaces in his Mercedes-Benz cars. Relations with the U.S. cooled after the collapse of communism in 1991. Through the 1990s, a cry for democratic reform swept the country, but Mobutu failed to carry out the reforms. By 1996, his rule was weakening and tension with his neighbors was mounting, resulting in the First Congo War (1996-1997). Although the war got little news coverage, it claimed more than 200,000 causalities, mostly civilians. It ended when rebel forces backed by neighboring powers overthrew President Mobutu. A rebel leader's son, Joseph Kabila, became president in 2001 and continues to rule over the country at the time of this writing.

The deadly Second Congo War (1998-2003) involved seven foreign armies and is sometimes called the "African World War." The war was the largest in modern African history with foreign nations and armed militia groups trying to control the country's rich natural resources. A 2003 peace agreement ended the war. By 2008, the war and its aftermath had killed 5.4 million people, mostly from disease and starvation, making the Second Congo War the deadliest conflict since World War II. Despite the peace accord, fighting continues in eastern Congo.

Contributing to this horrible crisis is the fact that the Congo holds a treasure of valuable minerals that are the country's greatest blessing and most lasting curse. The Congo should be one of the world's richest countries, if the government honestly used all the mineral wealth and distributed it evenly to its citizens. It has about a thousand mineral varieties: 10 percent of the planet's known copper; 30 percent of its cobalt; and 80 percent of its coltan. Industry uses coltan in everything from PlayStations and iPods to magnets, cutting tools, and jet engines. The country also has bauxite and zinc, cadmium and uranium, gold and diamonds. The electronics and computer industries use cassiterite, a derivative of tin and the most desirable Congolese mineral, to solder circuit boards in cell phones and laptops. The industry also purchases high demand minerals such as tin, tantalum and tungsten for the manufacture of cell phones, iPods and digital cameras. Batteries in cell phones, videogame consoles and laptops use tantalum. Tungsten, from wolframite, creates the vibrations in cell phones.

Various factions are fighting over the country's mineral wealth. Rebels have occupied two entire eastern provinces, where they mine the bulk of the valuable minerals. Congo's national army has cooperated in the illegal trade. Forced laborers mine the minerals. There are 1.5 million "diggers" in the Congo who mostly claw for nuggets with pickaxes or their bare hands.

Northeast part of the DR Congo is home to one of the world's richest goldfields, but its people live in poverty, scraping a living from small-scale gold mining.

Civilians have suffered in this long and brutal conflict. Even though the UN has sent a 17,000-strong peacekeeping mission, it is spread very thin across the vast territory. Children under the age of five are the hardest hit, making up nearly half of all deaths. They are especially at risk of diseases like malaria, measles, dysentery, and typhoid, which can kill when medicine is not available. The aftermath of the war has gutted the country. Paradoxically, over a century of natural resource exploitation of this mineral-rich country has left the Congolese people one of the poorest people in the world. Of Congo's 66 million inhabitants, 80 percent live on 50 cents a day or less. Annual per capita income is about $300, or less than a dollar a day. The Congo remains a humanitarian tragedy and a place of human rights violations.

The Hope of Bhutan

There is a glimmer of hope in the tiny nation of Bhutan. My partner in the Center for Global Awareness, Nancy Harmon, has traveled to the country several times with her tour leader husband, Roger Harmon. The following are her experiences traveling in the country:

In the fall of 2010, my husband and I first visited the kingdom of Bhutan. Its beauty and charming people enchanted us. Mainly a Buddhist country, its colorful traditional culture is alive and well. Perhaps most interesting of all, this tiny country is in the frontline of a new way of looking at economics and its relationship to well-being and happiness – the Index of Gross National Happiness (GNH).

Bhutan is a tiny country nestled in the beautiful valleys and on the slopes of the towering Himalaya Mountains between India and China. Its rugged geography kept it isolated from the rest of the world for centuries. Most people lived in villages and worked the land for wealthy landowners in exchange for food and protection. In the 1950s, the king recognized Bhutan's need to modernize. He pushed through a bloodless land reform. As a result, most Bhutanese villagers own some land. Modernization efforts continued in the 1970s. But the king realized by observing development in other countries that along with technology and higher living standards came environmental damage, urban nightmares, family problems, loss of traditional values, and community breakdown.

The king recognized that Bhutan had a choice in trying to prevent the mistakes many countries had made in their push for modernization, and he helped create the Index of **Gross National Happiness** (GNH). He based GNH on the principle that wealth alone does not lead to happiness. Under the GNH plan, economic growth and modernization would not put at risk the peoples' quality of life, their traditional values or the environment. Leaders use research on happiness to create, carry out and evaluate their plan. They described GNH in measurable ways and divided it into the following nine domains.

1. Psychological Well-Being includes life satisfaction and spirituality. Studies find that people with a spiritual practice have more positive feelings than those without. We saw the importance of spirituality throughout Bhutan – prayer wheels turned by rushing rivers, prayer flags draped over mountain passes and bridges, religious festivals attended by thousands, and whole families making pilgrimages to holy places. Many schools begin the day with a few minutes of quiet meditation during morning assembly. A common prayer/chant is, "May all beings be at peace."

2. Health includes physical and mental health. There is a school of traditional healing, as well as a hospital of Western medicine. The government supports both. Health care is free to all. Bhutan has great biodiversity, and they use many of the plants in traditional healing. Life expectancy has increased from 44 to 65 in one generation, thanks to health care and vaccinations. Tobacco is illegal. Although imported junk food is beginning to appear in packages, fast food restaurants are still unheard of.

3. Education is free for all through the 10th grade and through post-secondary for those who pass a qualifying exam. The schools post information about GNH, and several schools had banned plastic bags and junk food. The government requires that all classes are taught in English. Although only 60 percent of men and 34 percent of women are able to read, continuing education programs in the evening help adults, especially women, become literate. But some Bhutanese worry that as more people become well educated, traditional values will disappear, and young people will leave the villages for the cities.

146

4. Cultural Diversity and Resilience includes language, artisan skills, culture, and a code of etiquette and conduct. Bhutan has a rich and colorful cultural tradition. We visited several festivals in which the whole community was involved. At these festivals young people performed folk songs and dances taught in schools. The government supports a school of traditional arts, where some young people can spend at least four years learning traditional arts such as painting, wood carving, sculpture, and embroidery. Bhutan's most skilled artisans teach there. While everyone now learns English in school, Dzongka, the national language, is also taught and spoken in everyday life.

Teschu dancers at a festival in Bhutan. Photo Roger Harmon

5. Time Use Life seems to move at a slow pace in Bhutan, especially in the rural areas. The government only introduced TV in Bhutan in 1999 because leaders feared the cultural changes and materialism it would bring. Now most Bhutanese have access to a TV, and already, some have found that the traditional stories are disappearing as people spend more time watching it. There is a group that educates Bhutanese about the effects of media in their lives.

6. Good Governance means greater "direct democracy" and a government that is effective and trustworthy. Governmental power shifted from the king to a democratically elected parliament in 2006. GNH is included in the constitution. Democracy has taken hold. Signs in cities and along the road encourage people, especially women, to vote and run for office. Enthusiastic support and respect for the king remains strong, though. We were there at the time of the royal wedding in 2011; photographs of the king and his new bride were everywhere, and the wedding was an elaborate and popular affair.

7. Ecological Diversity and Resilience The Bhutanese know that their beautiful environment is a national treasure, and government policies protect it. More than 50 percent of all land in Bhutan is in parks or refuges, forests must always cover 60 percent of the land. Tourism, which leaves a big ecological footprint, is a growing source of income. But the government carefully controls the numbers – only 23,000 tourists visited in 2011. Fishing and hunting are illegal, and Bhutan is a refuge for tigers and other wild animals. Hydropower, mostly sold to India, will soon provide nearly 95 percent of Bhutan's GDP, but the first generating plants were built underground to limit environmental impact.

8. Community Vitality includes safety, community relationships, family, and donation of time and money. Happiness studies shows that people who feel a strong sense of community and have social connections are happier than those who are more isolated. Young and old from miles around attended festivals. In the fall, harvesting in many places is still a communal event, as is the building of traditional houses.

9. Standard of Living Happiness studies show that once basic needs (shelter, food and safety)

Tiger's Nest Temple, Bhutan. Photo Roger Harmon

are met, more money does not lead to more happiness. We didn't see evidence of grinding poverty, although 23 percent of the people live below the poverty line. Life is still hard in rural areas, but the new prime minister wants to put a rototiller in every village. In the city, many people live in apartment buildings that have running water and electricity. The goal is for every village to have electricity by 2014. Markets are busy and full of a large variety of vegetables, grains and yak meat.

Almost all of what we experienced supported the claim that Bhutan is walking its talk about GNH. Bhutan's leaders are optimistic, and as one said, "Bhutan still has the luxury of ethical choices."

Questions to Consider

1. What do you think are the biggest challenges the Bhutanese people face as they implement GNH?

CONCLUDING INSIGHTS:
THE IMPACT OF ECONOMIC GLOBALIZATION

With the spread of economic globalization, certain tensions have come to play out at the family, local, national, and global level. Four tensions are listed below.

1. Local/National Authority and Global Authority. Local and national authorities are yielding to the pull of economic globalization.

2. Neoliberalism and Managed Capitalism. Economic globalization rips apart national, managed capitalism and makes it behave according to neoliberal principles.

3. State Capitalism and Neoliberalism. Because of state support and planning, state capitalists have the economic might to manipulate neoliberal economies and shape economic globalization to their advantage.

4. Rural and Urban Forces. Migration from rural areas to cities has overwhelmed cities and contributed to the decline of rural areas. With economic globalization governments have channeled resources to cities while ignoring or taking resources from rural areas.

Questions to Consider

1. What tensions do you think result from economic globalization?
2. In your opinion, has economic globalization been beneficial or detrimental?

148

CHAPTER SEVEN

The Financial Sector of the Global Economy: Ten Fatal Flaws

"When the capital development of a country becomes a by-product of the activities of a casino, the job is likely to be ill-done."

--- *John Maynard Keynes*

Charles Ponzi, a well-dressed, five-foot-two-inch rascal, emigrated from Italy to the United States in 1903. Born in 1882, in Lugo, Italy, he was from a well-to-do family. He was a postal worker in his early years and later attended the University of Rome. He decided to try his luck in America. When he arrived, Ponzi had $2.50 in his pocket, having gambled away the rest of his life savings during the trip. He quickly learned English and spent the next few years doing odd jobs. He was a waiter for a while but was fired for theft and shortchanging the customers. Next, Ponzi suckered investors into a scheme to buy international postal-reply coupons. Money poured in, until an investigation found that his business was a fake, and the company collapsed owing $4 million to investors.[1]

Charles Ponzi circa 1920

Ponzi's next big scheme was nothing more than the age-old game: "Borrow from Peter to pay Paul." It lured innocent investors with visions of easy riches. It was a scam that would bear his name for decades: the Ponzi scheme. For their money Ponzi's investors received 50 percent interest in 90 days and later he promised them 50 percent interest in 45 days. The money rolled in. Ponzi trained sales agents, who received 10 percent sales commissions. Word of the financial "wizard" on School Street in Boston spread like wildfire when Ponzi paid off his first round of investors. Many people simply reinvested their profits with Ponzi. At its height around 40,000 people joined the feeding frenzy operated out of offices from Maine to New Jersey.[2] The Ponzi scam needed a constant supply of new investors to provide cash to pay returns to existing investors. The smooth-talking con-man raked in an estimated $15 million in eight months by persuading trusting Bostonians that he had unlocked the secret to easy wealth. They believed him, at least for a while. Ponzi's success at swindling was so remarkable that the public attached his name to his method.

Questions to Consider

1. What lessons can we learn from the Ponzi scheme?

THE FINANCIAL SECTOR: AN OVERVIEW

I am starting out this chapter on the financial sector describing a scam! I am making a point that, indeed, parts of the financial sector are scams and that we need to be aware of them. There are many parts of the financial sector that are lawful and run by trustworthy people, but when the scam part of the financial sector gets out of hand, as it did with the financial crisis of 2008 – it can hurt millions of people. Thus, these last two chapters will focus on the scam part of the financial sector. Neoliberal policies helped bring about the rise of the financial sector over other sectors, such as manufacturing and farming. The concentration of wealth in a nearly unregulated financial sector has contributed to the instability and inequality found in the U.S. today, as well as the entire world. After a brief overview of the financial sector, this chapter will describe its 10 fatal flaws.

The financial sector of the economy isn't just banks; it is a broad range of businesses that deal with money. These include banks

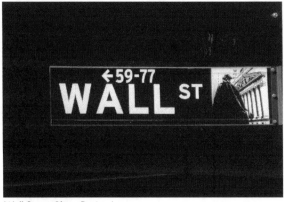

Wall Street. Photo Denise Ames

(commercial and investment), stock brokers, investment funds, foreign exchange services, real estate, and credit card, insurance, and consumer finance companies. One of the global centers of finance is Wall Street, located in lower Manhattan, New York City. As a physical place, Wall Street houses some of the powerhouses in the financial industry, including the New York Stock Exchange and multi-billion dollar firms. Wall Street represents the financial sector as a whole. But first let's briefly look at the different sectors of the global economy to see how the financial sector fits in.

Five Sectors of the Global Economy

1. **The Primary Sector** changes natural resources into primary products. The raw materials and their processing include agriculture, mining, forestry, farming, grazing, hunting, fishing, and quarrying.

2. **The Secondary Sector** manufactures finished goods using machinery and labor to do the job. It includes metal working, smelting, textile production, chemical industries, engineering, automobile and aerospace manufacturing, energy utilities, breweries and bottlers, construction, and shipbuilding.

3. **The Tertiary Sector** provides services that include retail and wholesale sales, transportation and distribution, entertainment (movies, television, radio, music, theater, YouTube) restaurants, clerical services, media, tourism, insurance, finance, banking, healthcare, and law.

4. **The Quaternary Sector** consists of informational and intellectual activities that include government, culture, libraries, scientific research and development, education, consultation, and information technology. This sector needs an educated workforce with advanced degrees.

5. **The Quinary Sector** includes nonprofit organizations that use revenues to achieve their mission rather than distributing them as profit. Education, culture, research, science, healthcare, media, police, fire service, and government are part of this sector. Our organization, the Center for Global Awareness, fits into this non-profit category.

The Rise of the Financial Sector

The financial sector is part of the tertiary or service sector. Yet, other sectors contribute to the national and global economy as well. The U.S. economy has moved from manufacturing (20 percent of the economy in 1980, to 11.5 percent today) to services.[3] But since the 1980s, the financial sector has grown to outsized proportions. Today it accounts for 40 percent of the total profits of U.S. corporations, up from 10 percent during the postwar era (1948-1973). Today, 7.7 percent of U.S. GDP consists of the financial sector, which has soared from 2.5 percent in 1947 to 4.4 percent in 1977 to 7.7 percent in 2005.[4]

The outsized growth of the financial system lined the pockets of financial managers. In 2008, one in every $13 in compensation in the U.S. went to people working in finance. By contrast, in the postwar years a mere one in $40 in compensation went to finance workers.[5] Since 1980, creativity fled from manufacturing to Wall Street. Finance has attracted an ever-growing number of highly educated workers. Among Harvard seniors surveyed in 2007, a whopping 58 percent of the men joining the workforce were bound for jobs not in medicine or public service but in finance or consulting.[6]

The U.S. has experienced a shift of investing in manufacturing to the financial sector. The economy flip-flopped from manufacturing to paper shuffling. The business of mergers and buy-outs rose, while the auto, steel, and other industries declined. Yet, a problem with much of the financial sector is it equates to squeezing value out of already created value. It may create profit, yes, but it does not create new value – only industry, agriculture, trade, and services create new value. Profits are not based on value that is created. For example, a stock, land, or other assets can keep going up, driven by upward speculation, then suddenly crash. Profits depend on taking advantage of the upward prices of the asset and selling before they go down. A **bubble** is the rise of prices of an asset far beyond its real value.[7]

It is important in a stable economy to maintain a balance between the different economic sectors. You may wonder how the financial sector grew into such a powerhouse. It is helpful to recall the events of the 1970s to understand this. The crisis of the 1970s had ended with a different economic landscape than before. Three dimensions of the global economy came out of the turmoil of the 1970s – neoliberalism, economic globalization, and financialization. Since we have already discussed neoliberalism and economic globalization, we will cover financialization in these last two chapters.

Financialization is a sector of the economy that specializes in creating financial products that can be traded and have a certain value. Some financial products are insurance, lending money, real estate sales, stocks, bonds, and others. Since the 1980s, the U.S. has shifted its policies from supporting manufacturing, small businesses and agriculture to favor large corporations and the financial sector. Because of a decline in the profitability of agriculture and industry as a result of over-capacity and competition, finance has been the engine for creating wealth and growth. Also, technology has made it easier to create and trade financial products. Since money in a capitalist system seeks the highest return on investment, there has been a shift from industries where profits were largely sluggish or low-yielding to the financial sector that channels capital towards financial products that have higher returns.[8] The result of these changes is an increased split between a financial economy and a sluggish real economy. A divide exists between the real economy known as **Main Street** and the financial economy known as Wall Street. This is not an accident the financial economy exploded to make up for economic stagnation owing to overproduction in the real economy.[9]

Share in GDP of US Financial Sector Since 1860

Source: Philippon, 2008

http://en.wikipedia.org/wiki/Financialization

Recklessness: The Master Narrative

I live in New Mexico. Native peoples make up about 10 percent of the population. In the last few decades they have built casinos on their land as a source of revenue. Even though New Mexico is the fifth largest state in area, it seems as though there are casinos everywhere. In fact, New Mexico has 20 of them, which ranks us 15th among all 46 states that have casinos, even though our population is less than 2 million. Albuquerque, where I live, boasts 4 casinos. That means a lot of gambling.

This gambling observation leads to a point I want to make about the 2008 financial crisis. Ever since the crisis, I have been thinking and rethinking the tragic chain of events. I keep coming back to the nagging question, "Why did the financial sector take such crazy risks in the first place?" What made them gamble? When asked what caused the financial crisis, many people answer greed, pure and simple. I don't disagree with the answer, but I think there is more to it than simple greed. After all, greed is part of the human condition and has been for a long time. But greed during the lead-up to the financial crisis seemed to be a different sort of greed than just bad behavior. In this case, greed was part of acceptable social values and behaviors. This is a far more harmful type of greed because it is largely a socially acceptable and encouraged type of behavior. But why does the U.S. promote extreme risk-taking, greed, and other behaviors? What is the underlying story or master narrative that helped shape this crisis?

Whether we know it or not, our national story shapes many of our views and behaviors, what I will call the master narrative. Since I have taught U.S. history for many years, I see the narrative unfold starting before the founding of the nation. It certainly helped shape the attitudes during the financial crisis. What is this narrative? Many Americans follow a "frontier mentality." There is always an unknown to discover, conquer, control, and rule. Settlers built the country by expanding westward, conquering new territories, and eliminating the native peoples. They led the way, fearless of danger and ready to risk everything for new opportunities. It was the Manifest Destiny of the American nation to conquer.

The narrative continued after World War II. Americans

This painting, (circa 1872) by John Gast called American Progress, is an allegorical representation of the modernization of the new west. Here Columbia, a personification of the United States, leads civilization westward with American settlers, stringing telegraph wire as she sweeps west; she holds a school book. The different stages of economic activity of the pioneers are highlighted and, especially, the changing forms of transportation.

boasted they were the nation with the highest standard of living, the first to reach the moon, and had the best political and economic system. President Johnson was intent on conquering poverty, as well as the moon and the North Vietnamese people. The narrative continued with President Reagan, who was ready to conquer a new enemy: the government itself. The heady days of the 1990s through the mid-2000s, except for the 9/11 tragedy, were a time of great triumphal optimism. The Soviet Union had collapsed. Neoliberal capitalism reigned supreme. The markets were the new "god." Overconfident, privileged men thought they were "born to rule" the marketplace, with limitless fame and fortune their destiny. Hubris, according to the ancient Greeks, leads to the downfall of man. Hubris was all around during this giddy time.

Risk-taking is part of the American story. But understanding the other side of risk is not part of it. There is no back-up plan if risk-taking goes awry. There is never a thought that the frontier may have limits, or technology might not save us from all our problems, or markets may not be right in all cases. If there is a mess up, so the story goes, something or someone will come along as the savior. We tell ourselves, it will always be so. In the 2008 financial crisis, it was the government that rode to the rescue.

Too many Americans don't want to understand that their national story is a lie. Nothing is limitless; with risks come consequences, Mother Nature always wins, what comes around goes around, with hubris comes humility, and with every action is a reaction. These sayings balance risk with the belief that failure can result from risk-taking, as well as success. And if failure does occur, there better be a back-up plan.

If the narrative is not changed, the same type of financial crisis will happen again. As I listen to the politicians or financial experts, I don't hear a different narrative. In fact, the narrative has gone into hyper-drive instead of stall mode. Our story of endless growth and high stakes gambling with Mother Nature has gone over the top. The economic crisis has tarnished the public's faith in markets, but only slightly. Our faith in technology is still sound. In fact, the narrative has shifted to one that government didn't ride to the rescue after the financial crisis, but government caused the problem in the first place! We are slamming our foot on the accelerator of unfettered markets, just when we should be putting on the brakes.

Excessive risk-taking without considering the consequences is the master narrative of the financial crisis. If we understand the narrative as part of the American national story, instead of merely a problem among a few "bad apples" on Wall Street, it is easier to see that we can change it. We need to replace the tired stories of limitless abundance and unending growth. I hope we can stitch together a new national narrative, one that does not follow a reckless path, but one more in keeping with our place in the larger human and natural community and with the well-being of the next generations in mind.

Questions to Consider

1. If you could write a new master narrative or story of the U.S. in the future, how would it read?

10 FATAL FLAWS IN THE FINANCIAL SECTOR

In my research, I have found ten fundamental flaws in today's financial system. The 2008 financial crisis and Great Recession revealed that in a big way. But the crisis was different from others since the 1980s – it was in the U.S. Most Americans like to think of their country as an engine of global economic growth and an exporter of sound economic policies – not recessions and bailouts.[10] Yet, that is exactly what happened. There are many reasons why the financial system has performed so badly since the 1980s, and especially in the 2000s. I have organized these reasons into what I call the 10 fatal flaws in the financial sector. Once again, these flaws are all interconnected and hard to separate. But, it is much easier to look at these flaws separately with the understanding that they all are part of a system – the financial system.

Organizing these fatal flaws into these 10 categories should give us a basic understanding of how and why we experienced the 2008 financial crisis and its lingering effects. I will be using the United States as the platform for how these 10 fatal flaws have played out. However, readers from outside the U.S. should be mindful that these flaws are also in many countries following neoliberal principles, including Europe.

Ten Fatal Flaws in the Financial Sector

Fatal Flaw #1. Too Big to Fail Banks (TBTF)
Fatal Flaw #2. Unchecked Deregulation
Fatal Flaw #3. A "Markets Know Best" Federal Reserve
Fatal Flaw #4. A Real Estate Bubble and Out of Control Lending
Fatal Flaw #5. A Mountain of Debt
Fatal Flaw #6. Dicey Financial Products
Fatal Flaw #7. Financial Speculative Mania
Fatal Flaw #8. Moral Hazard and Lack of Transparency
Fatal Flaw #9. Deceptive Rating Agencies
Fatal Flaw #10. Bloated Compensation Plans

FATAL FLAW #1: TOO BIG TO FAIL BANKS (TBTF)

I would bet that almost 100 percent of you have some type of bank account. It seems a necessity in our high-tech, cashless society. We have our non-profit organization's checking account at a credit union in Albuquerque, New Mexico. I like the idea that they are a non-profit credit-union that helps its members with loans and low-cost checking. But it is big and has many branches. No one knows my name, and they always ask for my identification when I make a transaction. In the late 1970s through the 1980s, I banked at Dewey State Bank in Illinois. It was a small, "no-frills" bank in a farming community. Everyone knew everyone else. When I did business at the bank, the president would come out of his office to say hello and personally give a treat to my toddler daughter. His wife, whose family started the bank in the early 20th century, was my son's English teacher. Their claim to fame was they survived the Great Depression. They have even survived the banking mergers of the last 30 years and several years ago celebrated their 100th anniversary. But Dewey State Bank is far from typical of the banking industry today.

At the heart of it, banking is a simple business. In the past, lenders lived in a straightforward world. There was a running joke that banks ran by the 3-6-3 rule. Bankers paid their depositors 3 percent interest, lent it out at 6 percent, and lined up to tee off at the golf course by 3 p.m. Customers deposited money in a bank in return for interest; the bank lent that money to other people at a higher rate of interest. It wasn't glamorous. However, the bankers had to be careful to whom they lent money. The quality of the loans was important. Banking customers wanted banking to be boring because they didn't want someone to take their money and gamble with it. They didn't want the bank's president to have a yacht and five lavish houses around the world. They wanted him/her to serve the needs of the community.

At the core of it, banking is creating more money by loaning it out. If you have a bank and your customers deposit

Senators Carter Glass and Henry B. Steagall, the co-sponsors of the Glass–Steagall Act in 1933.

$100 in the bank, you can double the money supply by simply loaning it to someone else. Maybe the person who borrowed it spends part of it and leaves the rest in his/her own bank account, which the bank then loans to someone else, and so it goes. An initial sum of currency can be "grown" into a much bigger money supply. In other words, banks take money and create new money by loaning it out.[11] They make money on the **spreads**, or the difference in what interest they pay depositors and the interest they charge borrowers for loans.

There are basically two types of banks: investment banks and commercial banks. **Investment banks** issue bonds and shares of stock, trade on capital markets, and put together mergers and acquisitions. **Commercial banks** lend out the money deposited in them. The two types of banks are called the piggy bank and the casino. The piggy banks are the commercial banks and the investment banks are the casinos. Investment banks issue stocks, and if a company whose stock they have issued needs cash, it becomes very tempting to make a loan, which can create a problem. If the casino activities of the investment banks get out of hand, it could endanger the piggy bank deposits of the general public. This is what happened during the 1920s, and contributed to the stock market crash of 1929 and the Great Depression.

The government passed the Glass-Steagall Act in the depths of the Great Depression in 1933. This act made retail banks split from investment banks and they successfully regulated banks for almost 70 years. As part of the act, the government set up the **Federal Deposit Insurance Corporation** (FDIC) to insure deposits. During the Depression, depositors were fearful that banks would close and all their hard-earned savings would be lost. With the FDIC, depositors felt that the government would protect their money. Once the government provided this insurance, it had to make sure that banks did not take too many risks with depositors' savings. To make sure that the banks didn't speculate and lose money, knowing they would have to pick up the tab, the government regulated the banks from too much risk-taking.

The government checked the banks for too much risk-taking in several ways. For example, in the post-war years, banks said homebuyers had to have a 20 percent down payment before they could purchase a house. The bank would then loan borrowers 80 percent of the value of the house they were purchasing. The bank hired an appraiser to estimate the price of the house compared to similar houses in the neighborhood. It was unlikely that an 80 percent mortgage would wind up more than the value of the house – prices would have to drop by 20 percent, which was highly unlikely, until recently. Bankers understood that an underwater mortgage (a mortgage more than the house is worth) had a large risk of nonpayment. The system worked pretty well. The fact that homeowners usually had to put up 20 percent of a home's value to get a loan dampened their dream of owning a home beyond their means.

Previously, regulated banking provided an important check on U.S. corporate activity. By carefully watching a corporation's loans, banks helped prevent bankruptcies and other problems. Accountants, rating agencies, and others also had a system of checks and balances, much like our three branches of government, in which each watched the others' activities and reduced risk. Things began to change in the 1980s with the phasing in of neoliberalism. Some bankers had been complaining that they were not earning high enough profits because of what they thought was too much regulation of their industry. The government gradually removed regulations on banking operations. As a result, since the early 2000s, the market share of the five largest banks – JP Morgan Chase, Citigroup, Goldman Sachs, Bank of America and Wells Fargo – grew from 8 percent in 1995 to 30 percent in 2008.[12] These 5 banks hold assets of more than 60 percent of U.S. gross domestic product (GDP): $8.6 trillion.[13]

Shadow banks, another part of the banking business, lend money just like traditional banks do. The difference between the two is that in a traditional bank money comes from depositors, while in shadow banking money comes from investors, who want to earn a return on their money. Also, the government regulates traditional banks, and it does not regulate shadow banks. The investors in shadow banking are corporations and money market funds, and the borrowers are financial firms. After 2000, the volume of transactions in the shadow banking system grew. By late 2007, these transactions were over $10 trillion.[14]

The financial sector is among the highest-contributing industries to U.S. political candidates.

156

They use their deep pockets to fund campaigns and congressional lobbying in order to influence public policies that benefit them. They receive many favors from government representatives, since many people from the financial industry go on to serve in key governmental posts. For example, one of the most powerful investment banks, Goldman Sachs, has had two of their former CEOs serve as Secretary of the Treasury: Robert Rubin (1993-1999, Bill Clinton) and Henry "Hank" Paulson (2006-2009, George Bush). This fact is why high-ranking Senator Dick Durbin from Illinois said of Congress, "The banks own the place."[15]

Questions to Consider

1. Describe the place where you bank. Where do they make most of their money?

FATAL FLAW #2: UNCHECKED DEREGULATION

Deregulation is the removal or simplification of government rules and regulations that manage market forces. It does not mean removing laws against fraud. Neoliberals say that fewer and simpler regulations will lead to more competition, productivity, efficiency, growth, and lower overall prices. Those who want regulations say they need them to rein in the excesses of the market that can cause instability. Since the 1980s, neoliberals have carried out a well-organized deregulation campaign. Below are a few of the many acts passed by the federal government to deregulate the financial sector.

Before the 1980s, American commercial banking was a small-scale affair. State and nationally chartered banks were not able to have branches outside their home state, or sometimes even outside their home county. In 1975, Maine and other states began passing laws allowing some interstate banking. The passage in 1994 of the Riegle-Neal Act capped the trend; the act allowed interstate banking mergers. Now a single banking company could operate across the U.S. In the 1990s, further deregulation of the financial sector took place. Banks saw the potential for earning huge profits. Bank lobbyists sprang into action. They said that regulations had kept the U.S. banking system from reaching its full potential for profits. President Clinton's Treasury Secretary, Robert Rubin, pushed for the repeal of the Glass-Steagall Act. He said that without its repeal, the U.S. would lose out in the global marketplace.[16]

The banks had won. November 12, 1999 marked the final death blow to the 66 year-old Glass-Steagall Act, which had contributed to banking stability and prosperity for decades. The new act, the **Gramm, Leach, Biley Act** or the **Financial Services Modernization Act**, was a result of the banking and financial-services industries' years-long lobbying campaign to reduce regulation. Banks could now offer investment, commercial banking, and insurance services all under one roof. With the repeal of Glass-Steagall, banks were now able to invest monies from checking and savings accounts into high-flying financial instruments, such as mortgage-backed securities. Problems that arose because of the repeal of Glass-Steagall would come to light a few short years later as corporate and banking scandals emerged.[17] Yet another bill to further deregulate the financial sector was just around the corner.

The passage of the **Commodity Future's Modernization Act of 2000** granted the financial sector another blessing. The high angel of giving out blessings to the financial sector was Senator Phil Gramm from Texas, who also helped pass the Gramm-Leach-Bliley Act in 1999. The act marked the deregulation of financial products known as derivatives (explained later). These derivatives would be at the heart of the financial crisis of 2008. The bill was not without its critics. One in particular stands out as a future seer of the problems that an unregulated derivative market could unleash: Brooksley Borne. She sought to regulate the derivatives market. But Rubin and Greenspan stopped

Brooksley Borne warned about the dangers of the derivatives market.

her efforts, and instead they pushed for more deregulation. With Borne out of the way, the scene was now set for the use of financial derivatives in many types of financial products (see flaw #6). The act prevented the federal government from regulating risky financial products. It even prevented the states from regulating these products using gaming laws – since so many of the new products were the same as racetrack bets.[18]

When deregulation allowed investment and commercial banks to merge together, the investment banks were more dominant. As ever, larger banks pushed out smaller banks, resulting in even less competition than in the past when America's banking system had been highly competitive with many banks serving different communities. This is no longer the case.

In 1975, there was a rule requiring investment banks to have a debt-to-net capital ratio of 15 to 1 or less. In simple terms, this meant that for every $15 borrowed, the bank had to have $1 in deposits to cover possible losses. This limited the amount of borrowed money the investment banks could use to lend out or for investments. In 2004, during the deregulation frenzy, the investment banks wanted higher debt to-net capital ratios. They were able to get ratios to as high as 40 to 1. This meant that a bank only had to have $1 in the bank for every $40 they borrowed. Neoliberals believed the marketplace would regulate itself. As speculation and costly bailouts kept repeating in the late 1990s and 2000s, it might seem as though regulators and legislators would have seen that deregulation was not working. But so much money was at stake that the political elite either cheered on the whole affair or looked the other way.[19]

Questions to Consider

1. Do you think regulation has a place in the banking industry? Explain.

FATAL FLAW #3: A "MARKETS KNOW BEST" FEDERAL RESERVE

We like to think that something of value backs up our money. It seems strange to think of money in the U.S. as simply debts of the Federal Reserve that are in circulation. The Federal Reserve (the Fed) is the central bank of the U.S. and is made up of a Board of Governors and 12 Federal Reserve Banks spread around the country. Although all 12 banks are supposedly equal, the New York Fed is more influential. It's the Fed's job to oversee the American banking system and manage the money supply with the goal of promoting full employment, steady economic growth, and stable prices. Since the U.S. is the world's largest economy, the Fed's policies have worldwide impact. In the past, it was common for national economies to back up their currency with something of market value, most commonly gold or silver. Those days are gone. Today governments have to manage their money according to the level of economic activity they engage in at home and abroad, and that can be tricky.

When I was a child I loved to play the game Monopoly. I coerced my grandmother to play the game with me for hours on end. I thought I was so smart, since I would usually win. But looking back, I am sure my grandmother was not as determined to win as I was, so she let me win most of the time. I always imagined the monopoly money as real money. I would wheel and deal until all the play money ended up in my stack. But the money actually had no real value, just as our currency today has no real value.

If our currency has no built-in value, what makes it more valuable than the Monopoly money I played with as a child? A combination of three things gives value to money: its status as money, its acceptability, and its scarcity. It is very tempting to politicians to try to slide more money into circulation. When the government expands the money supply too much, the value of money decreases and inflation may occur. **Inflation** is when price levels rise and the value of money drops. When inflation occurs, the public needs more money to buy the same amount of goods and services than in the recent past. Moderate inflation isn't a real problem if incomes rise faster, as well. In most of the world's economies, economists assume that there will be some inflation. Economists consider inflation of 2 to 3 percent well within an acceptable rate.[20] If inflation spirals out of control, it can wreak disaster on a nation's economy.

I visited Brazil in 1987, amidst one of its inflationary spirals. Upon arriving we had time to browse through the airport gift stores. In one of the stores, I spotted several moderately priced but unusual pieces of jewelry I wanted to buy as gifts for family and friends. I wanted to purchase them right away but decided against it since we hadn't even started our trip yet. I thought, "I will keep these in mind if I don't see anything better on the tour." Back at the airport after the tour, I decided to go back to the same store to pick up some of the jewelry items I liked so well two weeks earlier. To my surprise, the jewelry had practically doubled in price! Inflation was out of control. Resentful that prices had spiraled upward so fast, I decided to forgo my purchases. I thought of the hardship inflation imposed upon the citizens of Brazil as they bought necessities such as food and shelter.

The government has tools to adjust the American economy. Congress and the president focus on **fiscal policy**, spending and tax decisions, while the Fed focuses on **monetary policy**, adjusting the availability of money and credit. "**Fine-tuning**" the economy is how people refer to the Fed's actions when they raise or lower interest rates. The Fed can "print" money, which actually isn't really printing money, but the Fed makes cash available for lending by buying bank securities, such as bonds, which expands the economy. At the time of this writing, the Fed wants to stimulate the economy and has set a low interest rate, now hovering around 0 percent for banks, which has flooded the economy with money. Where does the Fed get the money? It creates it out of thin air. (Money does grow on trees if it is the Fed tree!) For example, the Fed writes a check for $10 billion and gives it to the sellers of government debt. These sellers deposit the money they've received from the Fed in various banks. Now these banks can use it to make loans worth several times that amount. Money is suddenly more available and credit is easier to get.[21]

On the other hand, if the Fed is worried about

The Marriner S. Eccles Federal Reserve Board Building in Washington D.C.

inflation and wants to keep the economy from over-expanding, often called overheating, it buys, for example, $10 billion worth of government debt. By doing so, it removes money from the economy. The purchasers of the debt have to write checks to the Fed, which the Fed then keeps. The banking system and the larger economy are now out that $10 billion. In this way, the Fed has tightened the money supply and made credit harder to get. Money responds to the laws of supply and demand, and now that the supply is lower, borrowing money costs more. Interest rates go up because lenders can now get a higher rate.[22]

At this point, you may wonder why the Federal Reserve is one of the fatal flaws in the financial sector. The reason I list it as a flaw is because of the actions of the Federal Reserve Chairman from 1987 to 2006, Alan Greenspan. Instead of regulating the economy, he thought the market knew best, better than the government or experts. Greenspan directed the Fed to follow "the market knows best philosophy." He was hesitant about government's role in regulating the financial industry, the very task the president appointed him to do. Greenspan seemed to have had little interest in long-standing central banking thinking that said it was best for the Fed to step in to prevent bubbles from forming. A former Fed chairman once said that the job of the central bank was "to take away the punch bowl just as the party gets going." Greenspan was unwilling to take away the punch bowl. In 1996, as the stock market shot into a giddy bubble of tech and Internet stocks, he did little to stop the bubble from inflating. When the dot-com bubble finally popped in 2000, Greenspan poured plenty more alcohol into the punch bowl, pumping more money into the economy, which helped form the next bubble – the housing bubble.[23]

In 2001, the economy was on the verge of serious recession. The dot-com bubble had burst and 9/11 had spooked markets, resulting in their steep decline. The administration of George W. Bush pushed for tax cuts, especially favoring the wealthy. But the tax cuts only helped stimulate the economy to a limited extent. Thus, the burden of restoring the economy to full employment shifted from the federal government to the Fed's "lose money" monetary policy. Greenspan lowered interest rates to flood the market with **liquidity** (money). The American economy was awash in money. With so much money in the economy, not surprisingly the lower interest rates did not lead to more investment in businesses and equipment. Since money is always looking for higher rates of return, a housing bubble replaced the tech bubble. A consumption and real-estate boom followed. [24]

FATAL FLAW #4: A REAL ESTATE BUBBLE AND OUT OF CONTROL LENDING

As we can see from the three previous fatal flaws, the ingredients for a housing bubble were forming. Do you or your parents own a house? It is considered to be the American Dream to own your own home. But not just any old house, a house with all the latest gadgets and decorating style. I recently watched a show on the HGTV channel where home buyers were searching for an upgraded house to buy. As the youngish, well-off couple toured a spacious home overlooking a golf course, they were constantly pointing out the slightly dated decorating details. When they reached the kitchen, the woman impatiently tapped on the kitchen countertop and insisted, "These have got to go!" The real estate agent protested that the homeowners had just installed them a few years ago. She quickly scolded him for his outdated taste in countertop design. He meekly took back his comments. The couple ended up buying the house, agreeing with each other that a sizeable amount needed to be set aside for a "cosmetic house face-lift."

I tell this story because it reflects the attitude that was central in creating the housing bubble.

160

Americans love home ownership; it serves as a status symbol, as well as their largest financial investment. Americans were willing participants in buying and selling real estate that contributed to the bubble. Yet for many decades, the public purchased homes according to the rigid lending standards set by mortgage lenders described in the banking section. I remember when my family built our first home. I was taken in, like the couple on HGTV, with all the latest home decorations. I wanted them all. I especially had my sights set on the brushed nickel bathroom faucets, instead of just the plain polished nickel. They looked so elegant in the showroom. Yet, our budget would not allow another upgrade. I already went over budget with purchasing the raised-panel oak

The Housing Bubble

cabinets built by the Amish in central Illinois, instead of the plain-faced cabinets they offered for the budget-minded shopper. Self-control was now in order. I grudgingly agreed to the polished nickel faucets. After a few weeks in the house I forgot about the texture of the bathroom faucets. Nor did my family or guests ever comment on their plain look. In hindsight, I wondered why I had been so obsessed with wanting them.

The real estate bubble, however, was not built solely on buyers purchasing homes that were beyond their means. Many politicians blamed the high foreclosure rates on individuals who simply bought too much house for their income. In my case, even if I wasn't able to finally rein in my costs, the lender would not approve a loan that was more than our income would allow. But during the housing bubble years, checks and balances on the system went out the window; the government had removed many regulations, and regulators ignored the ones remaining. The motto was: "the market knew best."

If it wasn't just individuals going house-wild, what really made this housing bubble the worst in recorded memory? Using a systems approach, there were many interconnected factors contributing to the housing bubble. Several decades ago banks that made home loans followed the "**originate and hold**" model. A would-be homeowner would apply for a mortgage, and the bank would lend the money, then sit back and collect payments on the principal and interest. The bank that originated the mortgage held the mortgage; it was strictly a business deal between the homeowner and the bank.[25]

To understand real estate lending even further, let's look at Fannie Mae and Freddie Mac. In 1938, during the Depression, the government created **Fannie Mae (Federal National Mortgage Association)**. Congress gave it authority to buy mortgages from lenders, thereby freeing up capital in order that those lenders could make more mortgages. Fannie Mae started to buy up mortgages. It soon sold bonds to investors in order to raise more capital and buy more mortgages. The bonds were an easy sell to investors because people were sure they would be paid back, since Fannie Mae was a government-sponsored entity (GSE). By 1982, Fannie Mae was funding one out of every seven mortgages made in the U.S.[26]

In 1970, Fannie Mae had company, a little brother, **Freddie Mac (Federal Home Loan**

Mortgage Corporation). The government decided to expand the secondary mortgage market. Well into the 1980s, Fannie and Freddie held most of the mortgages they bought and had strict lending rules. Mortgages which conformed to their rules were "conforming loans." But this "originate and hold" model changed in the 1970s. Another GSE, a sister with a cute name, in the mortgage lending business was born.

The Government National Mortgage Association (Ginnie Mae) put together the first mortgage-backed securities. Ginnie Mae bought mortgages on the secondary market, pooled the mortgages it had originated, issued them as bonds, and then sold these pools of bonds as a mortgage-backed security to investors. Ginnie Mae received a lump sum up front from the purchasers of the bonds. Investors buying these new bonds got part of the revenue stream from the thousands of homeowners paying off their mortgages. This secondary mortgage market seemed like a win-win situation for everyone – more money was available for home mortgage lending, and it was a sound investment choice.[27]

Financiers called this ground-breaking new method **securitization**. Now **illiquid assets** – not easily or quickly turned into cash, like mortgages – could be pooled and made into **liquid assets** – easily and quickly turned into cash – that were tradable on the open market. They were called **mortgage-backed securities**, since the collateral (guarantee) backing the loans were home mortgages. Investment banks and others jumped on the securitization band wagon to gobble up home mortgage bonds. Investors around the world snapped them up with the comforting knowledge that home prices never went down in the U.S. Now the mortgage model was called "**originate and distribute**" rather than "originate and hold."[28]

This securitization method was sound as long as the buyers of the securities knew the risk. But there were flaws. A bank selling new mortgages through the securitization pipeline wants to unload as many mortgages as quickly as possible. Each sale gives the bank more money with which to make more loans. If the bank makes a bad loan it doesn't need to worry, since bankers sell the loans into the securitization pipeline. The bank has much less reason to analyze the riskiness of the mortgages it originates. Thus, it is more likely to pass a bad mortgage down the line like a hot potato.[29]

U.S. Subprime Lending Expanded Dramatically 2004–2006

The "nonconforming" loan customers that Fannie Mae shunned were another thorny issue in the real estate industry; they had no place to go for lending. This changed too. It started with the **Community Reinvestment Act** in 1977, which encouraged banks to help meet the needs of all borrowers, including those in low-and-moderate-income neighborhoods. A huge new market in nonconforming mortgages, which didn't fit Fannie and Freddie's strict borrowing rules, grew. The banks gave lower-income, higher-risk groups, mostly minorities, a chance to get mortgages if they qualified. Banks found a new market in riskier but more profitable lending among less creditworthy borrowers. Lenders began extending mortgages – known as "**subprime**" mortgages – to this new group of creditors. From 2002 to 2006, subprime loan originations went from 8.6 percent of all mortgages to 20.1 percent.[30]

As securitization became more commonplace in the 2000s, many different types of mortgages were available. One was the 100 percent mortgage, in which banks would lend 100 percent or more of the value of the house. With no money down, homeowners were tempted to buy houses more expensive than what they could afford. Homeowners were posed to make a killing in the booming real estate market – at least they thought they were. Like the financial experts, they too thought that house prices would never go down. And because bankers and mortgage originators collected fees regardless of the outcome, they had little reason to curb this recklessness. Among the strangest of the new loan products were the so-called "liar loans." To get one of these loans, individuals were not required to prove their income, and in many cases borrowers lied about their incomes. The worst of all were the "NINJA loans" for which a borrower had "No Income, No Job, and no Assets." In many cases, borrowers were encouraged by loan officers to overstate their income. In other cases, the loan officers did the overstating for them.[31]

Low interest rates and lax regulation fed the housing bubble. Lenders had plenty of funds to lend out. If some loans didn't go well, it wouldn't matter. If banks had to foreclose, lenders bet that they could sell a foreclosed home for a higher price than the loan amount. Lending practices had gone wild.

As housing prices soared, homeowners could take money out of their houses in the form of **home equity loans** or by refinancing. Mortgage lenders encouraged borrowers to refinance their mortgages and withdraw their excess equity. **Equity** is the difference between the market value and unpaid mortgage balance on a home. Although some people chose to keep

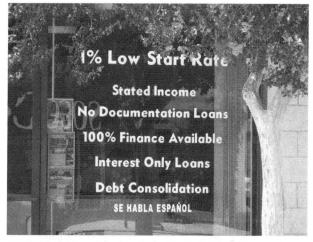

A mortgage brokerage company in the US advertising subprime mortgages on their door in July 2008.

their mortgages the same size and simply lower their monthly payments, many others wanted to get the equity that had built up in their homes by increasing the size of their mortgages. They found themselves with a pile of cash they could spend. These home equity loans gave borrowers money for a down payment on a new car or whatever they wanted. Homeowners had their own ATM machine with seemingly no limit: their home.

It was cheaper than ever for a family to buy a first home. In response, mortgage companies

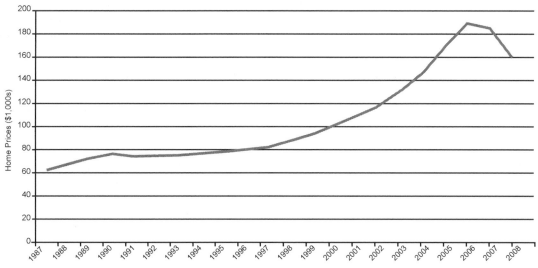

House Price Trend (1998-2008) as Measured by the Case-Shiller Index

http://en.wikipedia.org/wiki/Real_estate_bubble

introduced new mortgage products: adjustable rate mortgages (ARMs), interest only mortgages (only interest on the loan was paid), and promotional "teaser rates" that had a low introductory rate and then it would go up in the next few years. With all this credit available and demand skyrocketing, prices began to go up by double digit rates. Run-ups were close to 80 per cent in the key bubble areas of Phoenix, Las Vegas, north of Washington, D.C., and Florida. The run-up in house prices created more than $5 trillion in real estate wealth compared to where house prices would follow their normal growth rate.[32] The rise in house prices made the owners feel rich and sparked a consumption boom in the mid-2000s.

Real estate offered a seemingly risk-free path to fortune. Eager buyers made a quick buck in real estate, mortgage lenders got rich on fees, and investment bankers cried for more mortgage-backed bonds to sell to investors. They were all giddy from the punch bowl that served up an endless supply of addictive intoxicants. But when the banks finally raised interest rates on many of the loans, and supply exceeded demand, the party was over. We are still cleaning up the confetti and streamers celebrating the big bash.

Questions to Consider

1. How did real estate prices spiral out of control? Who do you blame for this occurrence?
2. Do you know someone whose house is "underwater"? What are they doing about it?

FATAL FLAW #5: A MOUNTAIN OF DEBT

What is debt? **Debt** is simply something that is owed or that one is bound to pay to another. There are different forms of debt, some of which we covered in chapter 4. In this section we will cover financial sector debt. Debt is important in a modern economy, but it may also spiral out of control.

During and after World War II, the U.S. had a large national debt and low interest rates, but the debt financed a war and later investment in productive assets, such as real homes, factories, and farms. Since the 2000s, debt has financed a speculative bubble of unproductive assets. This cycle of debt and bubbles is not new in world history. The basic message is no matter how different the latest financial crisis appears to be, there are usually similarities with past experience from other countries and from history. A common theme is that excessive debt – by government, banks, corporations, or consumers – often poses great risk. Debt-fueled booms all too often provide false confidence in a government's policies, a financial institution, or a country's living standard. Most of the booms end badly.[33]

Too much debt in the private sector often pushes an economy towards a crisis. The use of debt in investment is **leverage**. The financial system is more fragile with the greater dependence on debt and leverage. Journalist Nomi Prins claimed, "It wasn't the subprime market collapse that wrecked the banks and the greater economy; it was all of the borrowing on top of the subprime loans that did the deed."[34]

As a result of the Gramm, Leach, Biley Act in 1999, the government removed the fire wall separating investment and commercial banks. Some investment banks didn't want to merge with commercial banks. But the investment banks couldn't compete with the money and leverage of the commercial banks, which had the right to use their customers' deposits as collateral. The solution for the investment banks was to raise their own leverage limits so they could borrow more money, without having to put up as much collateral. But investment banks felt restrained by a rule that capped their debt-to-net capital ratio at 12 to 1. In 2004, the investment banks got the government to approve leverage ratios to 30 to 1. Some banks even increased their debt-to-net capital ratios, as in the case of Merrill Lynch, to as high as 40 to 1.[35] This high debt load by investment banks contributed to the crisis in 2008.

Questions to Consider

1. Would excessive debt create instability in a household? Explain.

FATAL FLAW #6: DICEY FINANCIAL PRODUCTS

For years, the financial sector was the way in which savers, who had funds, joined with entrepreneurs, who needed money to start or expand a business. Since the 1970s, speculative capital circulating around the world tried to find ways to make the highest returns. This burst of speculative activity has made finance the most profitable sector of the global economy, but it is also a source of economic instability. In the 1980s and 1990s, financiers created ever more sophisticated financial instruments, such as futures, swaps, options, and other derivatives. Profits came from trading assets and also from speculation. If you thought that the financial industry was all about financing businesses, such as Apple, Paramount Pictures, Microsoft, General Motors, home purchases, or basketball franchises, think again. Unfortunately, it is not as simple as that. These financial products are complicated. This creates layer upon layer of different products that financiers have chopped up, repackaged and sold to investors around the world. The rest of this section describes the different financial products. It is a difficult section. I have tried to make it as understandable as possible without over-simplifying. If you don't understand every detail, that is fine. If you grasp the fact that these financial products were (and still are) so complex that it is nearly impossible to know what they are and the risk involved, then you are getting the point of this section.

As described earlier, banks securitized mortgage loans made during the housing bubble. As a refresher, securitization is making illiquid assets like mortgages into liquid assets. The securities were sliced and diced, packaged and repackaged, rated by rating-agencies, and sold to banks and investment funds around the world. With securitization, investors could easily share bundles of mortgages and thus share the risk. But securitization did not see all risk. For example, information about the origination of the mortgage was unclear. The buyer of the security knew little about the borrower or about the bank that had originated the mortgage. And because the originator of the loan didn't bear the short-term consequences of his/her lending mistakes, s/he might not do a good job of evaluating the borrower. Yet, lenders ignored these risks as the feeding trough of riches brought out the greedy urge to make money anyway and anyhow.

Securitizing was not just in home mortgages, but also in commercial real estate mortgages, in consumer/credit card debt, and in car, student, and corporate loans. The bonds securitized from these loans – asset-backed securities – proved popular, and securitization soon spread. By the time the crisis hit, bankers had applied securitization to airplane leases, timber revenues, delinquent tax liens, radio tower revenues, boat loans, state and local government revenues, and even the royalties of rock bands.[36]

The banks sold the securities as bonds. Bonds have been around for many years. For governments and for many corporations, bonds are the single most important way to raise money. A **bond** is a debt security in which the issuer of the bond owes the holder of the bond a debt and is required to pay interest and to repay the principal at a later date. A bond repays an agreed upon rate of interest until it matures, and all of these facets are fixed – the price of the bond, the rate of interest it pays, and the date when it matures. Bonds vary widely as to whether they are a risky or a safe form of investment. Bonds that are safe carry a lower interest rate than high risk bonds that carry a higher rate of interest. Wall Street was eager to put together the mortgage-backed securities into packages that returned a higher rate of interest than ordinary low-yielding bonds. Around 2008, the total value of the global bond market was around $50 trillion.[37]

Since the demand for mortgage-backed securities was so strong, the banks even targeted the poor as borrowers. By the mid-2000s, a wave of **"predatory lending"** occurred. Mortgage lenders were madly searching for borrowers, anybody with a pulse, to sign up for a loan, especially for subprime mortgages. The mortgage lenders then sold these loans to investment banks for securitization, which were finally sold to investors. Some of this took place in the UK, Ireland, and Spain, but most happened in the U.S.[38]

Some in the media said people buying houses they couldn't afford caused the 2008 crisis. It was not. If sub-prime mortgage defaults only caused the crisis, the government could easily solve it. They could have bought and paid off every single sub-prime mortgage in the country and it would have only cost $1.4 trillion. This seems like a big amount, but the government spent about $13 plus trillion on bailouts and guarantees.[39] Financers piled debt onto the sub-prime mortgages; this was the actual cause of the economic meltdown. Now that is hard to wrap our heads around. There was debt on top of debt.

In order to understand this a little better, let's look at some of the Wall Street players and the financial products they invented that contributed to the financial crisis of 2008.

1. **Hedge Funds** are a private pool of capital managed by an investment adviser. They are only open to a limited number of investors who invest a minimum of $250,000 to over $10 million. Investors can be pension funds, university endowments and foundations, sovereign wealth funds, or wealthy individuals. In 2011, investors put $1.917 trillion into hedge funds around the world.[40] Hedge fund managers typically make 2 percent management fees based on the value of investments, plus performance fees.

2. **Derivatives** are a long-standing feature of financial markets. A derivative is a security whose price is dependent upon or derived from one or more underlying asset. Price changes in the underlying asset determine the derivative's value. The most common underlying assets

166

include stocks, bonds, currencies, interest rates, commodities, and market indexes. Most derivatives are highly leveraged. Traders use derivatives to lessen risk, but they are also used for speculation.[41] Speculation on tulip derivatives was a feature of the Dutch tulip bulb bubble in 1637 (see chapter 8). One of the oldest derivatives is rice futures, which were traded on the Dojima Rice Exchange, located in Osaka, Japan, since the 1700s.

In 1864, the Chicago Board of Trade (CBOT) listed the first ever futures contracts. At their simplest, **futures trading** is where a farmer will agree to a price for his/her next harvest months in advance. The future price of the harvest is thus a derivative, which farmers can sell. The name comes from the fact that a derivative's value derives or comes from an underlying product, the farmer's crop in this case. For years, derivatives have existed as a useful trading tool. The market assures farmers a price for their harvest, long before the crops are in. They are practical, and basically not too complicated.[42]

It quickly became obvious in Chicago and elsewhere that there was a huge potential market in the field of financial derivatives. But a major drawback was that no one could work out how to price them. The factors of time, risk, interest rates, and price instability were so complex that they defeated the best mathematicians, until Fischer Black and Myron Scholes figured

The Chicago Board of Trade Building was Chicago's tallest from 1930 until 1965.

out a formula in 1973. It was an important moment in applying mathematical formulas to market pricing. Within months, traders were using these new inventions, and the worldwide derivatives business took off like a rocket.

Derivatives are a double-edged sword. On one hand, a company can use them to manage risk. If Southwest Airlines, for example, is worried about the rising price of fuel, it can insure against that risk by buying oil on the futures market, locking in a price today for oil to be delivered in six months. Using derivatives Southwest can, in effect, take out an "insurance policy" against the risk that the price will go up. On the other hand, a derivative is a speculative bet. For example, the bet that the price of a stock will be greater than $10 next Monday is a derivative. A bet that the market value of a bet that a stock will be greater than $10 next Monday is a derivative based on a derivative. A bet that a Hollywood film will be a blockbuster is a derivative. There are countless products that one could invent.[43] And, indeed, in the 2000s, the financiers had a heyday in inventing speculative derivatives that were far removed from their mission of helping businesses grow and prosper. The total market in derivative products around the world is counted in the hundreds of trillions of dollars.

In recent years derivatives have gone from being a means of managing risk to pure speculation. It is akin to making wagers and bets in Las Vegas. Yet, the activities in Las Vegas are pure and simple gambling – gamblers do not promote them as a safe financial investment for a secure retirement. Traders buy and sell more than a $1 trillion worth of derivatives every day. In the words of the billionaire investor Warren Buffet, "The range of derivatives contracts is limited only by the imagination of man (or sometimes, so it seems, madmen). Say you want to write a contract speculating on the number of twins to be born in Nebraska in 2020. No problem – at a price, you will

Gambling at a pachinko parlor in Tokyo, Japan.

easily find an obliging counterparty." Buffet doesn't like derivatives. He prefers to know what's going on in the companies he invests in.[44]

3. A **Collateralized Debt Obligation** (CDO) is a pool of debt that financiers add together and then sell as a set of bonds paying a range of interest rates. I first introduced CDOs when explaining the function of Ginnie Mae. There are two streams of revenue from bonds, one from the fees to set up the deal and another from the debt and interest repayment. Financiers created the first CDO in 1987, but the years from 2002 to 2006 saw a wave of CDO stuffing with risky subprime mortgages. It was impossible to get to the bottom of exactly what was inside a CDO – which meant that no investor could possibly know either. Nevertheless, the CDO market climbed from nearly nothing in 1996 to $2 trillion by 2008.[45]

If the regular CDO market was not complicated enough, investment wizards began to design CDOs of CDOs, pools of pools of securitized debt, chopped and sliced and then chopped and sliced again; the underlying assets were none other than people with shaky credit who were struggling to pay back their loans. The new CDOs of CDOs were known as CDO^2, or CDO squared.[46] It is a good exercise to try and think for a moment what makes up a typical CDO^2. Warning, this may scare you. Start with a thousand different individual loans – commercial mortgages, residential mortgages, auto loans, credit card receivables, small business loans, student loans, or corporate loans. Package these loans together into an asset-backed security (ABS). Take that ABS and combine it with 99 other ABSs so that you have a hundred of them. That's your CDO. Now take that CDO and combine it with another 99 different CDOs. Want to pour your retirement savings into this "investment"? Do the math; in theory, the purchaser of this CDO^2 is supposed to somehow get a handle on the health of ten million underlying loans. Is this going to happen? Of course not![47] But for Wall Street, the CDO scheme was a machine that turned lead into gold.

4. **Credit Default Swap** (CDS), a form of insurance, is another murky financial product. The buyer of a credit default swap receives credit protection, whereas the seller of the swap guarantees the credit worthiness of the product. By doing this, the holder of the security shifts the risk of default to the seller of the swap. It gives the CDS buyer insurance against the risk of default, whether it is a corporate bond, an auto loan, or a subprime mortgage. The CDS market made sense before it spun out of control.[48]

Insights: Financial Products

The financial products Wall Street sold to investors leading up to the crisis in 2008 is like a house of cards. The cards do not have real value – like a bushel of wheat or barrel of oil, or a Main Street business – and when the reality set in that the house of cards had no value, they collapsed. Everyone who owns individual cards then tries to sell their cards, but, alas, since everyone knows that the cards are now worthless, no one will buy them. Those who made a profit bought the cards when the price was climbing upwards and then sold their cards at a higher price before everyone knew they were

CDS and General Electric

General Electric logo

In its simplest form, a CDS is an insurance policy, typically on a corporate bond. For example, an investor purchasing $100 million in General Electric (GE) bonds might worry that the company could default on its bonds. The investor decides it would be wise to purchase a type of insurance policy to make sure that s/he doesn't lose the whole $100 million if the company defaults on its bonds. The investor decides to pay $200,000 a year to buy a ten-year credit default swap on $100 million in GE bonds. In case the company, General Electric, does not default on its bonds, the most the investor could lose would be $2 million: $200,000 a year x 10 years. In the case the company does default on its bonds, the insurer of the credit default swap would then have to pay the investor $100 million. The most the investor who bought a CDS could make would be $100 million if GE defaulted on its debt any time in the next ten years and the bondholders received nothing. But the CDS insurer knows that GE is a good company, and the risk of default is slim. Therefore, the CDS insurer feels pretty secure that s/he will make $200,000 of easy money each year with little risk of losing the whole $100 million.[49]

worthless. The cards ended up worthless, but the lucky investor who sold at the right time made a profit. Wall Street's financial games added no value to the world economy, but the profits were excessive. When the house of cards finally collapsed, the crisis did not stop at the U.S. border. Wall Street sold these CDOs around the world, and they turned out to be toxic for banks and investment funds as far away as Norway, Bahrain, and China.[50] Warren Buffet compared the financial products to weapons of mass destruction – first because they are lethal, and second because no one knows how to track them down. The trouble with the securitization model was that it broke with the principles

House of cards.

that a bank had to individually assess and monitor every loan. The whole idea that a banker looks a borrower in the eye and makes a decision on whether s/he can be trusted seemed very old fashioned.[51]

FATAL FLAW #7: FINANCIAL SPECULATIVE MANIA

There is a gap between the productive economy of Main Street and the non-productive, speculative, yet profitable economy of Wall Street. Since the 1980s, there has been a political policy shift from the productive economy to favoring the speculative financial sector of Wall Street. If credit provides funding for some productive activity, such as transportation or medical research, it can be beneficial. But in the past 30 plus years, money has been concentrated in speculation.

Now here is something to ponder. Economist Nomi Prins says that finance today is based on the creation of absolutely nothing. It is continuously pushing nothing for something throughout the system. It may create profit, but it does not create new value – only industry, agriculture, trade, and services create new value. In other words, the financial products created did not contribute to the real economy.[52]

169

To be fair, the financial sector has done a good job in some areas, and has helped the country's economic growth. Innovations in centuries past, such as insurance and commodity options, have proven their value. Also, procedures for making home loans improved. Homeowners in the pre-World War II era had to save a whopping 50 percent to purchase a home. Financial firms have provided capital to many companies and community banks, credit unions, and local banks that supply consumers and small to medium-sized enterprises with the credit they need.[53] However, these examples show the difference between productive and speculative investments. Speculative financial products in the U.S. have taken money that businesses could have invested in the real economy because investors made more money in speculation on Wall Street than they could in the real Main Street economy.

FATAL FLAW #8: MORAL HAZARD AND LACK OF TRANSPARENCY

Moral hazard and transparency are two similar concepts. **Moral hazard** is simply someone's willingness to take risks that s/he would normally avoid, simply because s/he knows someone else will shoulder the consequences. For example, someone who has auto theft insurance may be more willing to park his car in a place where a thief might steal it than someone who lacks insurance. The car owner knows the insurance company will cover the loss. Moral hazard also played a role in the economic crisis.

The market badly misjudged the risk of subprime mortgage defaults. It made an even worse mistake trusting the rating agencies and the investment banks when they repackaged the subprime mortgages with a good AAA rating. Yet, the banks forged ahead with their risky decisions because of moral hazard. American International Group (AIG), a multi-billion dollar commercial insurance company in the U.S., is an example of moral hazard. In 2005-2006, AIG was the single biggest player in the CDS market. It had an excellent AAA credit rating. But as the companies it insured started to collapse, the downturn forced AIG to pay premiums on its insurance policies. It did not have enough money to do so. The federal government bailed out AIG because it had the entire economic system over a barrel.[54]

Financial markets lack transparency and are complex. **Transparency** is another word for information. For example, global capital flows through places like the Cayman Islands – a $2 trillion banking center in the Caribbean Sea. The U.S. can't regulate these places that launder money, evade taxes, and participate in other shadowy activities. The big banks don't like transparency. A fully transparent market would be highly competitive, and competition would drive down fees, as well as profits. Complexity also played a role in the 2008 crisis. The financial products were so complex that no one fully understood their risk. Computers running models couldn't possibly include all of the needed information to value the complex products.[55] With complexity and lack of transparency, banks have the power to exploit the uninformed.

FATAL FLAW #9: DECEPTIVE RATING AGENCIES

There would have been no credit crisis and, therefore, no economic crisis if not for the involvement of the credit rating agencies. They were the oil that greased all the moving parts in the great machine Wall Street assembled to package and sell U.S. subprime mortgages around the world. Their supposed job was to protect investors when the machine went haywire. Instead, they protected the profits they were making.[56]

A **credit rating agency** (CRA) is a company that assigns credit ratings for issuers of certain types of debt. Debt issues with the highest credit ratings – AAA – will have the lowest interest rates. Credit ratings influence the investors' confidence in the borrowers' ability to pay back the loan. The credit rating agencies do similar work as consumer credit bureaus, which calculate credit scores for individuals that may influence the interest rate at which the borrower pays. Perhaps some of you know your credit score. If it is high, then perhaps you can borrow money at a lower interest rate than if you had a low score.

The top three credit rating agencies dominate the business. These companies are Standard & Poor's (42.2% market share), Moody's Investors Service (36.9%), and Fitch Ratings (17.9%). Standard & Poor's (S&P) is owned by the McGraw-Hill Company (they publish textbooks as well). Fimilac, a French company, owns Fitch.[57]

Until the early 1970s, the bulk of the credit agencies' revenues came from investors. They published rating manuals and offered advisory services. But this changed when the agencies realized they could make more money with the issuer-pays model. For many years they paid little attention to the conflict of interest raised by the issuer-pays model that had become standard practice 30 years later. Unsurprisingly, the rating agencies gave high ratings for mortgage-backed securities to the same firms who paid them and whose bonds they rated. The banks that originated the securities were paying the rating agencies to rate their securities.

McGraw Hill, known for its textbooks to educators, owns Standard & Poor's. On November 26, 2012 McGraw-Hill agreed to sell its education division to Apollo Global Management for a reported $2.5 billion.

The rating agencies had a financial reason to satisfy those who were paying them. And cut-throat competition among the rating agencies just made matters worse. If one rating agency didn't give the grade that the banks wanted, they could turn to another.[58]

It is important that ratings of financial products are accurate. Managers of pension funds, for example, have to be sure the securities they buy are safe, and the credit rating agencies play a vital role by declaring their safety. However, this was not what was happening in the run-up to the financial crisis of 2008. The credit rating agencies were out to make a profit. At Moody's, profits quadrupled between 2000 and 2007, and it boasted the highest profit margin of any company in the S&P 500 for five of those years.[59] The credit rating business was very profitable.

Questions to Consider

1. How would you fix the issuer-pays model of compensation?

FATAL FLAW #10: BLOATED COMPENSATION PLANS

Wall Street doesn't produce anything of lasting value. The financial world does not create anything beyond the short-lived profits that it makes. Management bases Wall Street pay on the deals it closes in a year, never mind whether the long-term effects of those deals are disastrous. The more competitive and complex the financial industry became, the more firms had to find ways to get more money from the products they created. Plain-vanilla securities, as they were called, didn't return as much to investors or make as much for Wall Street bankers at year's end.[60]

Few people resent Bill Gates or the late Steve Jobs for their wealth because they made it by creating actual products and services that people actually use. An actor or actress might get paid millions for a film, but at least the film has entertainment value. But for the most part, when Wall Street pushes money around and takes huge profits, these are not activities that make Americans better, safer, or even more entertained. Management paid Wall Street financiers annual bonuses related to the fees they helped to bring in. In 2005, the major investment banks – Goldman Sachs, Morgan Stanley, Merrill Lynch, Lehman Brothers, and Bear Stearns – paid $25 billion in bonuses; in 2006, $36 billion, and in 2007, $38 billion. Even after the federal government bailed out these firms, they shamelessly continued to pay bonuses. The executives found ways for the company to pay them well, even when the firm didn't make money. Pay is high when work is good and when it is poor. And the bonus system, which focuses on short-term profits, made over the year, encouraged risk taking and too much leverage.[61]

Hedge fund managers have made outrageous compensation. There were just 610 hedge funds with $39 billion in assets in 1990. By the end of 2006, there were 9,462 hedge funds with $1.5 trillion in assets. In 2009, the 25 best-paid hedge-fund managers together earned $25.3 billion, an average of $1 billion each.[62] The financial crisis has not curbed these excesses. Compensation has continued to climb to all-time highs.

CONCLUDING INSIGHTS: THE 10 FATAL FLAWS IN THE FINANCIAL SECTOR

As we have seen from the ten fatal flaws in the financial sector, the industry has been able to create its own financial Wall Street economy separate from the Main Street economy. The two economies operate on separate planes. But the Wall Street economy feeds on the Main Street economy; it would not be able to exist without it. To be fair, there are still many valuable actions that Wall Street performs. But as we have seen, the excesses of Wall Street are so deep that purging the glut will not be an easy chore. They will use their riches and political influence to resist efforts to pry open their treasure chest of financial tricks for full examination and reform. It will not be an easy task, but it must be done.

Questions to Consider

1. How does Main Street suffer from Wall Street's actions?
2. What can be done to stop this pattern of wealth flowing to Wall Street at the expense of Main Street?

CHAPTER EIGHT

The Financial Sector:
Crisis and Its Aftermath

"Ideas, knowledge, art, hospitality, travel – these are the things which should of their nature be international. But let goods be homespun whenever it is reasonably and conveniently possible; and above all, let finance be primarily national."

--- John Maynard Keynes

PATTERNS OF FINANCIAL CRISES

Economist Nouriel Roubini believes the patterns of financial crises are remarkably predictable. He thought that the 2008 financial crisis was not an unusual event but that these crises actually happen quite often. It is because we are short-sighted in our thinking and don't know the lessons of history that we would say the 2008 crisis was a unique event. It followed patterns that have been repeated through history, only under slightly different circumstances.

---

10 Financial Crisis Patterns

1. A popular or valuable asset is in short supply while its demand is high.
2. Prices for the asset rise as demand increases.
3. Outsiders enter the market and buy popular assets, seeking quick and high returns.
4. Over-investment in the desirable asset leads to a bubble.
5. When supply is greater than demand, the bubble bursts.
6. There are more panicked sellers than buyers, and asset prices swiftly decline.
7. Those who bought the inflated asset are unable to repay their loans to lenders.
8. Either the government bails out the lender or their loans go into default.
9. If severe enough, the total economy collapses, resulting in a recession or depression.
10. Unless the government takes steps to curb abuses, the bubble can be repeated.

FINANCIAL CRISES

I have included in this section several different financial crises that have occurred in the past. There were many to choose from, each following the 10 basic patterns outlined above with slight variations. The first I have included is one of the most interesting and the earliest known financial crises: tulip mania.

Tulip Mania

I have a deal for you. I have a beautiful tulip bulb that will cost you a mere year's salary! Are you interested? If you were carried back to early 17th century Netherlands, your answer might be yes. You may think that the Dutch seem like sensible people. Could they be so foolish as to engage in such gambling? With the Netherlands as the world's first capitalist economy in the 16th and 17th centuries, a new kind of financial crisis appeared: the asset bubble. In 1630, **tulip mania** gripped the country. During this time the prices for tulip bulbs reached high levels and then suddenly collapsed. It is the first recorded speculative bubble. The term "tulip mania" refers to any large economic bubble.

The Ottoman Empire introduced the tulip to Europe in the mid-16th century, and it became very popular in the Netherlands. The flower became a prized luxury item and a status symbol. As the flowers grew in popularity, professional growers paid higher and higher prices for certain bulbs. Soon speculators began to enter the market. In 1636, the Dutch created a type of formal futures market where contracts to buy bulbs at the end of the season were bought and sold. The popularity of tulips caught the attention of the entire nation,

A tulip, known as "the Viceroy", displayed in a 1637 Dutch catalog. Its bulb cost between 3,000 and 4,200 guilders depending on size. A skilled craftsman at the time earned about 300 guilders a year.

and people eagerly took part in the tulip trade. Some individuals suddenly grew rich. By 1635, a sale of 40 bulbs for 100,000 florins was recorded. By way of comparison, a ton of butter cost around 100 florins, a skilled laborer might earn 150 florins a year, and "eight fat swine" cost 240 florins.[1]

Every one imagined that the love for tulips would last forever and that the wealthy from every part of the world would buy tulip bulbs from the Netherlands. They believed the riches of Europe would flow to their country. Poverty would be a thing of the past. At the peak of tulip mania in February 1637, some single tulip bulbs sold for more than 10 times the annual income of a skilled craftsman.[2]

People were buying bulbs at higher and higher prices, planning to re-sell them later for a profit. But such a scheme could not last unless someone was willing to pay the high prices. In February, 1637, tulip traders could no longer find new buyers for their bulbs. Panic set in, the demand for tulips collapsed, and prices plunged – the speculative bubble burst. The collapse left some traders holding futures contracts to purchase tulips at prices now ten times greater than those on the open market. Others found themselves owners of bulbs worth a fraction of the price they had paid for them. The panicked tulip speculators sought help from the Dutch government. But the judges said the debts were gambling debts and thus not enforceable by law. The mania finally ended with many individuals stuck with worthless tulip bulbs.[3]

The Roaring 1920s and the Stock Market Crash of 1929

The Roaring Twenties, the decade that led up to the stock market crash of October 1929, was a time of wealth and excess. A speculative boom had taken hold in the late 1920s, during which thousands of Americans invested in the stock market. In 1929, the president of what would later become Citibank had made it popular to sell stocks and high yield bonds directly to smaller investors. The public loved it. But a small group of bankers, brokers, and speculators manipulated the stock market and grew wealthy.

Almost everyone believed the stock market was a no-risk investment, where everything went up. By August 1929, brokers were lending small investors more than two-thirds of the face value of the stocks they were buying. Over $8.5 billion was out on loan at the time, it was more than the entire amount of money circulating in the U.S. economy. The rising share prices encouraged more people to invest, hoping share prices would continue to go up. Speculation fueled an economic bubble. It was a crisis waiting to happen. Although there were a few critics, most people said that America would soon enter a time when there would be no more poverty – a "New Era" when everyone could be rich.[4]

Many people poured all their savings into the stock market without learning about the companies they were investing in. With the flood of inexperienced investors into the market, it was ripe for manipulation. Investment bankers, brokers, traders, and sometimes owners banded together to influence stock prices. They did this by buying up large chunks of stock between them and then trading the stocks with each other for slightly more gains each time. When the public noticed the rising stock prices, they decided it was time to buy. The manipulators would then sell off their overpriced shares for a profit. They left the public holding stocks worth less than they paid for them.[5]

The stock market had been on a six-year run that saw it increase in value fivefold, peaking at 381 points on September 3, 1929. Shortly before the crash, economist Irving Fisher said, "Stock prices have reached what looks like a permanently high plateau." A string of terrible days followed, with more than a 40 percent drop in the market at the end of October 1929. In fact, the market continued to decline until July 1932, when it bottomed out, down nearly 90 percent from its 1929 highs.[6]

Crowd at New York's American Union Bank during a bank run early in the Great Depression.

The Stock Market Crash had a major impact on the U.S. and world economy. As the crisis got worse, the Federal Reserve stood idly by. Rather than pumping money into the economy, an expansionary monetary policy, it pushed austerity measures, making a bad situation even worse. As a result, the money supply shrank between 1929 and 1933, leading to a severe liquidity and credit crunch. This turned a stock market bust into a banking crisis and eventually into a severe economic depression. The U.S. Treasury secretary Andrew Mellon believed that the financial panic would "purge the rottenness out of the system. High costs of living and high living will come down. People will work harder, live a more moral life."[7]

The roaring 1920s captured the unbounded optimism of the age; it was a time when the stock market symbolized the false promise of permanent prosperity. It did not last forever.

The Dot-Com Bubble (1995-2000)

The **dot-com bubble** was a speculative bubble from around 1995 to 2000. A new technology – the Internet – was the craze in the 1990s and promised many possibilities. The period was marked by the founding and, in many cases, failure of a group of new Internet-based companies known as dot-coms. Companies were seeing their stock prices shoot up if they simply added an "e" prefix to their names or a ".com" to the end. Many confident investors ignored typical ways of measuring a successful business. One of the most disreputable dot-com companies was World-Com, a long-distance telephone and Internet-services provider that used illegal accounting practices to increase its stock price. The company filed for bankruptcy in 2002, and the courts convicted the CEO of fraud and conspiracy.

The Pets.com sock puppet was a casualty of the dot-com bubble. The company was founded in Aug. 1998, and defunct in Nov. 2000.

The disconnect between the real economy and the finance economy was on display during the dot-com bubble. With profits in the real economy stagnating, the money flocked to the financial sector. For example, there was a rapid rise in the stock values of Internet firms which, like Amazon.com, still had not returned a profit. The U.S. economic expansion became too dependent upon the stock market's rise. But finally reality set in and the market forced a "correction" of stock prices. On March 10, 2000, the stock market peaked. The dot-com bubble fully burst in 2001, wiping out $5 trillion in market value from March 2000 to October 2002. The tragic events of 9/11 added to the stock market decline. When the bubble popped, only 50 percent of new companies survived through 2004.[8] The economy escaped a long recession, but it was only by encouraging another bubble to form: the housing bubble.

Japan's Asset Price Bubble (1980s onward)

World War II devastated Japan's economy. However, with American assistance and the hard-work of its citizens, it launched a remarkable recovery to become the third largest economy in the world today. After the war, Japanese industry competed in a low-tech world market, offering low prices and poor quality products. In the 1960s, the American public called Japanese-made products "junk." However, the economy quickly improved by sharpening workers' skills and importing technology from around the world. By the 1980s, Japanese brands such as Toyota and Sony had become famous for their high quality and low prices. In the 1980s, America thought of Japan much as it does China today – as a rival for global economic dominance. Then, in 1990, the Japanese economy entered a period of economic stagnation.

In 1952, Finance Minister Hayato Ikeda created a model of growth for companies to follow. In this model, banks, rather than the stock exchange, were the main source of capital for industry. The joint stock company, a 17th century Dutch invention, formed the basis of the British and American capitalist model. In this Western model, companies raise money through the sale of shares of stock on stock exchanges. The stock exchange publicly lists most large corporations in order to get capital for their business. Ikeda thought that this system focused too much on short-term profits to satisfy shareholders, rather than on the long-term. He reasoned that the Japanese model of bank lending to corporations was better.[9]

The Japanese government directed Japan's banks to establish close relationships with their industrial borrowers. Banks freely lent to them for the long term. For lending, banks used the funds from Japanese citizens, who were savers rather than consumers.[10] Despite Western doubt, Ikeda's model seemed to be working. Japan ran trade surpluses year after year as it pushed export-led growth, much like China does today. By the 1980s, Japan was the world's largest creditor nation, a distinction once held by the U.S. This growth was achieved by the government's policy to keep the value of the yen low and Japanese exports competitive on the world market. The U.S. was importing more than exporting to Japan resulting in large trade deficits. The U.S. wanted Japan to raise the value of the yen in order to balance its trade.[11] In 1985, Japan agreed to the American request and allowed the value of its currency to rise steadily against the dollar. As a result, the spending power of Japanese companies heated up. Since the yen was now worth more overseas, it sparked a wave of real-estate and other purchases abroad. Fearing a rising yen would lead to an economic slump, the Bank of Japan cut interest rates. This move also meant cheap credit was available to industry. Driven by cheap and plentiful credit, a bubble in Japanese shares of stock and real estate started to inflate.

In keeping with neoliberal principles, the U.S. pressured the Japanese to deregulate their financial sector. As a result Japanese banks, looking for new ways to make money, invested heavily in real estate. They also began using speculative derivatives. At the same time, the banks continued to lend to their long-established clients without regard for their credit worthiness. Asset prices in Japan spiraled upward. By 1990, the value of all shares traded on Japanese stock exchanges was greater than that of those traded in the U.S., a country with an economy twice Japan's size. Real estate prices soared as well. At the peak of Japan's real estate boom, the land beneath and surrounding Tokyo's Imperial Palace – several hundred acres in total – had by some estimates value equal to all the real estate in California! Real estate in Tokyo was so valuable that it was selling by the square meter. Choice properties, such as in Tokyo's Ginza district, were fetching over 100 million yen (approximately $1 million) per square meter ($93,000 per square foot).[12]

At the end of 1989, the Bank of Japan finally decided to pop the inflated bubble. It began to raise interest rates. The strategy worked. By October 1990, the Nikkei 225 Stock Exchange had fallen by nearly 50 percent from its peak and real estate prices were in a tailspin, eventually falling 70 percent. As the economy slowed, Japanese companies that had invested heavily in real estate turned to their banks seeking short-term loans to ease their cash-flow woes. Fearing the possible bankruptcy of their clients, the banks lent freely, even though the real estate market was sinking. The banks were now in trouble; real-estate collateral that was declining in value backed 80 percent of their loans.[13]

Nikkei 225 (1970-2015)

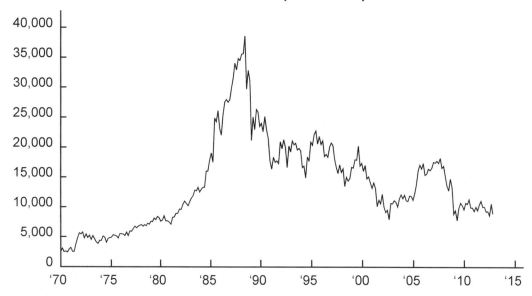

The Nikkei 225, Japan's stock market index, peaked on December 29, 1989 at 39,957. It closed on March 10, 2009 at 7,054.

Toxic assets were piling up in Japanese banks. Yet bank managers refused to do anything. Instead, they decided to wait until the crisis blew over and real estate prices would rise again. This meant hiding the true size of their losses. Worried Japanese savers took their money out of the banks and put it in postal savings banks (government banks) or under their futons. This only deepened the banking crisis. Neither the banks nor the government had the willpower to clean up the toxic assets.[14]

Unlike the U.S. in the 1930s, the Japanese economy did not melt down. It experienced stagnation, not depression. The bubble's deflation lasted for more than a decade with stock prices bottoming out in 2003, although they would go down even further during the global crisis in 2008. On March 10, 2009, the Japanese stock market Nikkei 225 stock index reached a 27-year low of 7054. The Japanese asset price bubble contributed to what the Japanese refer to as their "Lost Decade."[15] Today, as a result of a stagnant economy, many young people cannot find jobs or must resort to part-time work. Because of their reduced earnings, many share living space with their parents.

THE FINANCIAL CRISIS OF 2007-2008
The Fall of Lehman Brothers

Monday morning broke on this beginning-of-fall day September 15, 2008, and like any other day, it seemed uneventful. But it was far from uneventful on Wall Street, located at the southern tip of the island of Manhattan in the financial center of the world: New York City. Some insiders refer to it as the 9/11 of the financial world – the fall of the respected 158 year old financial firm, Lehman Brothers. The firm was at the center of the financial crisis gripping the nation. It had lost billions of dollars in the sub-prime mortgage crisis. Its fall was swift.

Lehman Brothers started small. In 1844, 23-year-old Henry Lehman emigrated to the U.S. from Bavaria, Germany. He settled in Montgomery, Alabama, where he opened a dry-goods store. His two younger brothers, Emanuel and Mayer, later joined him in the business. In 1850, the firm changed its name to "Lehman Brothers." Eventually the business started to trade the profitable cotton commodity, and soon after the end of the Civil War, the firm moved its headquarters to New York City. Emmanuel became a member of the New York Stock Exchange in 1887. His son, Philip, expanded his father's investment bank business and became managing partner from 1901 until his retirement in 1925. Upon Philip's retirement, management of the company passed on to his son, Robert. Under Robert's leadership, the bank financed enterprises in retailing, airlines, and entertainment. He guided his company through the stock market crash and Great Depression of the 1930s. After World War II, he expanded the company's international operations and became one of the country's wealthiest people. After 44 years as manager of the firm, he died in 1969, leaving no member of the Lehman family involved with the partnership.

With no clear successor, the firm floundered in the early 1970s. But the company returned to profitability later in the 1970s under new leadership. The company was sold in 1984 and reincorporated as Lehman Hutton in 1988. During the 1980s and early 1990s, the company rebuilt a successful financial business.

In 1994, Lehman Brothers was spun off as a separate company, and Richard S. Fuld was appointed CEO. In 1969, the year Robert Lehman died, Fuld began his career with Lehmans as

CEO Dick Fuld, former chair of bankrupt Lehman Brothers, after testifying before Congress on October 6, 2008.

a commercial paper trader and rose rapidly through the ranks. By 2008, at the time of Lehman's bankruptcy, Fuld had been with the company for almost 40 years. Lehman's did quite well under Fuld's leadership and the industry awarded him many honors for his management of the firm. In March 2008, Fuld appeared in *Barron's* list of the 30 best CEOs and they dubbed him "Mr. Wall Street." He received nearly half a billion dollars in total compensation from 1993 to 2007. But there was also a darker side to Fuld's personality. One magazine ranked Fuld as their Worst American CEO of All Time list. Fuld's shadier, nastier personality came into full public view as the drama of Lehman's fall unfolded.

Almost overnight the successful investment bank and CEO turned from the darlings of Wall Street to the whipping dog with the added humiliation of filing for the largest bankruptcy in U.S. history. In the years leading up to its bankruptcy in 2008, Lehman had borrowed significant amounts of money to fund its investing strategies, a process known as leveraging. A large portion of this investing was in housing-related assets, making it at risk to even the slightest downturn in the housing market. Its risky leverage ratios increased from 24:1 in 2003 to 31:1 by 2007. The profits rolled in during the boom time, but its highly leveraged position meant that just a 3 – 4 percent decline in the value of its assets would result in disaster. In 2008, Lehman faced a huge loss on its holding of dicey subprime tranches (categories) that had plunged in value. In the first half of 2008 alone, Lehman stock lost 73 percent of its value. In August 2008, Lehman released 6 percent of its work force, 1,500 people. In September, Lehman's stock lost even more of its value. The U.S. government was not planning on rescuing the ailing giant.

On September 13, 2008, Timothy F. Geithner, then president of the New York Federal Reserve Bank and future Treasury Secretary, called a meeting to discuss the future of Lehman. Leaders of major Wall Street banks and high-ranking government officials met on September 14 to try to prevent Lehman's bankruptcy. The banks agreed to purchase Lehman's toxic assets and there was a slim hope that Barclays of London would purchase the firm. But Barclays's backed out at the 11th hour, leaving bankruptcy the only option. Lehman Brothers filed for Chapter 11 bankruptcy protection on September 15, 2008.

The fall of Lehman Brothers alone did not cause the financial crisis, nor did just the sub-prime mortgage market. There was a lot more to it than simply a "few bad apples" – bankers making unwise loans to foolish homeowners, who bought houses they couldn't afford. There is a lot more to the financial system than meets the eye. The financial crisis of 2008 is no exception.

Finance: The Circulatory System

Finance is like the circulatory system in the human body, and the banking system is the heart of the economy. Ideally, the banking system pumps the lifeblood of the economy – money – to the places where it needs it most. If the banking system is the heart of the financial sector, in 2008, it suffered a heart attack, a massive one. This heart attack could have caused the death of the Too Big To Fail (TBTF) banks because of the way they were structured, and hence, the death of the U.S. economy, but the U.S. government revived the banks on their deathbed. The government administered massive shocks to the dying heart, frantically trying to revive the comatose banking system. They put it on life supports, infused with government loans and guarantees and paid for by the taxpayers. Slowly it began to revive. At the time of this writing, the government revival of the TBTF banks has perhaps saved the system from financial collapse. But the whole circulatory system – the financial sector – has many plugged arteries that need tending. Will the patient – the financial sector – return to its old ways of undisciplined living that caused its heart attack in the first place or has it changed its habits to a more sober and simple life style that will unclog the arteries and prevent another heart attack?

Next, we will examine some of the highlights of what took place during the financial crisis of 2008. Keep in mind these questions: "What are the prospects for the patient? And is there a chance of recovery?"

The Financial Crisis: Setting the Stage

In a short period, Wall Street had gone from celebrating its most profitable age to finding itself on the edge of ruin. Trillions of dollars had vanished. Some of the most prized principles of capitalism were shattered. The idea that financial wizards had invented a new era of low-risk profits and that American-style finance was the global gold standard was now officially dead – at least for the moment.[16]

In 2007, at the peak of the economic bubble, the financial services sector had ballooned to more than 40 percent of total corporate profits. Financial products – too complex to understand – were driving the nation's economy. The mortgage industry provided the loans that served as the raw material for Wall Street's elaborate cre-

An Ameriquest Mortgage Company blimp flying over San Francisco, CA.

ations, repackaging and then reselling securities as many times as needed to generate fees and then selling them to an unsuspecting world. Financial titans were confident that they had invented a new financial model that they could successfully export around the globe. "The whole world is moving to the American model of free enterprise and capital markets," said Sandy Weill, the CEO of Citigroup in 2007. But the financial firms had built their shaky empire on a pile of enormous debt.[17]

The following is a story about how one mortgage company, Ameriquest, turned the old-fashioned field of mortgage lending into one in which money was as abundant as flies on a carcass and those involved as predatory as vultures searching for a fresh kill.

Ameriquest: A Tale of a Shady Mortgage Business

It was the 2004 holiday season in Sacramento, California. Bob, a college student, was home for the holidays. One night, out on the town, he met a 26-year-old young man – Slickdaddy G, who was a "larger-than-life personality type," Bob recalls. "He had perfectly highlighted blond hair, short and gelled, perfect white teeth, and perfectly bronzed skin." He also had his own limo driver and a seemingly endless supply of cash. Bob joined Slickdaddy G for a night of lavish partying. The next morning, Bob asked Slickdaddy G, "What do you do?" "Ameriquest," came his reply. "I'm in the mortgage business."[18]

The subprime bubble was as wild as anything ever seen in American business. Slickdaddy G told Bob that in one good month, he took home $125,000. In some places, like Ameriquest's Sacramento offices, drug usage was an open secret, so that the loan officers could sell 14 hours a day. The money poured in.[19]

Ameriquest was the U.S. leader in subprime lending in 2003, having driven its volume to $39 billion, up from $4 billion in 2000. Investigators found in file after file of Ameriquest's loan applications that borrowers listed their occupation as "antiques dealer." Borrowers told of signing a loan application and finding out at the closing that an entire financial record – tax forms and everything – had been made-up for them, including their occupation. In 2007, Ameriquest was the object of major lawsuits filed by more than 20 state attorneys general, while federal regulators did nothing.[20]

Questions to Consider

1. What is your reaction to the story about Ameriquest? Were you surprised about these events?

Events of the Financial Crisis

By the spring of 2006, the financial system with its dependence on leverage – and its belief that asset prices would continue to rise – was ready for a collapse. Housing starts had leveled off, and home prices stopped rising. The supply of new homes began to outstrip the demand, and a rise in interest rates made mortgages more expensive. The hundreds of unregulated nonbank mortgage lenders relied on short-term financing from larger banks. Since subprime mortgage borrowers were defaulting at a higher rate, the larger banks refused to renew these lenders' lines of credit. The nonbank lenders began to fail.[21]

By late summer of 2007, the balance sheets of many financial firms showed that they held a large number of toxic assets. The question was, "Which banks had toxic assets buried off their balance sheets?" Since the financial system lacked transparency, no one knew for sure. Two hedge funds run by investment bank Bear Stearns sank billions of short-term loans into their supposedly high-quality, triple A rated, subprime collateralized debt obligations (CDOs). But once demand dried up for these types of securities, their values dropped. This meant that their value as collateral for borrowing also dropped. To make up for this difference, creditors started to ask Bear Stearns to post more collateral for their loans, but at the same time investors were pulling out. The only way for the investment bank to come up with the money to post as collateral was to sell the declining assets at bargain-basement prices, which further decreased the value of the funds. In the end, the funds completely ran out of cash.[22] Bear Stearns was the weakest and most leveraged of the pre-crisis big five investment banks. It was the first to fall.

In the spring of 2008, the crisis was gathering steam. Loans for ordinary mortgages, credit cards, automobiles, and other consumer products dried up. Even the federal government-sponsored entities (GSE), Fannie Mae and Freddie Mac, started to falter. Traders had stuffed their investment portfolios with toxic subprime mortgages securities. Latecomers to the securitization club, they had leveraged themselves at the ratio of 40 to 1 by issuing debt that benefitted from the understood backing of the U.S. government. The GSEs cast aside their tried and true conservative lending principles of the past. From 2007 onwards, as housing prices started to decline, delinquencies and foreclosures began rising sharply. The GSEs recorded $14.9 billion in combined net losses in 2007.[23] Concerns about their

Fannie Mae headquarters at 3900 Wisconsin Avenue, NW in Washington, D.C.

solvency grew. The economy was grinding to a standstill. There was a cry for the government to do something.

On July 30, 2008, President George W. Bush gave the U.S. Treasury Department authority over Fannie Mae and Freddie Mac. In September 2008, the government placed the companies into a conservatorship, with the commitment to keep both corporations solvent. The two companies needed cash, which was in short supply because of billions of dollars in mortgage losses. A **conservatorship** is like a Chapter 11 bankruptcy, with new leadership appointed to the bankrupt company.

A conservatorship has temporary government control, while **nationalization** is where the government completely takes over a private enterprise. The Treasury Department gave $200 billion to keep both GSEs operating in exchange for stock in the companies. Together, the two GSEs had more than $5.2 trillion in outstanding mortgage-backed securities in 2008.[24] In 2009, they held almost half of the estimated $12 trillion U.S. mortgage market.[25]

As Lehman Brothers and Merrill Lynch slid toward bankruptcy, Treasury Secretary Hank Paulson called a meeting of the city's financial elite to the office of the Federal Reserve in Lower Manhattan on Saturday, September 13, 2008. Paulson told the bankers that dealing with the panic would rest with all of them. He told them to figure out a way of dealing with Lehman. After an all-night session, they decided on a deal to buy Lehman's toxic assets while Barclays of London bought the rest of the bank. However, British regulators ruined the deal; the government would force Lehman to file for bankruptcy.[26]

Lehman's bankruptcy on September 15, 2008, sent shock waves through the financial markets. The global economy was headed for difficulties. The following are 6 of the many tense developments that occurred as a result of the financial crisis in the fall of 2008:

1. American International Group (AIG)

Lehman's bankruptcy shock waves first hit the insurance giant AIG. The credit rating agencies downgraded AIG's credit rating. Its losses had been mounting for months, but the downgrade called into question the guarantees they had on half a trillion dollars' worth of AAA rated CDO tranches. It was unable to survive on its own, and had to accept a bailout from the federal government. In effect it was more than a bailout of AIG; it was a bailout of all the banks that had purchased insurance from it.[27]

2. Money Market Funds

Money market funds were in trouble. Even though they are part of the shadow banking system, the public considers them a safe place to put money. Although the FDIC does not insure most money market funds, there is the assurance that they will not decline. A dollar will be worth a dollar no matter what. The no-matter-what day arrived on September 16, 2008, when a fund "broke the buck." The value of the money market fund dipped below $1, meaning that a dollar invested with the fund was no longer worth a dollar. This was almost unheard of in the $4 trillion money market industry.[28] But the government stepped in to insure money market funds and ended depositors' fear of losing all their money.

3. The Commercial Paper Market

Corporations go to this market for their short-term borrowing needs, such as for payroll. They can borrow billions of dollars for 30, 60, or 90 days, and when those debts come due, most corporations simply roll them over for another term. The problem comes when no one wants to buy a company's commercial paper, and it is unable to roll over its debt. Money market funds generally buy commercial paper, but they were now in trouble. AIG, for example, was unable to borrow on the commercial paper market and it simply ran out of money. The Fed came to the rescue and created a fund with $1.8 trillion worth of commercial paper for the borrowing needs of companies.[29]

4. The Federal Reserve: The Lender of Last Resort

If need be, the Fed could step in to loan banks money in an emergency. In return, the banks would post safe assets, such as Treasury bonds, as collateral. The better the collateral, the more favorable were the loan terms for the borrowing bank. The Fed halted this practice during the crisis. As the bailout unfolded, banks began to borrow heavily from the Fed and post all sorts of toxic junk assets as collateral. For a few weeks during the fall of 2008, corporate borrowing and lending collapsed. Even good corporations found themselves short of cash. In order to avoid further disaster, the Fed extended loans to nonfinancial firms. This had never happened before. It was an expansion of government support of the financial system.[30]

After the initial credit crunch, money from the Fed freely flowed to the banks at very low interest rates, sometimes even 0 percent. But even though the banks had the cash to loan, they still refused to do so. Banks were getting no-interest loans from the Fed, but interest rates for everyone else were high. Banks sank the money into the safest investments around: government debt. The banks had little risk and made a modest return. This strategy was disastrous for the Main Street economy, since small businesses could not get loans. But Wall Street profited.[31]

5. The Federal Reserve's Quantitative Easing

By the fall of 2008, it was clear the government would not allow the banks to fail outright because of their poor business decisions. The Fed was lending lots of money, but the credit market was still dead. The Fed would attack the problem of increasing the flow of capital by quantitative easing. When I heard the term quantitative easing, I thought of the times when I may overeat and

the waistband on my pants becomes too tight. If I had a really good elastic waistband on my pants, then an expanding elastic waistband could ease my quantitative overeating. End of my over-eating misery. In a way, that is what the Fed did in the financial crisis. The overeating, though, was the wild gluttony exhibited by bankers, lenders, and home-buyers, which led to a situation where the Fed had to step in to ease the pain they caused to the global economy.

The Fed might not like my waist band comparison, so here is a more technical definition. **Quantitative easing** is used by Central Banks (the Fed) when interest rates are at or very near zero, and they cannot be lowered any further. In such a situation, the central bank may perform quantitative easing by purchasing bonds from banks. This act puts liquidity into the markets because the Fed would pay for those bonds by creating money essentially out of thin air. As it purchased hundreds of billions of dollars' worth of bonds, cash flowed to the banks that sold them. Supposedly the banks had even more cash and were more likely to lend it. The goal of this policy is to increase the money supply rather than to decrease the interest rate, which is already around 0 percent. Economists say this is a "last resort" to stimulate the economy.[32]

The Fed basically granted subsidies to the banks in their time of need. The Fed used a sleight of hand trick to take on trillions of dollars in useless toxic assets from the banks, giving cheap loans in return to the very banks that had created the financial crisis in the first place. While the Fed was pumping trillions into the economy, the general public was largely distracted by the fray taking place in Congress over the much less expensive $700 billion Treasury bailout package that would be known as TARP.[33]

6. The Troubled Asset Relief Program (TARP)

Let's review a moment – this can get confusing. In March 2008, JP Morgan Chase acquired the huge investment bank Bear Stearns. In September 2008, in the midst of the 2008 presidential election,

Lehman Brothers had declared bankruptcy. Fannie Mae and Freddie Mac, the two mortgage giants, were on federal life support. The federal government bailed out AIG, the country's largest commercial insurer. At this point, Merrill Lynch, Morgan Stanley and Goldman Sachs, the three remaining independent investment banks, all faced runs that would quickly bankrupt them without government support. Bank of America quietly acquired Merrill Lynch for $50 billion. In the same month JP Morgan Chase took over the failing Washington Mutual Bank (WaMu) for $1.9 billion. In October 2008, Wells Fargo bought Wachovia in a $12.7 billion deal. Many other banks also faced ruin.[34] The industry was now more concentrated than ever.

An important secretive meeting took place in mid-September between leading Wall Street executives and government officials. The Wall Street bankers had billions of dollars of toxic assets on their books with no buyers, and they thought it would be great if the U.S. Treasury would buy them. Treasury basically agreed. Over the weekend, Treasury put together a short three-page memo outlining plans that would allow them to purchase banks' toxic mortgage-backed assets; the banks that made the bad bets in the first place.[35] Treasury officials told Congress that if they did not immediately rescue the banks the economy would collage.

The **Troubled Asset Relief Program (TARP)**, signed into law by President Bush on October 3, 2008, was a government program to purchase assets from the banks with the intended purpose to strengthen the banks. The TARP's $700 billion was the smallest part of the whole government bailout of the financial sector. There was no Congressional uproar about the trillions of dollars of Fed guarantees and loans. Wall Street was delighted with the government program to buy their bad assets. It was great for them to offload their junk to the government at inflated prices. The banks could have sold many of these assets on the open market at the time, but not at prices they would have liked.[36]

Secretary Henry "Hank" Paulson was nominated by President Bush (left) to be Secretary of Treasury. Paulson guided the nation through the initial stages of the financial crisis.

Insights: The 2008 Financial Crisis

The public did not appreciate the arrogant attitude displayed by many Wall Street financiers during the financial crisis. They did not appear to regret the damage they had done. Journalist Dan Schecter writes about an example of one of these unapologetic attitudes. "I went to a dinner party early in August [2011] and met a financial executive who worked at one of Wall Street's top investment firms. He [told] me that the people shoveling out those sub-prime loans KNEW many of the borrowers couldn't afford to pay back. They knew what misery they'd cause, but that didn't stop them. I asked: 'So, what happened …to the market disciplines that these bankers are always preaching? He shrugged, indicating that there was so much to be made that normal safeguards and standards were pushed to the side or forgotten."[37]

THE AFTERMATH OF THE 2008 FINANCIAL CRISIS
The New Normal: The 5 Rs

We are still experiencing the aftermath of the financial crisis of 2008. It is tricky to write about it because it is still going on. What problems are still not solved? What leaders are providing sensible solutions? Should we return to the type of economy that brought about the financial crisis, reform it, or make it more conservative? Should we stage a revolution and overthrow the existing economy? Should we send out more petitions and hold more rallies or should we rebuild a more equitable and sustainable economy? These are just a few of the many questions that I am thinking about as I write this final section.

We are at a very critical juncture in our human history. Our planet is in crisis. Pressing economic needs have eclipsed the environmental issue for the past several years. Yet, the issue has not gone away. Our U.S. economy is built upon the foundation of a system devised over 150 years ago. It is no longer adequate for a complex nation such as the U.S., nor is it good for the global community bursting at the seams with 7+ billion plus people and critical environmental concerns. No wonder we, as a collective people, are confused, angry, and ready for real answers and solutions to the problems we are facing. Our political leaders, who we turn to for guidance, are as unsure as the rest of us. They have no idea which way to turn. In fact, many are merely clinging to the past system that got us into trouble in the first place. How can we sort out the global economy amidst such turmoil, indecision, stalemate, and fear? The shrillness of the debate masks the uncertainty people feel.

In researching the topic of the global economy and the financial sector over the last couple of years, I have come to the conclusion that we have responded in different ways to our current economic problem. Each of these responses views the economy differently. Since the teacher in me is always trying to simplify complex ideas, I have called these responses or movements the 5 Rs. I am listing the 5 Rs in what I consider a logical order. The rest of this chapter is devoted to explaining each of the 5 Rs.

The 5 Rs: Movements in Response to the Economic Situation

1. **Revolt** – violently overthrow the whole system for a different system.
2. **Restore** – keep the same neoliberal system as before the crisis.
3. **React** – keep the same neoliberal system as before the crisis except make it more conservative.
4. **Reform** – keep basically the same capitalist system but reform or regulate its excesses.
5. **Rebuild** – gradually work to build a new economic model.

Revolt

When the economic and political structures of a country break down, as is happening in some countries in Europe, Africa, and the Middle East, then a country is ripe for a possible revolution. A **revolution** is an overthrow and replacement of an established government or political system by the people governed.[38] Revolutionaries are eager to overthrow the government that they blame for all problems. But they often do not have a clear plan for what should follow once the government is toppled. Revolutions usually result in more chaos, violence, and instability, rather than solving the issues leading to the revolution in the first. They are not a sensible way to bring about change.

Greece has been in the news in 2010-2012 for experiencing many problems. It is deeply in debt and struggling to avoid a debt default. No country is under more pressure to cut back on spending than near-bankrupt Greece. The downturn has saddled a once booming nation with 35 percent youth unemployment and years of depressed growth up ahead. Buckling under a culture of tax evasion by elites and public sector overspending, Greece received a $170 billion bailout from the International Monetary Fund (IMF) and European Union in 2010.[39] Some people say, Greece is ripe for a revolution.

Restore

The chaotic events of 2008 have settled down. There is a desire by many to return to what they see as "normal," whatever that means anymore. I once lived in Normal, Illinois, home of Illinois State University where I taught history. When people asked where I was from, I would reply Normal, Illinois, always waiting for the giggles

Demonstrators in the plaza in front of the Greek parliament, May 25, 2011.

that would follow. Although normal was poked fun at in the past, today many people want a return to what they think is normal. When people are faced with an unknown future or the safety of restoring what they knew in the past, many choose the safer path. Restoring the past is a powerful vision for many people at this time.

In 2012, Republican presidential candidate Mitt Romney had as one of his campaign slogans, "Restore America." Economically, Romney wanted to restore the principles of neoliberalism and, in particular, the primacy of the financial sector from which he made his sizable fortune. President Obama wanted some reforms of the financial sector, but not enough to curb its economic dominance. Romney's running mate, Republican Congressman Paul Ryan of Wisconsin, on the other hand, followed a reactionary path.

Since we have already discussed in some depth in this book the policies of neoliberalism and economic globalization, I will not add to the information. However, many of the restorers in America have turned to a reactionary movement, in which there is a push to make neoliberal policies even more conservative.

React

Reaction is a movement that favors extreme conservatism or right wing political views. Reactionaries oppose political, economic, or social reforms and are at one end of the political continuum, opposite of revolution. Reaction is a third movement since many politicians and business leaders are moving even further to the right of the restore movement. They want more concentration of corporate power, smaller government, austerity programs to reduce the deficit, tax cuts – including capital gains, vouchers for Medicare and schools, more deregulation, and more privatization of public institutions such as schools, prisons, government services, the military, electricity, federal lands, and Social Security. The following are 4 ways in which reactionaries are pushing for a more conservative economy and government.

1. React: Austerity

The austerity camp sees the deficit as a bigger problem than stagnation and unemployment and refuses to consider any more stimulus spending. Aside from the military, they want to cut government spending through **austerity** measures targeted at social programs, especially education,

Tea Party protesters walk towards the United States Capitol during the Taxpayer March on Washington, September 12, 2009.

Medicare, social security, infrastructure, and programs for the poor. For example, Paul Ryan wants to turn Medicare into a voucher system which restricts health care spending to a specific amount. The reduce-the-deficit slogan has gained strength in the U.S, by appealing to the anti-big government feelings of many Americans. Also, Wall Street has shifted the debate from it to the deficit. It says that big government is the problem, not big banks. And the vocal Tea Party movement supports austerity.[40]

2. React: The Banks

The financial crisis and bailout led to further concentration of the financial sector. The crisis gave stronger firms an opportunity to pick up weaker firms in a wave of mergers mentioned earlier and made them bigger, stronger, more profitable and more politically influential. Since the crisis of 2008, the big six U.S. mega-banks – Bank of America, Citigroup, J.P. Morgan Chase, Goldman Sachs Group, Wells Fargo, and Morgan Stanley – have staged a comeback. Profits and stock prices and executive pay are up, and government bailouts have been paid back. But, critics say that a closer look shows big-bank stability is just skin-deep, hiding a powder keg of bad debt. Smaller banks have had a different experience. Despite some TARP bailout crumbs, they have gone under in record numbers – 140 failed in 2009.[41]

3. React: Housing and Consumption

Millions of poor Americans have lost or are losing their homes – by one estimate, 2.3 million in 2008 alone. In 2007, foreclosure actions stood at almost 1.3 million, while almost 3 million home-owners received at least one foreclosure filing during 2009, setting a new record for the number of people falling behind on their mortgage payments.[42] Lenders filed a record 3.8 million foreclosures in 2010, up 2 percent from 2009 and an increase of 23 percent from 2008.[43]

4. React: Labor and Social Inequality

In much of the non-financial sector, workers have increased their productivity, but the gains have largely been added to corporate profits and higher CEO salaries rather than rising wages. This means that labor produces more goods and services for less income. For example, the General Motors (GM) factory in Orion Township, Michigan, negotiated a deal with the United Auto Workers (UAW) union that pays 40 percent of the workers crawling through cars on the assembly

General Motors (GM) automobile manufacturing workers.

line only $15 an hour. That's about half the traditional UAW wage.[44] Depressing the pay of labor is part of the reactionary movement.

As of this writing, the country has suffered unemployment rates around the range of 7.0 to 10 percent since the beginning of the financial crisis, with more than 25 million people unemployed, underemployed or who have given up looking for work altogether. The soaring unemployment caused tax revenues to tank, touching off fiscal crises in nearly every state. In reaction, governments cut spending and axed tens of thousands of teachers. For example, about 75 percent of the non-supervisory workforce in the U.S. has seen an 18 percent drop in real wages since the mid-1970s. Meanwhile, productivity has increased by more than 90 percent.[45] Yet, top hedge fund managers continue to pull in more than 26,000 times the pay of teachers in 2009. Are 25 hedge fund managers worth 658,000 teachers?[46] It is easy to trace where the money from higher productivity went: into the hands of the few.

> **Questions to Consider**
> 1. Do you think the reactionary policies are the right approach to solving economic problems?

Reform

Reform, the fourth movement, means to put or change into an improved form or condition. It means fine tuning the existing system, without changing its fundamentals. Reform seeks to improve the system as it stands.[47] Thus, reformers do not want to overthrow capitalism but correct the problems of neoliberalism.

The big question for reformers is, "If there is a role for government in the global economy, what will that role be?" Neoliberals say the best role of government is to govern least. But the financial crisis showed that there is an important role for government. If there is a reform effort to undo some of the neoliberal policies, clearly the government will need to take the lead.

Reformers still promote economic growth as the path to prosperity. They see it as the way to end high unemployment. But many reformers support a more managed form of capitalism, which has an important role for government. These reforms include a more equal tax system, targeted regulations, a stimulus to encourage consumer demand, and a curb on the excesses of neoliberalism. Next, I'll describe a few of the proposed and already passed reforms. However, those in the reactionary camp are pushing back against reforms. Although Obama's health care bill survived a 5-4 vote by the Supreme Court in the summer of 2012 and 2015, efforts continue to overturn the bill. The Dodd-Frank Wall Street Reform Bill is a case in point.

1. Reform: Stimulus

The reform camp thinks stagnation is a threat to the economy and suggests more **stimulus** (government spending). The fear of burdening future generations with debt is odd to them, since they think the best way to help future citizens is to make sure that they have a healthy economy. They believe that austerity measures will not reduce the deficit but hurt growth and the economy in the long run. Government spending has a **multiplier effect**, which is about 1.5 in the U.S. economy. For example, if the government spends a billion dollars now, GDP this year will go up by $1.5 billion. If stimulus money is put into assets that increase the country's long-term productivity, the country will be in better shape in the long run as a result of a stimulus. However, not all spending has the same multiplier effect. Spending on foreign contractors working in Iraq has a low multiplier, because much of the consumption takes place outside the U.S.; so do tax cuts for the wealthy, who save much of what they receive. Unemployment benefits have a high multiplier, because the unemployed spend almost all they receive.[48]

189

2. Reform: Break Up the TBTF Banks

America's major banks are too big to fail. The solution is to break them up. Yet, when reformers try to break them up, tax them or impose regulations on them, the financial sector lobbyists spring into action to prevent the government from passing and putting the reforms into action. Wall Street lobbyists have spent over $700 million in the years after the financial crisis to stop reforms.[49]

3. Reform: The Financial Reform Bill

Signed into law by President Barack Obama on July 21, 2010, the 2,300 page **Dodd – Frank Wall Street Reform and Consumer Protection Act** is a federal law that is supposed to reform the

financial sector. On one hand, critics say the reforms are not enough to prevent another financial crisis. On the other hand, the financial sector says the reforms have gone too far and impose too many restrictions on banks. Reformers see the bill as going a long way towards regulating the banks and their financial products. Others question whether the bill does enough to curb the giant financial sector, which gobbles up more of the nation's economic activity than other economic sectors. Also, new regulations won't do anything to stop the financial sector from exerting its influence over Washington. Interestingly, even though the Congress passed and the president signed the Dodd-Frank Bill, the government has had difficulty putting the reforms in place, especially

President Barack Obama meeting with Rep. Barney Frank, Sen. Dick Durbin, and Sen. Chris Dodd, in the Green Room at the White House prior to a financial regulatory reform announcement on June 17, 2009.

if the reforms clash with powerful financial interests. The financial sector has called out its legions of lobbyists and lawyers to wage war against financial regulators over every line of the bill in the rulemaking process.

Questions to Consider

1. How can reformers change the economy when confronted with such obstacles as described above?

Rebuild

The fifth response to the financial crisis is to rebuild the economy. **Rebuild** means to develop an alternative economy that takes into consideration the environment, social and economic justice, and human well-being. It is largely about changing the mix in a mixed economy. Markets are a big part of rebuilding the economy, but not the only part.[50] Because communism failed so miserably, many say that the best economic system is neoliberal capitalism. But many think it is failing, too. It has not been ushered out on its deathbed, as was the case with communism, but it is drawing its last breadth on the hospital's gurney, only kept alive with intravenous feeding from the government.

Some people want to rebuild a mixed economy. But what is the mix in a mixed economy? A **mixed economy** is a diverse economy in which a mix of different economic sectors prevents the concentration of wealth and power and cushions the downturn in one economic sector from freezing up the entire economy. It means breaking up large corporations, such as TBTF banks. Regulations make sure that corporations follow existing laws. It means government policy favors small businesses and small agriculture, instead of large corporations and agri-business firms. Public ownership of certain large utilities achieves efficiencies of scale and offers reasonable prices for consumers. Tax rates are more equitable and encourage investment in companies and the creation of jobs rather than just consumption. And, most importantly, the government gears policies to protect and preserve the environment.

I have organized this last section into five ways in which rebuilding can take place. I have tried to make the list positive. Inspired individuals and groups can put in place some of these five actions. Although it takes more effort than changing light bulbs to energy-saving ones, it doesn't take a huge effort to start a community or school garden or buy fresh local produce at the grower's market. These are merely suggestions in starting to rebuild a more sustainable, equitable, and life-affirming economy.

Rebuilding Actions

1. Emphasizing Small and Local
2. Challenging the Consumer Growth Model
3. Renewing Public Ownership
4. Healing Our Planet
5. Creating Shared Values

1. Emphasizing Small and Local

Our economy, society, institutions, and way of life have become so complex they are overwhelming our capacity to deal with them. One way to deal with this overpowering complexity is to simplify – simplify everything! This means emphasizing the local and small – from business, utilities, health care, banking, housing, education, transportation, and shopping to agriculture. Small, local, and diversified is the motto. There are different models for implementing this strategy; in this brief section I have highlighted two. Yet, there are many more possibilities emerging every day.

A **farmers market** is a collection of individual vendors – mostly farmers – who sell produce, fruits, meat products, and sometimes prepared foods and beverages. The local community benefits from farmers markets because farmers sell directly to consumers, keeping dollars

A Farmers' Market

circulating in the locality instead of flowing to large corporations. Consumers can buy direct from the farmer/producer and enjoy fresh, seasonal food grown within a drivable distance from their homes. In addition, local, fresh food is much healthier than heavily processed foods.

The Bank of North Dakota (BND) is a state-owned bank based in Bismarck, North Dakota. At the time of this writing, it is the only state-owned bank in the nation. Although state agencies are required to place their funds in the bank, local governments are not required to do so. Another 14 states are considering creating state banks, following the long-established North Dakota model.[51] This trend is likely to continue since money stays in the local and state economy instead of flowing to banking giants.

2. Challenging the Consumer Growth Model

The economic notion of constant economic growth is widespread, yet we are living on a planet where continued, unlimited growth is impossible. After all, we are exploring the last frontier for precious resources, such as oil in inhospitable climes, such as the far Arctic and dangerous deep water drilling. Countries such as Saudi Arabia and China that cannot grow enough food for their people are snapping up valuable agricultural land in Africa.[52] Can our environment survive in a system that requires unlimited growth to continue? Who is demanding that economic growth continue? What part of our economy is demanding growth year after year? The dominant economic model today is a particular brand of corporate capitalism in which shareholders who aren't involved in the business itself demand that their investments grow. That part of our economy has to shrink, and that is frightening to the people who are part of it.[53] For example, locally-based businesses don't need to grow year after year. Business needs to provide enough revenue to pay salaries, expenses, and stash away enough for hard times. Described below are locally-based business models that don't need to grow and in which distant shareholders and corporate owners do not siphon off the revenues. These models are not new; they have a long history in the U.S. and Europe, but neoliberalism has overshadowed them since the 1980s.

Worker ownership is where workers have an equal stake in the company they are working for and share common goals. This model benefits from lower overhead costs and offers benefit plans, such as healthcare and pensions.[54] Interestingly, the United Steel Workers Union once dismissed this model in the past, but now it has become a strong supporter of worker ownership. One model is based upon the Mondragón Cooperative Corporation in the Basque country of Spain. Groups of worker-owned cooperatives employ 85,000 people in fields ranging from sophisticated medical technology and the production of appliances to large supermarkets and a credit union.[55]

The Green City Growers greenhouse under construction in September 2012. Green City Growers Cooperative (GCGC) was conceived in 2008 an entirely worker-owned, year-round, hydroponic food production greenhouse that could supply Cleveland-area retailers and wholesalers with fresh produce.

In the hard-hit city of Cleveland, Ohio (US), a worker-owned initiative is the "Cleveland Model." It involves a number of worker-owned cooperative businesses targeted at the $3 billion purchasing power of three large anchor institutions; one is the Cleveland Clinic. The association includes a fund so that profits made by the businesses help establish new ones. The first of the worker-owned companies, Evergreen Cooperative Laundry, is a state-of-the-art commercial laundry that provides clean linens for area hospitals, nursing homes, and hotels. It uses energy-saving design for its building and uses much less water per pound of laundry than its competitors. It includes 50 worker-owners, pays above-market wages, provides health insurance, and is able to compete against other commercial laundries. Another enterprise, Ohio Cooperative Solar (OCS), provides weatherization services and installs, owns, and maintains solar panels. Each year, the association plans to open two to four new worker-owned ventures.[56]

A "fourth sector" of the economy, different from the government, business, and non-profit sectors, is "**social enterprises**." These enterprises contribute to human and environmental well-being, rather than maximizing profits for outside shareholders. They support programs such as drug rehabilitation and job re-training. Another 130 million Americans are members of social enterprises, including urban food and housing co-ops, traditional agricultural cooperatives and credit unions. Other models include more than 4,500 members of not-for-profit community development organizations that run affordable housing and community-building programs. In many cities "community land trusts," use nonprofit or municipal ownership to develop affordable housing. I like this model because our non-profit organization, the Center for Global Awareness, is one of approximately 1.5 million non-profits providing more than 10 percent of the nation's employment.[57]

3. Renewing Public Ownership

Rebuilders make a case to renew public ownership in certain industries. But, this does not mean public ownership of small, medium-sized or even large businesses. Some would say that those supporting public ownership are socialist. But looking closely, the U.S. has a mixed economy in which there already is public ownership. Most people would not want to see the Grand Canyon turned over to private land developers or mining interests. For example, the Tennessee Valley Authority (TVA), a public enterprise, established in 1933, is one of the largest energy companies in the nation. Local public utilities and cooperatives supply more than 25 percent of the electricity in the U.S. And the government owns timber, mineral, oil and other resources on public land covering almost 30 percent of the nation. The government runs two of the most cost-effective health care providers in the U.S. – Medicare and the Veterans Administration. The largest pension manager in the country is the publicly owned Social Security Administration. The US Postal Service, which employs 645,000 men and women, is a public enterprise that is generally regarded as well-run by most experts.[58]

Public enterprises do not spend large amounts on advertising to sell their products, they do not add a profit margin to their prices, nor do they pay huge executive salaries. The government-run Medicare administrator made a base salary of approximately $170,000 in 2010 while, the CEO of the privately-held United Health Group, made a base salary of $1.3 million and received $101.96 million in total pay that same year. Thus, our private healthcare system costs the nation up to twice the share of GDP as in other countries. These inefficiencies waste perhaps a trillion dollars a year. Public enterprises do not force cities and states to pay millions in "incentives" to encourage businesses to locate in their locality. Often these private businesses take these incentives and then move on when they expire. Public enterprises do not spend huge amounts of money lobbying public officials, as do corporate interests. And public corporations are open to public scrutiny, while private corporations keep most of their activities secret.[59]

Many core and middle nations have found large-scale, publicly-regulated companies beneficial in such key operations as energy, transportation, and banking. In energy, publicly-owned corporations produce 75 percent of all oil. Saudi Aramco, the national oil company of Saudi Arabia, was estimated to be worth $781 billion in 2005, making it the world's most valuable company, almost twice that of ExonMobil, the largest private sector company.[60] In transportation, many governments run high-speed rail systems and airlines. For example, France holds 16 percent of Air France-KLM, and Singapore owns 56 percent of Singapore Airlines, which is one of the world's best. In banking, there are more than 200 public and semi-public banks and 81 funding agencies, accounting for one-fifth of all bank assets in the European Union. Japan Post Bank is the world's biggest public bank and one of its largest employers. Brazil has more than 100 state-owned or state-controlled enterprises, including the oil company Petrobras. In some countries with public ownership, there is better and faster Internet service than in the U.S.[61]

4. Healing Our Planet

The fate of our planet hangs in an unstable position. The earth's atmosphere, which cannot safely absorb the amount of carbon we are pumping into it, is only one of a number of significant environmental crises facing all of us. We are also exploiting the oceans, freshwater supplies, the topsoil and biodiversity. An expansionist mindset assumes that resources are limitless and there for endless human taking. Scientific research shows we have pushed nature beyond its limits. To heal the planet we need more than just new green products and market-based solutions; we need a new civilizational model grounded not in dominance over nature but in respect for nature and its limits.[62] The neoliberal model of continuous expansion and exploitation of the environment is simply and clearly unsustainable. Therefore, we must change it.

China's largest open-pit coal mine is located in Haerwusu in the Inner Mongolia Autonomous Region.

5. Creating Shared Values

The values and beliefs of a society shapes how it is organized. In this interacting dance, a society holistically forms such cultural traits as an economy, ways of living, technology, politics, religions, the way it treats the environment, and, thus, its worldview or civilizational model. Most of us were raised according to a modern worldview in which Enlightenment ideals of progress taught us that our ambitions could not be confined by nature's limits. This is true for the progressive left, as well as the neoliberal right. What we need is a re-evaluation of our values and attitudes, from the long cherished belief in rugged individualism and cut-throat competition to an ethic of more collective action, an ethic of sharing and cooperation. Climate change is a message from the earth, screaming to us all that many of our culture's most cherished ideas and values are no longer working. It is a wake-up call that we must heed.[63]

Questions to Consider

1. What do you think about the rebuild ideas presented in this short section?
2. Do you think they are a viable alternative to neoliberalism? What others might you include?

CONCLUDING INSIGHTS: THE AFTERMATH OF THE 2008 FINANCIAL CRISIS

America will likely remain the world's largest economy for years to come. But it is not inevitable that the American standard of living will continue to increase as it did, for instance, in the years following World War II. The U.S. is no longer operating within the confines of a national economy, where the nation primarily determines policies and wages. Now our standard of living and job opportunities compete with 7+ billion people on the planet. Many Americans have been living in a fantasy world of easy credit and limitless opportunities, and that world is over. The country as a whole will face a drop in living standards. Not only is the country living beyond its means, but so are many families.[64] This is a stunning shift from what we thought life should be like in America. Each generation, we have been told, would have a better life than the previous generation, in a spiral of upward progression. These are intensely challenging eye-openers, shaking us to the very core.

We are deeply embedded in our current way of life. But we need to change. We must heed the call of the planet. Either we change the economy with planning and insight to a way of life of our choosing that is within nature's limits and more equitable for all, or we will have changes forced upon us by an angry planet ravaged by our excesses.

This brings us back to the rebuilding response described above. Rebuilding a more just, equitable and sustainable economy may be the most difficult and yet the most important challenge we face as a human species. It involves changing the way we think, work, act, what we prize, and what we believe in. This profound and deep examination of who we are as a people and what type of economy we want to leave for the next generations is not an easy shift. But there are many signs of hope sprouting up amongst us. From the community banks, cooperatives, worker-owned businesses, and land trusts mentioned above, to individual acts of supporting local businesses and buying fewer consumer items, many people are becoming more aware that our economy needs fundamental change, and they want to participate in these changes. Many of us are joining with others to explore and take action in implementing options for a more just, sustainable, and peaceful world community. The choice is ours to make.

Questions to Consider
1. What do you think are the choices we need to make?

Endnotes

Endnotes with no website references.
To see endnotes with website references and full bibliography please visit the website:
www.global-awareness.org/globaleconomybrief

Endnotes Chapter 1: The Global Economy: An Overview

[1] Richard H. Robbins, *Global Problems and the Culture of Capitalism* (Boston: Allyn and Bacon, 1999) 11-12.
[2] Aidan Rankin, "Double Trouble: Capitalism and Communism," *Ecologist* (June, 2001).
[3] Rankin, "Double Trouble," *Ecologist.*
[4] "Neoliberalism," *World English Dictionary*, ret. 10/10/10.
[5] Robbins, *Global Problems*, 100.
[6] Jane Hiebert-White, "Health Affairs Blog," *Health Affairs* (June 2, 2009) ret. 10/10.
[7] Ian Bremmer, *The End of the Free Market: Who Wins the War Between States and Corporations?* (New York: Portfolio, 2010) 33 and 40.
[8] Bremmer, *Free Market*, 21 and 42.
[9] Bremmer, *Free Market*, 20-21.
[10] Ranking information, see website endnotes.
[11] O'Conner, Joseph and McDermott, Ian, *The Art of Systems Thinking: Essential Skills for Creativity and Problem Solving* (London: Thorsons, 1997) 3-13 and John Goekler, "Teaching for the Future: Systems Thinking and Sustainability," *Green Teacher 70* (Spring 2003) 8-14.
[12] John Goekler, "Teaching for the Future," *Green Teacher*, 8-14.
[13] Donella Meadows, Dennis Meadows, Jorgen Randers, *Limits to Growth: The Thirty Year Update* (White River Junction, Vermont: Chelsea Green Publishing, 2004) 4.
[14] "Indigenous Peoples and the United Nations System" *United Nations*, Office of the High Commissioner for Human Rights, United Nations Office at Geneva, ret.9/09 and "Indigenous issues," *International Work Group on Indigenous Affairs* ret. 9/09. The 5% is based on a population of 7 billion people.

Endnotes Chapter 2: Historical Roots of the Global Economy

[1] Peter N. Stearns, *World History: Patterns of Change and Continuity,* (New York: Harper Collins Publishers, 1995) 297.
[2] Philip J. Adler, *World Civilizations,* (Minneapolis/St. Paul: West Publishing, 1996) 541-542.
[3] Kevin Phillips, *Wealth and Democracy: A Political History of the American Rich,* (New York: Broadway Books, 2002) 180-181.
[4] Phillips, *Wealth and Democracy*, 175-176 and 190.
[5] Jeffrey Frieden, *Global Capitalism: Its Fall and Rise in the Twentieth Century,* (New York and London: W.W. Norton, 2006) 4.
[6] Frieden, *Global Capitalism*, 52.
[7] Rondo Cameron, *A Concise Economic History of the World: From Paleolithic Times to the Present,* (New York: Oxford University Press, 1993) 189-190 and Peter Stearns, *The Industrial Revolution in World History,* (Boulder: Westview Press, 1993) 27 and L.S. Stavrianos, *Lifelines from Our Past: A New World History,* (New York: Pantheon Books, 1989) 125.
[8] Frieden, *Global Capitalism*, 52-53.
[9] Frieden, *Global Capitalism*, 6-7.
[10] Frieden, *Global Capitalism*, 120.
[11] Frieden, *Global Capitalism*, 121.
[12] Harry Magdoff, "Capitalism as a World Economy," *Monthly Review*, Vol. 55, Issue 4 (2003), interview with Huck Gutman.
[13] Richard H. Robbins, *Global Problems and the Culture of Capitalism,* (Boston: Allyn and Bacon, 1999) 93-94.
[14] Frieden, *Global Capitalism*, 90-91.
[15] Frieden, *Global Capitalism*, 16, 19, and 24.
[16] Frieden, *Global Capitalism*, 26.
[17] Frieden, *Global Capitalism*, 59-60.
[18] Phillips, *Wealth and Democracy*, 184-185 .
[19] Phillips, *Wealth and Democracy*, 186 and 189.
[20] Frieden, *Global Capitalism*, 130, 131 and 133.
[21] Frieden, *Global Capitalism*, 135-137.
[22] Frieden, *Global Capitalism*, 171.
[23] Frieden, *Global Capitalism*, 169.
[24] Frieden, *Global Capitalism*, 173-174 and179.
[25] Frieden, *Global Capitalism*, 182, 183-184 and 190.
[26] Frieden, *Global Capitalism*, 192 and 195.
[27] Frieden, *Global Capitalism*, 192.
[28] Frieden, *Global Capitalism*, 217 and 219.
[29] Frieden, *Global Capitalism*, 221 and 223.
[30] Frieden, *Global Capitalism*, 276.
[31] Frieden, *Global Capitalism*, 300.
[32] Frieden, *Global Capitalism*, 327 and 337.
[33] Frieden, *Global Capitalism*, 302-305 and 317.

[34] Alejandro Reuss, "That 70s Crisis: What can the crisis of U.S. capitalism in the 1970s teach us about the current the crisis and its possible outcomes?" *Dollars & Sense* (Nov./Dec., 2009).

[35] Frieden, *Global Capitalism*, 340 and 342.

[36] Frieden, *Global Capitalism*, 343.

[37] Walden Bello, "Drop Till We Shop," *The Nation* (October 21, 2002).

[38] Reuss, "70s Crisis," *Dollars & Sense* and William Grieder, "Goodbye Keynes, Hello Hoover," *The Nation* (June 21, 2010).

[39] Reuss, "70s Crisis," *Dollars & Sense*.

[40] Frieden, *Global Capitalism*, 365.

[41] Reuss, "70s Crisis," *Dollars & Sense*.

[42] Reuss, "70s Crisis," *Dollars & Sense*.

[43] Frieden, *Global Capitalism*, 359.

[44] Frieden, *Global Capitalism*, 360.

[45] Reuss, "70s Crisis," *Dollars & Sense*.

[46] Reuss, "70s Crisis," *Dollars & Sense*.

Endnotes Chapter 3: The Neoliberal Stew: A Dozen Essential Ingredients

[1] William Greider, "The One-Eyed Chairman," *Nation* (Sept. 1, 2005).

[2] Greider, "Chairman," *Nation*.

[3] Ha-Joon Chang, "Kicking Away the Ladder: An Unofficial History of Capitalism in Britain and United States," *Challenge* (Sept.-Oct., 2002): 5.

[4] Thom Hartmann, *Threshold: The Crisis of Western Culture*, (New York: Viking, 2009) 52.

[5] Jeffrey Frieden, *Global Capitalism: Its Fall and Rise in the Twentieth Century*, (New York: W.W. Norton, 2006) 66.

[6] "Export" *Export.gov* ret. 9/28/2011.

[7] Francisco Gil-Diaz, "The Origin of Mexico's 1994 Financial Crisis," *The CATO Journal* Vol. 17, No. 3.

[8] "The World Bank, Poverty in Mexico fact sheet," *World Bank*, ret. 10/10.

[9] Marcy Kaptur, "You think NAFTA is bad now? *C-Span*, speech before Congress (Sept. 2008).

[10] John Locke, *The Second Treatise on Civil Government*, (New York: Prometheus Books, 1986) Chapter 5 "Of Property."

[11] Susan George, "A Short History of Liberalism," *Conference on Economic Sovereignty in a Globalizing World* (March 24, 1999).

[12] Ellen J. Dannin, "White Paper on Privatization." *California Western School of Law*, ret. 10/10/11.

[13] "Water Privatization Threatens Workers, Consumers and Local Economies," *Food and Water Watch* (May 21, 2009).

[14] Allison M. Jaggar, "Is Globalization Good For Women?" *Comparative Literature* (Fall 2001): 2.

[15] "Enron Scandal," *Answers*.com and "Enron" *BBC News at a Glance* (Aug. 22, 2002).

[16] Christopher Weare, "The California Electricity Crisis: Causes and Policy Options," (San Francisco: Public Policy Inst., 2003): 1-3.

[17] "Enron Scandal," *Answers* and "Enron," *BBC News at a Glance*.

[18] Joseph E. Stiglitz, *The Roaring Nineties: A New History of the World's Most Prosperous Decade* (New York: W.W. Norton, 2003) 277.

[19] "Grover Norquist," *Brainy Quote*, ret. 9/2010.

[20] David Schaper, "Not so Fast, Future of High Speed Rail Uncertain," *National Public Radio* (Nov. 12, 2010).

[21] Jaggar, "Globalization Women" *Comparative Literature*, 2.

[22] Chang, quoted in Hartmann, *Threshold*, 50.

[23] Walden Bello, "A Primer on the Wall Street Meltdown," *Focus on the Global South* (2008).

[24] John Perkins, *Hoodwinked: An Economic Hit Man Reveals Why the World Financial Markets Imploded – and What We Need to Do to Remake Them*, (New York: Broadway Books, 2009) 84 and Robert Kuttner, *The Squandering of America: How the Failure of Our Politics Undermines our Prosperity*, (New York: Alfred A. Knopf , 2007) 201.

[25] Kuttner, *Squandering America*, 199, 201 and 204.

[26] Warren E. Buffett, "Stop Coddling the Rich," Opinion Pages, *New York Times* (Aug. 15, 2011).

[27] Rick Wolff, "Deficits: Real Issue, Phony Debates," *Dollars & Sense* (2010).

[28] "Social Security Trust Fund Report," Bureau of the Public Debt, *United States Department of the Treasury* (Sept. 2008).

[29] "Social Security," *U.S. Department of the Treasury*.

[30] David Leonhardt, "America's Sea of Red Ink Was Years in the Making," *New York Times* (June 10, 2009).

[31] Kuttner, *Squandering America*, 191.

[32] Kalle Lasn and Tom Liacas, "Birth of the Corporate 'I.'" *Adbusters* No. 31 (Aug/Sept 2000): 1.

[33] Lasn and Liacas, "Birth Corporate," *Adbusters*, 1-2.

[34] Hartman, "Railroad Barons," *Common Dreams*.

[35] Kuttner, *Squandering America*, 254-255.

[36] Alexandro Reuss, "Do Lower Tax Rates Really Increase Government Revenue?" *Dollars & Sense* (June 2011): 2.

[37] Ayn Rand, *Atlas Shrugged*, (New York: Signet, 1992) 1065.

[38] Stiglitz, *90s*, 271.

[39] Kuttner, *Squandering America*, 68.

Endnotes Chapter 4: The Impact of Neoliberalism in the United States: Ten Consequences

[1] Robert Kuttner, *The Squandering of America: How the Failure of Our Politics Undermines our Prosperity*, (New York: Alfred A. Knopf, 2007) 199, 201 and 204.

[2] Kuttner, *Squandering America*, 200.

[3] Alejandro Reuss, "That 70s Crisis: What can the crisis of U.S. capitalism in the 1970s teach us about the current the crisis and its possible outcomes?" *Dollars & Sense* (Nov./Dec., 2009).

[4] Warren E. Buffett, "Stop Coddling the Rich," Opinion Pages, *New York Times* (Aug. 15, 2011).

[5] Rick Wolff, "Deficits: Real Issue, Phony Debates," *Dollars & Sense* (2010).

[6] "Social Security Trust Fund Report," Bureau of the Public Debt, *United States Department of the Treasury* (Sept. 2008).

[7] "Social Security," *U.S. Department of the Treasury.*

[8] Michelle Caruso-Cabrera, "Greece Still Faces High Debt to GDP Ratio," *CNBC* (July 25, 2011).

[9] Carmen M. Reinhart, "Testimony Senate Budget Committee," Senate Budget Committee, *U.S. Senate* (Feb. 9, 2010), ret. 2/9/2011.

[10] Paul Krugman, "Bad analysis at the deficit commission," Conscience of a Liberal Blog, *The New York Times: The Opinion Pages* (May 27, 2010) ret. 2/9/2011.

[11] Stiglitz, *90s*, 270.

[12] David Leonhardt, "America's Sea of Red Ink Was Years in the Making," *New York Times*, (June 10, 2009).

[13] Al Auerbach with William G. Gales, "(Still) Tempting Fate," working paper, Univ. of California, Berkeley (August 2011).

[14] Martinez and Garcia, "What is Neoliberalism," *CorpWatch*, 1-2.

[15] Alexia Eastwood, "Revisiting Economic Man," *Share the World's Resources* in *Common Dreams* (Apr 16, 2010).

[16] Joseph E. Stiglitz, *The Roaring Nineties: A New History of the World's Most Prosperous Decade* (New York: W.W. Norton & Co., 2003) 272-273.

[17] William Greider, "The One-Eyed Chairman," *Nation* (Sept. 1, 2005): 5.

[18] Kuttner, *Squandering America*, 191.

[19] Kalle Lasn and Tom Liacas, "Birth of the Corporate 'I.'" *Adbusters*, No. 31 (Aug/Sept 2000): 1.

[20] Lasn and Liacas, "Birth Corporate," *Adbusters*, 1-2.

[21] Thom Hartman, "The Railroad Barons Are Back – And This Time They'll Finish the Job," *Common Dreams* (Dec. 11, 2002): 1.

[22] S. President Abraham Lincoln, Nov. 21, 1864 (letter to Col. William F. Elkins) Ref: Archer H. Shaw, "The Lincoln Encyclopedia," (New York: Macmillan, 1950), as cited in Hartman, *Railroad Barons*, 2.

[23] Hartman, "Railroad Barons," *Common Dreams.*

[24] Lasn and Liacas, "Birth Corporate," *Adbusters*, 1.

[25] Hartman, *"Railroad Barons,"* 2-3.

[26] Greider, "One-Eyed Chairman," *Nation*, 4.

[27] Keith Bradsher, "House Votes to Request Clinton Data on Mexico." *BusinessWeek Online* (Mar. 2, 1994), ret. 6/4/2011.

[28] Kuttner, *Squandering America*, 254-255.

[29] "Market Dispatches," *MSN Money Central* (Oct. 12, 2010).

[30] "Labor," Dictionary.com and *The American Heritage® New Dictionary of Cultural Literacy, Third Edition*, Houghton Mifflin Co., (2005), ret. Sept. 24, 2010.

[31] Rondo Cameron, *A Concise Economic History of the World: From Paleolithic Times to the Present*, (New York: Oxford University Press, 1993) 189-190 and Peter N. Stearns, *The Industrial Revolution in World History*, (Boulder: Westview Press, 1993) 27.

[32] Cameron, *Economic History*, 190.

[33] L.S. Stavrainos, *Lifelines from Our Past: A New World History*, (New York: Pantheon Books, 1989) 125-126.

[34] Alejando Reuss, "Do Lower Tax Rates Really Increase Government Revenue?" *Dollars & Sense* (June 2011): 2.

[35] Ayn Rand, *Atlas Shrugged*, (New York: Signet, 1992) 1065.

[36] Stiglitz, *90s*, 271.

[37] Kuttner, *Squandering America*, 68.

[38] Eastwood, "Economic Man," *Share the World's Resources.*

[39] Stiglitz, *90s*, 278.

[40] Kuttner, *Squandering America*, 11-12.

[41] Doug Hall, "Weak economic recovery reflected in high state-level poverty and child poverty rates," *Economic Policy Institute*, (Sept. 22, 2011).

[42] Tom Turnipseed, "Hunger and Homelessness in America," *Common Dreams* (Nov. 28, 2010).

[43] Susan George, "A Short History of Neoliberalism," *Conf. Economic Sovereignty in a Globalizing World* (March 24-26, 1999).

[44] Kuttner, *Squandering America*, 68.

Endnotes Chapter 5: The Economic Globalization Puzzle: Ten Pieces

[1] "How many farmers in the world," *Answers.com.*

[2] Erik Assadourian, "State of the World, Transforming Cultures: From Consumerism to Sustainability," *World Watch Institute*, 2010.

[3] *California Council on Science and Technology*, ret. 2/1/2007.

[4] Eugene Rotberg, "Financial Operations of the World Bank," in *Bretton Woods: Looking to the Future*. ed. Bretton Woods Commission (Washington, D.C.: Bretton Woods Commission,1994).

[5] George Monbiot, "I'm With Wolfowitz," *Monbiot Website* (Mar. 4, 2005): 9.

[6] Robert Kuttner, *The Squandering of America: How the Failure of Our Politics Undermines our Prosperity*, (New York: Alfred A. Knopf, 2007) 245.

[7] Kuttner, *Squandering America*, 247-248.

[8] Robin Hahnel, "Capitalist Globalism in Crisis: Part III: Understanding the IMF." *Z Magazine* (Feb. 1999): 2-3.

[9] Kevin Danaher and Jason Mark, *Insurrection: Citizens Power to Corporate Challenge*, (New York: Routledge, 2004) 242 and Craig Hovey with George Rehmke, *The Complete Idiot's Guide to Global Economics*, (New York: Alpha, 2008) 96.

[10] *WTO* official site.

[11] Danaher, *Insurrection*, 271.

[12] Thom Hartmann, *Threshold: The Crisis of Western Culture* (New York: Viking, 2009) 46 quoted from Ha-Joon Chang, *Bad Samaritans: The Myth of Free Trade and the Secret History of Capitalism.*

[13] Hartmann, *Threshold*, 45-46.

[14] Paul Beingessner, "Monsanto Sues and Sues and Sues," *Keep Maine Free* (July 14, 2003).

[15] Beingessner, "Monsanto Sues," *Keep Maine Free.*

[16] "Percy Schmeiser," *Percy Schmeiser website.*

[17] "Richest Man in the World," *Economics* (Mar. 2010).

[17] "Privatization in Mexico: Telemex," *50 Years is Enough.*

[19] Peter H. Gleick, Gary Wolff, Elizabeth L. Chalecki, Rachel Reyes, "The new Economy of Water: The Risk and Benefits of Globalization and Privatization of Fresh Water," *Pacific Institute Executive Overview* (2004): 1-5.

[20] Tony Clarke and Maude Barlowe, "The Battle for Water," *Yes Magazine* (Winter 2004): 2.

[21] William Finnegan, "Leasing The Rain," *The New Yorker.*

[22] Benjamin Blackwell, "From Coca To Congress," *The Ecologist* (Nov. 11, 2002).

[23] Clarke, "Battle for Water," *Yes Magazine*, 3.

[24] James Speth, *The Bridge at the Edge of the World: Capitalism, the Environment, and Crossing from Crisis to Sustainability*, (New Haven: Yale University Press, 2008) 173.

[25] "Multinational Corporations," *Share the World's Resources.*

[26] Scott DeCarlo, "The World's Biggest Companies," *Forbes.com* (Apr. 2, 2008).

[27] "Multinational Corporations," *Share the World's Resources.*

[28] "Multinational Corporations," *Share the World's Resources.*

[29] "What Is the Meaning of Specialization in Economics?" *eHow.com.*

[30] Richard C. Longworth, *Caught in the Middle: America's Heartland in the Age of Globalism*, (New York: Bloomsbury, 2008) 62-63.

[31] Longworth, *Caught in the Middle*, 64-65.

[32] Longworth, *Caught in the Middle*, 65.

[33] "Economics," *About*.com.

[34] Thomas Palley, "Labor Threat," *Tom Paine* (Oct, 4, 2005): 1.

[35] Nayan Chanda, *Bound Together: How Traders, Preachers, Adventurers, and Warriors Shaped Globalization*, (New Haven: Yale University Press, 2007) 294.

[36] Immanuel Wallerstein, "Empire and the Capitalists," *ZMagazine* (May 21, 2003): 1-2.

[37] David Korten, *When Corporations Rule the World*, (Hartford, CT: Kumarian Press, 1995) 251.

[38] Jerry Meldon Long, "U.S. Dance with Mobutu Ends," *The Consortium* (1997).

[39] Raj Patel, *The Value of Nothing: How to reshape market society and redefine democracy* (New York: Picador, 2009) 79 and "Military Expenditure Database," *Stockholm International Peace Research Institute* (SIPRI).

[40] Chalmers Johnson, *Dismantling the Empire: America's Last Best Hope*, (New York: Macmillan, 2010) 121.

Endnotes Chapter 6: The Global Impact of Economic Globalization

[1] Lester Brown, *World on Edge: How to Prevent Environmental and Economic Collapse*, (New York: W.W. Norton & Co., 2011) 78.

[2] "Why Population Matters," *World Overpopulation Awareness* (Sept.10, 2007) and Michele L. Swartz and Jessica Notini, "Desertification and Migration in Mexico and the United States," *US Commission on Migration* (2000): 7.

[3] Donella and Dennis Meadows, Jorgen Randers, *Limits to Growth: the Thirty Year Update*, (White Rive Junction, Vermont: Chelsea Green Publishing Company, 2004) 75.

[4] "Deforestation," *Earth Observatory/NASA.*

[5] Mark A. Sircus, "Water: The World is Facing a Dire Shortage of this Essential Element," *Natural News.com* (May 20, 2008).

[6] Tony Clarke and Maude Barlowe, "The Battle for Water," *Yes Magazine* (Winter, 2004): 1.

[7] George J. Bryjak. "Does the World Face a Future of Water Wars?" *Ecology* (Sept., 2002) and Lester Brown, "Rising Temperatures and Falling Water Tables Raising Food Prices," *Earth Policy Institute* (Aug. 21, 2002).

[8] "Food and Agriculture Organization of the United Nations report" reported in *Age* (Mar. 22, 2007).

[9] Lester Brown, "Water Deficits Growing in Many Countries," *Earth Policy Institute* (Aug. 6, 2002).

[10] "Environmental Fact Sheet," *Environmental and Energy Study Institute.*

[11] "Why Population Matters," *World Overpopulation Awareness* (Sept. 10, 2007).

[12] Meadows & Rander, *Limits to Growth*, 57 and 61. From 1950 to 2000 world grain production more than tripled, from around 590 to more than 2000 million metric tons per year.

[13] Meadows & Rander, *Limits to Growth*, 1 and 3.

[14] Living Planet Report, *World Wildlife Foundation* (Oct. 24, 2006).

[15] *The Columbus Dispatch* (Feb. 20, 2007).

[16] *The Columbus Dispatch* (Feb 20, 2007).

[17] Meadows & Rander, *Limits to Growth*, 174-175.

[18] "World Clock," *Poodle Waddle.*

[19] "United Nations News," reported in *World Overpopulation Awareness* (Mar. 19, 2007).

[20] Karen Gaia, "World's Expected Carrying Capacity in a Post Industrial Agrarian Society," *The Oil Drum: Europe* (Nov. 1, 2007).

[21] "Species Extinction," *Rainforest Action Network.*

[22] "Species Extinction," *Rainforest Action Network.*

[23] Meadows and Rander, *Limits of Growth*, 42 and 43.

[24] Don Peck, "Can the Middle Class be Saved?" *The Atlantic* (Sept. 2011): 63.

[25] Mai Ling, "Housing," *MSN Real Estate* (Oct. 14, 2010).

[26] Globalization and Inequality, *Business Maps of India.*

[27] Sam Pizzigati, "Mapping Global Wealth," report from Credit Suisse, *OtherWords* (Sept, 2011).

[28] Pizzigati, "Mapping Global Wealth," *OtherWords.*

[29] Pizzigati, "Mapping Global Wealth," *OtherWords.*

[30] Jon Jeter, *Flat broke in the free market: how globalization fleeced working people*, (New York: W.W. Norton & Co., 2009) xiii.

[31] Chen, Shachua, Ravallion, Martin and Sangraula, Prem. "A Dollar a Day Revised." and "The developing world is poorer than

we thought," *World Bank* (Aug. 2008), found in globalissues.org.
[32] "Globalization and Inequality," *Business Maps of India.*
[33] Pizzigati, "Mapping Global Wealth," *OtherWords.*
[34] Jeter, *Flat Broke*, xii.
[35] "Poverty Facts and Stats," *Global Issues* (Sept. 2010) ret. 10/11and "State of the World's Cities 2008/2009," *UN Habitat*, ret. 10/11.
[36] Meadows and Rander, *Limits of Growth*, 27, 41, and 42.
[37] Rajesh Makwana, "The Follies of Growth and Climate Denial," *Share the World's Resources* (June 2, 2010).
[38] Andrew Simms, Victoria Johnson, and Peter Chowla, "Growth Isn't Possible," *New Economic Foundation* (Jan. 25, 2010): 38.
[39] Simms, "Growth," *NEF* and Meadows and Rander, *Limits of Growth*, 49.
[40] "Well-being," *Dictionary*.com.
[41] Simms, "Growth," *NEF*, 45.
[42] Simms, "Growth, *NEF*, 45 and 47-48.
[43] "Genuine Progress Indicator," *Redefining Progress.*

Endnotes Chapter 7: The Financial Sector of the Global Economy

[1] Matthew Bishop and Michael Green, *The Road from Ruin: How to Revive Capitalism and Put America Back on Top* (New York: Crown Business, 2010) 32.
[2] Mary Darby, "In Ponzi We Trust," *Smithsonian* magazine (Dec. 1998).
[3] Joseph E. Stiglitz, *Freefall: America, Free Markets, and the Sinking of the World Economy,* (New York: W.W. Norton, 2010) 65.
[4] Nouriel Roubini and Stephen Mihm, *Crisis Economics : A Crash Course in the Future of Finance,* (New York : Penguin Press, 2010) 190 and Robert Reich, *Aftershock: the Next Economy and America's Future,* (New York: Alfred A. Knopf, 2010) 56.
[5] Roubini, *Crisis Economics*, 190.
[6] Roubini, *Crisis Economics*, 191.
[7] Walden Bello, "A Primer on the Wall Street Meltdown," *Focus on the Global South* (2008).
[8] Walden Bello, "The Global Financial System in Crisis," Speech at *People's Development Forum*, Univ. Philippines, (Mar. 25, 2008).
[9] Bello, "Primer," *Focus on the Global South* and David C. Korten, *Agenda for a New Economy: From Phantom Wealth to Real Wealth,* (San Francisco: Berrett-Koehler, 2010).
[10] Stiglitz, *Free Fall*, 1 and 6.
[11] Craig Hovey with Greg Rehmke. *The Complete Idiot's Guide to Global Economics*, (New York: Alpha, 2008) 136.
[12] Stiglitz, *Free Fall*, 163 and Nomi Prins, *It Takes a Pillage: Behind the Bailouts, Bonuses, and Backroom Deals from Washington to Wall Street,* (Hoboken, NJ: Wiley Press, 2009) 179.
[13] Thom Hartman, "Is the Fix in on Derivatives?" *Thom's Blog* (May 17, 2010), ret. 1/12/12.
[14] "Shadow Banking," *Wikipedia*, ret. 1/12/12.
[15] Larson, Not Too Big, *Dollars & Sense* (July/August, 2010).
[16] Larson, Not too Big, *Dollars & Sense* and Stiglitz, *90s*, 222-223.
[17] Robert Weissman, "12 Deregulatory Steps to Financial Meltdown," *CommonDreams.org* (March 7, 2008).
[18] Matt Taibbi, *Griftopia,* (New York: Spigel & Grau, 2010) 67.
[19] Robert Kuttner, *The Squandering of America: How the Failure of Our Politics Undermines our Prosperity*, (New York: Alfred A. Knopf , 2007), 157 and Weissman, "12 Steps," *CommonDreams.*
[20] Hovey, *Global Economics*, 131-132.
[21] Roubini, *Crisis Economics*, 144.
[22] Roubini, *Crisis Economics*, 143.
[23] Roubini, *Crisis Economics*, 73.
[24] Kuttner, *Squandering America*, 157 and Stiglitz, *Free Fall*, 4.
[25] Roubini, *Crisis Economics* 63.
[26] David Faber, *And Then the Roof Caved In: How Wall Street's Greed and Stupidity Brought Capitalism to its Knees,* (Hoboken, NJ: John Wiley & Sons, 2009) 61.
[27] Roubini, *Crisis Economics*, 64.
[28] Roubini, *Crisis Economics*, 64-65.
[29] Roubini, *Crisis Economics*, 65.
[30] John Lanchester, *IOU: Why Everyone Owes Everyone and No Once Can Pay*, (New York: Simon & Schuster, 2010) 113 and Nomi Prins, *It takes a pillage: behind the bailouts, bonuses, and backroom deals from Washington to Wall Street*, (Hoboken, NJ: Wiley, 2009) 53.
[31] Stiglitz, *Free Fall*, 86 and Roubini, *Crisis Economics*, 65.
[32] Dean Baker in Bello, Global Financial System Crisis, *People's Development Forum.*
[33] Carmen M. Reinhart and Kenneth S. Rogoff, *This Time is Different: Eight Centuries of Financial Folly,* (Princeton, NJ: Princeton University Press, 2009) preface.
[34] Prins, *Pillage*, 177.
[35] Prins, *Pillage*, 146.
[36] Roubini, *Crisis Economics*, 65.
[37] Lanchester, *IOU*, 61.
[38] Lanchester, *IOU*, 122.
[39] Taibbi, *Griftopia*, 123.
[40] Christine Williamson, "Institutional share growing for hedge funds," *Pension and Investments* (Feb. 10, 2011) ret. 12/5/11 and "Hedge fund industry assets swell to $ 1.92 trillion," *Daily Financial Services* (Jan. 24, 2011) ret. 12/5/11.
[41] "Derivatives," *Investopedia*, ret. 12/5/11.

[42] Lanchester, *IOU*, 46-47.
[43] Stiglitz, *Free Fall*, 169.
[44] Warren Buffet in Lanchester, *IOU*, 56-57.
[45] Michael Lewis, *The Big Short: Inside the Doomsday Machine*, (New York: W.W. Norton, 2010) 258.
[46] Lanchester, *IOU*, 119.
[47] Roubini, *Crisis Economics*, 194.
[48] "Credit Default Swap," *Investopedia*, ret. 12/7/11, and Faber, *Roof Caved In*, 5.
[49] Lewis, *Big Short*, 29.
[50] Stiglitz, *Free Fall*, p. 77.
[51] Lanchester, *IOU*, 74.
[52] Prins, *Pillage*, 146.
[53] Immanuel Wallerstein, "Empire and the Capitalists," *Z Magazine* (May 21, 2003).
[54] Lanchester, *IOU*, 78.
[55] Stiglitz, *Free Fall*, 160-161.
[56] Faber, *Roof Caved In*, 81.
[57] Faber, *Roof Caved In*, 81 and market share % by Mark Kolakowski, *About*.com, ret. 12/10/11.
[58] Faber, *Roof Caved In*, 87 and Stiglitz, *Free Fall*, 92.
[59] Faber, *Roof Caved In*, 85.
[60] Prins, *Pillage*, 152 and 157.
[61] Stiglitz, *Free Fall*, 151-152 and Roubini, *Crisis Economics*, 69.
[62] Prins, *Pillage*, 13 and Reich, *Aftershock*, 57.

Endnotes Chapter 8: The Financial Sector: Crisis and its Aftermath

[1] Mike Dash, *Tulipomania: The Story of the World's Most Coveted Flower & the Extraordinary Passions It Aroused*, (New York: Crown Publishing, 2010).
[2] Dash, *Tulipomania*.
[3] Dash, *Tulipomania*.
[4] "The Crash of 1929: Timeline: A selected Wall Street chronology," *PBS* ret.10/31/29.
[5] Andrew Beattie, "Market Crashes: The Great Depression 1929," *Investopedia*, ret. 10/31/11.
[6] Beattie, "Market Crashes," *Investopedia*.
[7] Nouriel Roubini and Stephen Mihm, *Crisis Economics : A Crash Course in the Future of Finance*, (New York: Penguin Press, 2010) 23-24.
[8] Walden Bello, "The Global Financial System in Crisis," Speech at *People's Development Forum*, Univ. Philippines (Mar. 25, 2008).
[9] Matthew Bishop and Michael Green, *The Road from Ruin: How to Revive Capitalism and Put America Back on Top*, (New York: Crown Business, 2010) 136.
[10] Bishop, *Road from Ruin*, 137.
[11] Bishop, *Road from Ruin*, 137.
[12] Bishop, *Road from Ruin*, 138 and Roubini, *Crisis Economics*, 27.
[13] Bishop, *Road from Ruin*, 138.
[14] Bishop, *Road from Ruin*, 139.
[15] Bishop, *Road from Ruin*, 140.
[16] Andrew Ross Sorkin, *Too big to Fail: The Inside Story of How Wall Street and Washington Fought to Save the Financial System from Crisis – and Themselves*, (London: Allen Lane, 2009) 3.
[17] Sorkin, *Too Big to Fail*, 4.
[18] Bethany McLean and Joe Nocera, *All the Devils are Here: The Hidden History of the Financial Crisis*, (New York: Portfolio/Penguin, 2010) 125.
[19] McLean and Nocera, *All the Devils*, 125.
[20] Charles Ferguson, *Predator Nation: Corporate Criminals, Political Corruption, and the Hijacking of America*, (New York: Crown Business, 2012) 60 and 72.
[21] Roubini, *Crisis Economics*, 88-89.
[22] Roubini, *Crisis Economics*, 91 and Nomi J. Prins, *It takes a pillage: behind the bailouts, bonuses, and backroom deals from Washington to Wall Street*. Hoboken, NJ: Wiley, 2009) 12.
[23] Roubini, *Crisis Economics*, 103 and 108 and Investopedia Staff, "How Fannie Mae And Freddie Mac Were Saved," *Investopedia* (Apr 17, 2009), ret. 12/15/11.
[24] Dawn Kopecki, "U.S. Considers Bringing Fannie, Freddie on to Budget," *Bloomberg News*, (Sept. 11, 2008) ret. 12/15/11.
[25] "Fannie and Freddie," *Investopedia*.
[26] Roubini, *Crisis Economics*, 110.
[27] Roubini, *Crisis Economics*, 111.
[28] Roubini, *Crisis Economics*, 111.
[29] David Faber, *And Then the Roof Caved In: How Wall Street's Greed and Stupidity Brought Capitalism to its Knees*, (Hoboken, N.J.: John Wiley & Sons, 2009) 5 and 10 and Prins, *Pillage*, 109.
[30] Roubini, *Crisis Economics*, 112 and 148.
[31] Roubini, *Crisis Economics*, 151.
[32] James Bullard, "Quantitative Easing – Uncharted Waters for Monetary Policy," *Federal Reserve Bank, St. Louis*, (Jan., 2010) ret. 12/14/11.
[33] Prins, *Pillage*, 112.
[34] Prins, *Pillage*, 180.

[35] Prins, *Pillage*, 27.

[36] Josephy Stiglitz, *Freefall: America, Free Markets, and the Sinking of the World Economy*, (New York: W.W. Norton, 2010) 123.

[37] Danny Schechter, "On the Third Anniversary of the Crash of the Economy: 'Those Were the Days, My Friend. I Thought They'd Never End.' They Haven't," *CommonDreams.org* (Aug. 3, 2010).

[38] "Revolution," *Dictionary.com* Unabridged, ret. 12/16/11.

[39] Anthony Faiola, "In Greece, austerity kindles deep discontent," *Washington Post* (May 13, 2011) ret. 12/16/11.

[40] Bello, "Political Consequences," *Foreign Policy*.

[41] Rob Larson, "Underwater: Profits and pay are sky-high, as bad loans are sinking the megabanks," *Dollars & Sense* (Nov., 2010).

[42] Les Christie, "Foreclosures, *CNN Money* (Jan. 14, 2010).

[43] Jon Prior, "Foreclosures," *Housing Wire* (Jan. 13, 2011).

[44] Robert Sheer, "Fail and Grow Rich on Wall Street," *TruthDig.com* in *CommonDreams.org* (Nov. 24, 2010).

[45] Les Leopold, "Help! What's the Cure for Financial Insanity?" *Huffington Post*, in *CommonDreams.org* (May 14, 2010).

[46] Leopold, "Help!" *Huffington Post*. 6

[47] "Reform," *Wikipedia*, ret. 7/11/12.

[48] Stiglitz, *Free Fall*, 60-61.

[49] Larson, "Underwater," *Dollars & Sense*.

[50] Naomi Klein, "If You Take Climate Change Seriously, You Have to Throw Out the Free-Market Playbook," *Common Dreams* (Feb.29, 2012).

[51] Gar Alperovitz, "America Beyond Capitalism," *Dollars & Sense* (Nov. 11, 2011).

[52] Michael T. Klare, *The Race for What's Left: The Global Scramble for the World's Last Resources*, (New York: Metropolitan Books, 2012).

[53] Klein, "Climate Change Seriously," *Common Dreams*.

[54] "Worker Ownership for the 99%," *United Steel Workers* (March 26, 2012).

[55] Alperovitz, "America Beyond Capitalism," *Dollars & Sense*.

[56] Alperovitz, "America Beyond Capitalism," *Dollars & Sense*.

[57] Alperovitz, "America Beyond Capitalism," *Dollars & Sense*.

[58] Alperovitz, "America Beyond Capitalism," *Dollars & Sense*.

[59] Alperovitz, "America Beyond Capitalism," *Dollars & Sense*.

[60] "Saudi Aramco," *Wikipedia*, ret. 7/20/12.

[61] Gar Alperovitz and Thomas Hanna, "Beyond Corporate Capitalism: Not So Wild a Dream," *The Nation* (June 11, 2012).

[62] Naomi Klein, "Capitalism vs. the Climate," *The Nation* (Nov. 9, 2011).

[63] Klein, "Capitalism vs. the Climate," *The Nation*.

[64] Stiglitz, *Free Fall*, 186.

202

Glossary

austerity cut government spending through austerity measures mainly targeted at social programs, especially education, Medicare, social security, infrastructure, and programs for the poor, in the U.S., military spending is not cut. (8)

bond a debt security in which the authorized issuer owes the holders a debt and is obliged to pay interest and to later repay the principal. (7)

bubble the radical rise of prices of an asset far beyond real values. (7)

capitalism is an economic system in which private parties make their goods and services available on a free market and seek to make a profit on their activities. Private parties, either individuals or companies, own the means of production – land, machinery, tools, equipment, buildings, workshops, and raw materials. Private parties decide what to produce. The center of the system is the free market in which business people compete, and the forces of supply and demand determine the prices received for goods and services. Businesses may realize profits from their endeavors, reinvest profits gained, or suffer losses. (1)

carrying capacity means humans are taking more from the earth than it can replace through natural processes. (6)

cash crops are crops, such as coffee, cotton, sugar, fruits, and tobacco, that are grown by farmers and plantation owners and sold in the commercial market place. (2)

classical economic order system of capitalism, which prevailed during the period of the 19th century to 1914, relied on flexible wages, laying off workers or lowering their wages during bust cycles. Supporters also advocated for minimal government interference in industry, which clashed with the demands of labor. Based on the gold standard, a limited government role in the economy, and the political influence of the business sector. (2)

climate change takes place when the climate is altered during two different periods of time, with changes in average weather conditions, as well as how much the weather varies around these averages. Humans also cause climates to change by releasing greenhouse gases and aerosols into the atmosphere. (6)

Cochabamba Water Wars were a series of protests that took place due to the privatization of the municipal water supply in Cochabamba, Bolivia in 2000. The protesters were successful in outlawing the privatization of their municipal water supply by foreign corporations. (5)

collateralized debt obligation CDO is a pool of debt that is added together and then sold as a set of bonds paying a range of interest rates. Those who issue the bonds pay interest and principal to the investors of the bonds. (7)

colonialism extension of a powerful country's control over a dependent, weaker country, territory, or people. (2)

commercial banks lend out the money deposited in them. Called the piggy banks. (7)

commercial paper market a part of shadow banking, what credit-worthy corporations do for their short-term borrowing needs, such as to meet regular operating expenses like payroll. Corporations can borrow billions of dollars for 30, 60, or 90 days, and when those debts come due, most corporations simply roll them over for another 30, 60, or 90 day term. (8)

commodification comes from the word commodity, used here as the process of turning something with little or no economic value into a product or service that has a specific value or a higher monetary value. (4)

Commodities Futures Modernization Act of 2000 officially marked the deregulation of financial products known as over-the-counter derivatives, spearheaded by Senator Phil Gramm of Texas. (7)

Community Reinvestment Act in 1977, designed to encourage banks and savings associations to help meet the needs of all borrowers, including those in low-and moderate-income neighborhoods. (7)

comparative advantage suggests that countries should specialize in the goods they can produce most efficiently rather than trying for self-sufficiency and argues strongly in favor of free international trade. (5)

conservatorship is essentially the equivalent of a Chapter 11 bankruptcy, with new leadership appointed to the bankrupt company. A conservatorship implies a more temporary control than nationalization, in which the government would more completely take over the enterprise.(8)

consumer debt are debts that are owed as a result of purchasing goods that are consumable and/or do not appreciate. (4)

consumerism is a social and economic order that is based on the systematic creation and fostering of a desire to purchase goods or services in ever greater amounts. In economics, it refers to economic policies placing emphasis on consumption. (4)

core areas are where intense and extensive modern developments in technology, military, society, politics, culture, and especially the economy have taken place. These areas are where wealth generation and accumulation are concentrated and also where rules for the system are devised and enforced. (1)

Corn Laws in Britain, the taxes imposed in the early 1800s on imports of grain (corn). The tariffs substantially increased the domestic price of grain. Farmers were eager to maintain very high tariffs on imported grain in order to protect their grain market, and rightly argued that repeal of the laws would doom British farming. (2)

corporate raiders during the 1980s they bought up a company's stock when it was undervalued, thus, the company's assets were worth more than their stock. The raiders would then sell off the assets of the company to make a profit, but then the companies taken over were no longer operational. (4)

corporation is a formal business association with a publicly registered charter recognizing it as a separate legal entity having its own privileges, and liabilities distinct from those of its members. (2)

cottage industries flourished alongside the domestic economy and guild system during the Middle Ages in Europe. Textile merchants moved production to the countryside, away from city guilds. They set up shop in rural cottages. (2)

credit default swap (CDS), a form of insurance, the buyer of a credit default swap receives credit protection, whereas the seller of the swap guarantees the credit worthiness of the product. The risk of default is transferred from the holder of the fixed income security to the seller of the swap. (7)

credit rating agency (CRA) is a company that assigns credit ratings for issuers of certain types of debt. Debt issues with the highest credit ratings – triple A – from the agencies will incur the lowest interest rates. The credit rating agencies' analyses highly influence the investors' confidence in the borrowers' ability to meet their debt payment obligations. (7)

Dawes Act 1887 spelled out the division of commonly held tribal lands in Oklahoma (US) into individually-owned parcels, while the remaining "surplus" lands were opened up for settlement and the railroads. (3)

debt simply something that is owed or that one is bound to pay to or perform for another. (7)

deficit an excess of expenditure over revenue. (3)

delay in feedback for example, we are not yet in a situation where the stresses on the earth have sent strong enough signals to force us to shrink our ecological footprint. Overshoot is possible because of resource stocks that can be drawn down. (6)

demand for goods and services by consumers determines the overall level of economic activity, and that inadequate demand could lead to prolonged periods of high unemployment. (2)

deregulation removal or simplification of government rules and regulations that regulate the operation of market forces by eliminating or reducing government control of how business is done, thereby moving toward a more free market. (3)

derivative a security whose price is dependent upon or derived from one or more underlying asset. Fluctuations in the underlying asset determine the derivative's value. (7)

desertification expanding deserts that are mainly the consequence of deforested land and also overstocked and overgrazed grasslands. (6)

devalue used in this book to mean make currencies worth less on the global market. (2)

Dodd – Frank Wall Street Reform and Consumer Protection Act passed in 2010, it is a federal statute instituting

reform of the financial sector. Passed in response to the recession after the financial crisis. (8)

dot-com bubble a speculative bubble based on a new technology, the internet, covering the years 1995–2000. (8)

ecological footprint is derived by calculating the amount of land required to supply needed resources, such as grain, food, water, and wood, and absorb the resulting wastes such as carbon dioxide and pollutants. (6)

economic development is the process of increasing the standard of living in a nation's population through sustained economic growth that requires a transition from a simple, low-income economy to a modern, high-income economy. (5)

economic gap disparities in allocation of economic resources to society, determined by governmental rules that tilt policies to favor those with more capital than those with less. It also ensures the continuation of the concentration of wealth through policies, such as a low inheritance tax, that perpetuates the concentration of wealth. (6)

economic globalization refers to the increasing integration and expansion of the capitalist economy around the world. In this economic system, trade, investment, business, capital, finance, production, management, markets, movement of labor (although somewhat restricted), information, competition, and technology are carried out across local and national boundaries on a world stage, bringing many national and local economies into one integrated economic system. There is a growing concentration of wealth and influence of multi-national corporations, huge financial institutions, and state-run enterprises. (1)

economic growth is the process by which wealth increases over time as new commodified value is added to goods and services in the economy. Growth is an essential component of the capitalist economic system, which must expand constantly to generate new wealth. (4)

Efficient Market Theory markets rather than government are able by their very nature to be more efficient and accurate in pricing and allocating resources. (3)

elite democracy in which elites manipulate the democratic process for their own self-interest and control. (4)

enclosure the process in which farms, as well as shared areas called "the commons," were first enclosed or converted to privately owned plots marked with clear boundaries and specific private ownership. (2)

equity is the difference between the market value and unpaid mortgage balance on a home. (7)

export-oriented industrialization (EOI) countries such as South Korea, Taiwan, Singapore, and Hong Kong pushed exporting manufactured goods to core countries. The East Asians turned to EOI in part because they had few natural resources to export to pay for necessary imports, and the only way to earn foreign currency was to export manufactures. They specialized in labor-intensive manufacturers for export. (2)

external areas are those that have not been incorporated into the core-and-periphery world system; they remain outside modern developments. (1)

external costs the cost(s) not paid for by the producer but which is imposed on others. (4)

externalities external benefits or external costs. (4)

factory are were numerous workers, sometimes hundreds, gathered under one roof, were paid a standard wage, divided tasks into individual parts, and worked under the close supervision of the owner or manager. (2)

Fannie Mae (Federal National Mortgage Association) authorized in 1938 by Congress, it gave the GSE a mandate to buy mortgages from lenders, thereby freeing up capital in order that those lenders could extend more mortgages. (7)

farmers market is a collection of individual vendors – mostly farmers – who sell produce, fruits, meat products, and sometimes prepared foods and beverages. The local community benefits because farmers sell directly to consumers, keeping dollars circulating in the locality instead of being siphoned off to large corporate conglomerates. (8)

Federal Deposit Insurance Corporation (FDIC), part of the 1933 Glass Steagall Act, it insured deposits in commercial banks. (7)

Federal Reserve (sometime called the Fed or central bank), is the central banking system of the United States. It was created in 1913 under the administration of President Woodrow Wilson Its duties today are to conduct the nation's monetary policy, supervise and regulate banking institutions, maintain the stability of the financial system and provide financial services to depository institutions, the U.S. government, and foreign official institutions. (3)

Financial Services Modernization Act or **Gramm-Leach-Bliley Act** of 1999, rescinded the Glass-Steagall Act of 1933. It was signed into law by President Bill Clinton. This act allowed commercial banks, investment banks, securities firms, and insurance companies to consolidate, which was prohibited by the Glass-Steagall Act. (7)

financialization is a sector of the economy that specializes in creating financial products that have a certain value and can be traded in the market place. Some financial products are insurance, lending money, real estate sales, stocks, bonds, derivatives, and many others. (7)

fine-tuning the economy typically refers to the Federal Reserve's actions in raising or lowering interest rates. (7)

fiscal austerity raising taxes and reducing government spending. (5)

fiscal policy relates to governmental decisions on spending and taxes. (7)

Freddie Mac (Federal Home Loan Mortgage Corporation) 1970, expanded the secondary mortgage market. (7)

free trade elimination of import and export quotas and tariffs that are considered to be "barriers to trade." (3)

fundamentalism refers to a belief in a strict adherence to a set of basic principles (often religious), sometimes as a reaction to perceived compromises with modern social, ideological and political life. (1)

futures trading is, for example, where a farmer will agree to a price for his/her next harvest months in advance. The future price of the harvest is thus a derivative, which can itself be sold. (7)

Genuine Progress Indicator (GPI) created by the organization Redefining Progress in 1995, measures the general economic and social well-being of all citizens. (6)

Government National Mortgage Association (Ginnie Mae) put together the first mortgage-backed securities. It bought mortgages on the secondary market, pooled the mortgages it had originated, issued them as bonds, and then sold these pools of bonds as a mortgage-backed security to investors on the open market. Rather than waiting 30 years to make back the proceeds from a mortgage. (7)

Glass-Steagall Act of 1933, part of the New Deal reforms in the U.S. that prohibited a single company from offering investment banking, commercial banking, and insurance services. (3)

global warming describe general shifts in climate. But actually it refers specifically to any change in the global average surface temperature. The world will not warm uniformly, even though the term implies that it will; some areas warm more than others, such as the North and South poles. Some areas will even become cooler. I have used the term climate change in this book. (6)

Global Wave is transforming our human story as this new millennium dawns. Within it is five often contentious and conflicting worldviews, with contradictory ways of knowing and understanding the world. In the United States and throughout the world, most people identify with one or a combination of these worldviews: indigenous, fundamentalist, modern, globalized, and transformative. (1)

globalization is a complex, dominant, phenomenon that interconnects worldwide economic, political, cultural, social, environmental, and technological forces that go beyond national boundaries. Greatly intensifying since the 1980s, it reflects the many ways in which people are being drawn together, through their own movements and through the flow of goods, services, capital, labor, technology, ideas, and information. Globalization refers to the worldwide shrinking of space and time and the reduction of the national government in importance. Globalization influences the way billions of people around the world conduct their everyday lives. (1)

globalized worldview differs from the modern worldview in that "time has speeded up," the pace of growth and development has intensified and spread to the farthest reaches of the earth. (1)

Gramm-Leach-Bliley Act or the **Financial Services Modernization Act** of 1999 rescinded the Glass-Steagall Act of 1933. It was signed into law by President Bill Clinton. This

205

act allowed commercial banks, investment banks, securities firms, and insurance companies to consolidate, which was prohibited by the Glass-Steagall Act. (7)

Gross Domestic Product (GDP) a measure of a country's overall official economic output. It is the market value of all final goods and services officially made within the borders of a country in a year. (4)

Gross National Happiness (GNH) is an indicator based on the principle that wealth alone does not lead to happiness. (6)

guild is where artisans who had a common business or trade banded together to carefully control and regulate the production and distribution of their products. They restricted membership, regulated standards of quality and price, discouraged competition, and resisted technological innovations. Guilds charged a just price not a market price for their products. A just price would cover the expenses of the guild member and a small, but not an exorbitant, profit. The guilds did not seek to realize profits as much as to protect markets and preserve their members' livelihoods and security. Guilds of the past do not follow capitalist principles. (2)

hedge funds are a private pool of capital actively managed by an investment adviser. Hedge funds are only open for investment to a limited number of investors who typically invest a minimum range from about $250,000 to $10 million. (7)

hegemony is the political, economic, ideological or cultural power exerted by a dominant group over other groups, regardless of the explicit consent of the latter. (5)

holistic means that all a society's cultural traits – political, economic, technological, cultural, religious, social, arts, values, attitudes, and environmental – reinforce and support each other. (1)

home equity loans homeowners refinance their mortgages and withdraw their excess equity in their homes for their purposes. (7)

hostile takeovers "corporate raiders" bought up a company's stock when it was undervalued; thus, the company's assets were worth more than their stock. The raiders would then sell off the assets of the company to make a profit, but then the companies taken over were no longer operational. (4)

illiquid assets not easily or quickly converted into money, like mortgages. (7)

imperialism 1873-1914, differentiated from colonialism. It describes political and economic control by a greater power over a less powerful territory or country. During this imperialist era much of Asia, the Pacific islands, the Middle East, and sub-Saharan Africa were the objects of an extensive land-grab by the more powerful nations of Europe – particularly Great Britain and France, and to lesser extent the Netherlands, Belgium, Russia, Portugal, Spain, and Germany – and the United States, Japan, and Australia. (2)

import substitution industrialization (ISI) is a trade and economic policy based on the principal that a country should attempt to reduce its foreign dependency through the local production of industrialized products. Primarily refers to 20th century economic policies adopted in many Latin American countries from the 1930s until the late 1980s, and in some Asian and African countries from the 1950s onward. Domestic production replaced goods that were previously imported. (2)

indigenous peoples are any ethnic group who share a similar ethnic identity and inhabit a geographic region with which they have the earliest known historical connection. (1)

inequality is used in this book to mean the disparity between rich and poor. (6)

Industrial Revolution is the industrialization process, which moved rapidly from Britain, its place of origin, to neighboring countries. (2)

industrialization is the process of change from an economy based on home production of goods to one based on large-scale, mechanized factory production with a wage-based labor force. (2)

inflation is when price levels rise and the value of money drops. When it occurs, more money is needed than before to buy the same amount of goods and services. (7)

International Monetary Fund (IMF) was established with the mandate to regulate an international monetary system based on convertible currencies (currencies were pegged to the US dollar), to use its reserve of funds to lend to countries experiencing temporary balance of payment problems, and to facilitate global trade while leaving sovereign governments in charge of their own monetary, fiscal, and international investment policies. (5)

investment banks issue bonds and shares of stock, issue other complex financial instruments, trade on capital markets, and put together mergers and acquisitions, called the casino banks. (7)

just price in the Middle Ages, guilds would cover the expenses of the guild member and they earned a small, but not an exorbitant, profit. The guilds did not seek to realize profits as much as to protect markets and preserve their members' livelihoods and security. They did not follow capitalist principles. (2)

Keynes, John Maynard (1883-1946) British economist who had the biggest impact on shaping the transition from laissez faire capitalism to the era of social democracy in the 1930s. His policies are referred to as Keynesian Economics. (1)

labor productive activity, especially for the sake of economic gain. It is also the body of persons engaged in such activity, especially those working for wages. This body of persons is considered as a separate class of people who are distinguished from management (employers, owners) and capital (those engaged in finance). (3)

labor productivity is the amount a worker produces in a unit of time, usually per hour. (4)

laissez faire capitalism a French term that describes free trade, deregulated, unfettered capitalism. (2)

leverage the use of debt to supplement investment. (7)

leveraged buyouts when companies would "go private" by buying up their own stock with borrowed funds to avoid the acquisitions of their corporation by another rival firm. (4)

liquid assets easily and quickly converted into money that were tradable on the open market. (7)

liquidity money. (7)

Long Depression of 1873-1896 often referred to as the Great Depression before the 1930s depression, it contributed to great dissatisfaction with free trade and the gold standard. (2)

Main Street considered the real economy, collectively the aggregate of the producing sector of the economy that produces real wealth, as opposed to the phantom wealth of the Wall Street economy. (7)

managed capitalism the government closely regulates the financial sector to prevent wild financial speculation and insures transparency of the system. Tariffs protect manufacturing jobs in the home country; therefore, wages and prices are set according to supply and demand at the national level rather than the global level. For the most part services such as education, health care, the military, and prisons are government run and paid for through taxes. The state sometimes owns large service providers such as utilities, airlines and transportation networks or closely regulates them. Private enterprise exists but is carefully regulated, with high tax brackets for the wealthiest individuals. Corporations also pay a larger share of their profits in taxes than in the neoliberal model. Labor unions have a powerful say in wages and other benefits, as long as their wages keep up with productivity. There is a more equal circulation of wealth with managed capitalism than neoliberal capitalism, hence the presence of a vital middle and working class and less of a concentration of wealth in the hands of the elite and corporations. (1)

Marx, Karl (1818-1883), critiqued capitalism, along with co-author Frederich Engels, proposed a socialist/communist alternative to capitalism in their short book, the *Communist Manifesto* in 1848. (1)

mercantilism was based on the economic relationship between a European country, called the "mother country," and its colonies. The colonial rulers strove to maintain a favorable balance of trade for their country by importing cheap raw materials from their colonies and in turn exporting back to them the more profitable manufactured goods that the mother country produced. (2)

middle of the core and periphery are simply middle countries or areas, or correspondingly people in the middle class (1)

mixed economy is a diverse economy in which a mix of different economic sectors prevents the concentration of wealth and power and cushions the downturn in one economic sector from paralyzing the whole economy. (8)

modern worldview traces its historical origins back more than 500 years to the expansion of Western European power and its influence and/or ultimate dominance around the world. The modern worldview has been especially powerful over the last two centuries and has today expanded to the farthest reaches of the world. (1)

monetary policy the Federal Reserve influences the flow or availability of money and credit. (7)

moral hazard someone's willingness to take risks – particularly excessive risks – that s/he would normally avoid, simply because s/he knows someone else will shoulder whatever negative consequences will follow. (7)

mortgage-backed securities, the collateral backing the securities were home mortgages. (7)

multinational corporations (MNCs) corporations that have services in at least two countries. (5)

multiplier effect of government stimulus infusions. On average, the short-run multiplier for the U.S. economy is around 1.5. If the government spends a billion dollars now, GDP this year will go up by $1.5 billion. (8)

nationalization the government completely takes over a private enterprise. (8)

neoliberalism is an economic theory favoring free trade, privatization, minimal government intervention in business, and reduced public expenditure on social services, etc. (1)

nonprofit sector (quinary) is an organization that uses surplus revenues to achieve its goals rather than distributing them as profit or dividends. While not-for-profit organizations are permitted to generate surplus revenues, they must be retained by the organization for its self-preservation, expansion, or future plans. (7)

North American Free Trade Agreement (NAFTA) was signed on January 1, 1994 by President Bill Clinton to create a trilateral free trade bloc between the U.S., Canada, and Mexico. The goal of NAFTA was to eliminate tariffs and regulations on investments between the three countries. (3)

open field system a form of agricultural organization in which peasants farmed large tracks of land for elite landlords. They produced food for their own subsistence needs, and paid a required amount of the surplus as tribute to the landowner. (2)

OPEC (Organization of Oil Producing Countries in 1961 the major oil producing nations – Iran, Iraq, Kuwait, Saudi Arabia, and Venezuela – had enough of supplying cheap oil to the core nations and formed a cartel to regulate the price of oil and production. (2)

originate and distribute, investment banks and others jumped on the securitization band wagon to gobble up profitable pools of the growing numbers of home mortgage bonds. (7)

originate and hold a prospective homeowner would apply for a mortgage, and the bank would lend the money, then sit back and collect payments on the principal and interest. The bank that originated the mortgage held the mortgage. (7)

outsourcing involves the contracting out of a business function to an external provider, usually to a low-wage country. (5)

overcapacity or overproduction. This means that there is a tendency for capitalist economies to build up tremendous productive capacity to produce goods and services that outruns the population's capacity to consume. (2)

overshoot the human species is taking more resources from the planet than can be replaced by natural processes in a given year. (6)

participatory democracy attempts to check the abuses of elite democracy and corporate economic and political power with regulatory legislation and careful oversight of the whole process. Increasingly, participatory democracy takes the form of involvement by citizen groups who are playing a "watchdog" role over giant corporations in an effort to curb their financial excesses and detrimental corporate policies. (4)

periphery areas are often drawn into a dependent interaction with the core regions; commercial wealth is extracted from the periphery in the form of cheap raw materials produced with cheap labor – or, more recently, manufactured goods produced with cheap labor. The wealth from this transaction is siphoned to core areas where it is concentrated or used to generate more wealth. (1)

predatory lending mortgage lenders were doing everything they could to sign up borrowers for subprime mortgages. (7)

primary industries (sector) a form of wealth creation that includes mining, agriculture, forestry, trapping animals, and fishing – that changed natural resources into primary products. The manufacturing industries that amass, package, clean or process the raw materials close to the primary producers are generally considered part of this sector as well. (1)

private sector businesses owned by individuals or corporations. (3)

privatization the sale of state-owned enterprises, goods and services to private investors. Put another way, it is the transfer of assets or service delivery from the government to the private sector. (3)

progressive tax rates increase as the taxable base amount increases, which means those who have a higher income pay more of their total income in taxes. Federal income taxes are progressive. (4)

public sector where ownership is collectively held by the government for the people. (3)

quantitative easing is used by Central Banks (the Fed) when interest rates are at or very near zero, and they cannot be lowered any further. They may purchase a pre-determined number of bonds or other assets from financial institutions. Money is pumped into the economy. The goal is to increase the money supply rather than to decrease the interest rate, which is already around 0 percent, often considered a "last resort" to stimulate the economy. (8)

quaternary sector of the economy consists of informational and intellectual activities. Services include government, culture, libraries, scientific research and development, education, consultation, and information technology. (7)

reaction is a movement that favors extreme conservatism or right wing political views. They oppose political, economic, or social change or reforms and are considered to be at one end of a political spectrum whose opposite pole is radicalism or revolutionaries. (8)

rebuild developing an alternative economic structure that takes into consideration the environment, social and economic justice, and human well-being. (8)

reform means to put or change into an improved form or condition. Distinguished from revolution which means radical change, whereas reform may be no more than fine tuning, or at most redressing serious wrongs without altering the fundamentals of the system. (8)

regressive tax rates decrease as the amount subject to taxation increases, which means those who have a higher income pay less of their total income on taxed items. Social security and medicare (FICA) taxes are considered regressive. (4)

revolution is an overthrow or repudiation and thorough replacement of an established government or political system by the people governed. (8)

Santa Clara County v. Southern Pacific Railroad 1886, the Supreme court's reporter, who was in cahoots with the railroad barons, secretly inserted into the Court Reporter's headnotes in the case the rule that the railroad corporations were persons in the same category as humans. It stood in subsequent cases. (3)

secondary industries (sector) manufacturing and construction industries processing raw materials into manufactured goods. Since value was added to the raw materials in the form of labor, expertise, and so on, these products generated even more wealth than primary industries. (1)

Securities Exchange Act of 1934, part of the New Deal reforms in the U.S., which is a law governing the trading of stocks and bonds. (3)

securitization illiquid assets – not easily or quickly converted into money, like mortgages – could be pooled and transformed into liquid assets – easily and quickly converted into money – that are tradable on the open market. (7)

self-reliance is trust in one's own capabilities, judgment, or resources; independence, reliance on one's own efforts and abilities. It is the opposite of dependence. (4)

shadow banks are organizations that lend money to people just like traditional banks, except traditional bank money comes from depositors, while in a shadow banking system the money comes from investors, who want to earn a return on their money. Traditional banks are regulated by the government, and the shadow banking system is not regulated. (7)

sixth extinction alarming extinction of species, following upon the five previous known extinctions in the Ordovician, Devonian, Permian, Triassic and Cretaceous periods. (6)

Smith, Adam an Englishman, he wrote the seminal book *The Wealth of Nations* in 1776, he opposed mercantilism and instead argued that a free market or free trade economy was better. (2)

social democracy alternative to laissez faire capitalism in Western democracies arising during the 1930s, where coalitions of workers and farmers demanded and got economic management, social insurance and social security, and labor rights. (2)

social enterprises are organizations applying commercial strategies to maximize improvements in human and environmental well-being, rather than maximizing profits for external shareholders. These businesses support missions such as drug rehabilitation and training programs. (8)

social gap refers to a situation in which individuals in a society do not have equal access to social programs provided by the government to its citizens. These include voting rights, freedom of speech and assembly, legal rights, security, and access to quality education, health care, job training, and other social goods. (6)

socialism advocates for collective or governmental ownership and administration of the means of production and distribution of goods and services. (1)

socioeconomic gap this definition in this book combines two concepts into one: the social gap and economic gap. (6)

specialization economic actors concentrate their skills on tasks they are the most skilled at. Specialized individuals and organizations focus on the limited range of production tasks they perform best. This specialization requires workers to give up performing other tasks at which they are not as skilled, leaving those jobs to others who are better suited for them. (5)

spreads or the difference in what interest is paid depositors and the interest banks charge borrowers for loans. Concept is applied to different scenarios as well. (7)

stagflation a combination of low economic growth and high unemployment ("stagnation") with high rates of high inflation. This phenomenon epitomized the 1970s. (2)

state capitalism a system in which the state plays the role of leading economic actor and uses markets primarily for political gain. Those nations that support a state-capitalist system believe that public wealth, public investment and public enterprise offer the surest path toward politically sustainable economic development. These governments will micromanage entire sectors of their economies to promote national interests and to protect their domestic political standing. (1)

stimulus government spending to counter economic stagnation and/or recession. (8)

Stolper-Samuelson theorem basically says that the effect of trade between a core nation and a periphery nation is that the wages for the unskilled labor force in the core nation will be lower because they are competing globally with the unskilled workers in a periphery nation. (5)

suprime mortgage, a new market of riskier but more profitable loans to less creditworthy borrowers. (7)

subsidy a form of financial assistance paid to a business or particular economic sector. (4)

supply and demand the relation between these two factors determines the price of a commodity. This relationship is thought to be the driving force in a free market. As demand for an item increases, prices rise. (2)

supply side economics. This school of macroeconomic thought emphasizes the importance of tax cuts and business inducements in encouraging economic growth, in the belief that businesses and individuals will use their tax savings to create new businesses and expand old businesses, which in turn will increase productivity, employment, and improve general prosperity. (3)

system is defined as something that maintains its existence and functions as a whole through the interaction of its parts. (1)

systems thinking is a way of thinking in which the whole system is understood and recognized as interconnected. Instead of analyzing the separate parts of the whole, we look at how the pieces or parts of the whole interact, interconnect, and affect each other. In a systems approach we attempt to see beyond what appears to be isolated and independent, unrelated incidents to see deeper patterns and understand the connections of these patterns. In other words, we see the interaction of the parts working together as a whole. In using this approach we can recognize reoccurring patterns in the system and the interrelationships of these patterns, as well as the underlying structures which are responsible for the patterns. (1)

tariffs are duties or customs imposed by government on exports or imports. (2)

Telecommunications Act 1996 passed under President Clinton, amended the Communications Act of 1934. Deregulation of the broadcasting market was the primary goal, which meant that media cross-ownership was now allowed. (3)

tertiary sector is the service industry. Services are intangible goods. Activities associated with this sector include retail and wholesale sales, transportation and distribution, entertainment (movies, television, radio, music, theater, YouTube) restaurants, clerical services, media, tourism, insurance, finance, banking, healthcare, and law. (7)

transformative worldview alternatives to prevailing notions of cultural uniformity, corporate dominance, consumer-driven values, unchecked individualism, oligarchic concentration of wealth and power, and environmental destruction. (1)

transparency is another word for information. (7)

Triangle Trade in the 18th century trade developed between Africa, Europe, and the Americas. European ships carried guns, knives, metal ware, manufactured items, beads, colored cloth, and liquor to the West African coast to be exchanged with African chieftains who dealt in captured slaves. The captured slaves shipped to the Americas were exchanged for raw materials, such as sugar, tobacco, furs, precious metals, and raw cotton that were in turn transported to Europe to be made into finished goods that were either shipped back to the colonies or to Africa to begin the trading network again. (2)

Troubled Asset Relief Program (TARP) was a $700 billion government program to purchase assets and equity from financial institutions in the fall of 2008 with the intended purpose to strengthen the financial sector. (8)

tulip mania first financial crisis or speculative bubble in modern history, occurred in 17th century Netherlands. Now sometimes used metaphorically to refer to any large economic bubble. (8)

Wall Street a street located in the financial district of lower Manhattan in New York City. It is a collective phrase to refer to the financial sector of the economy, the phantom economy. It is opposition to Main Street that is considered the real economy.

Washington Consensus, named for the three institutions that shaped neoliberal policies, all located in downtown Washington D.C.: IMF, World Bank, and the U.S. Treasury. (5)

welfare capitalism   corporations in the Western social democracies of the 1930s largely backed the economic, social, and labor reform agenda. (2)

well-being is a kind of contentment, happiness, or a state of life-satisfaction. (6)

worker ownership is where the workers have an equal equity stake in the company they are working for; they share common goals and adhere to common principles. (8)

World Bank provides loans to developing countries for capital programs with the stated goal of reducing poverty. By law, all of its decisions must be guided by a commitment to promote foreign investment and international trade, and assist in capital investment. (5)

World Trade Organization (WTO) deals with regulation of trade between participating countries; it provides a framework for negotiating and formalizing trade agreements, and a dispute resolution process aimed at enforcing participants' adherence to WTO agreements. (5)

worldview is an overall perspective from which one sees and interprets the world, a set of simplifying suppositions about how the world works and what is seen and not seen. It is an internal collection of assumptions, held by an individual or a group that are firmly believed to be self-evident truths. (1)

List of Commonly Used Acronyms

AAA triple A rated securities, the best
ABS asset-backed security
AIG American International Group
AU African Union
BP British Petroleum
CDO collateralized debt obligation
CDS credit default swap
CEO Chief Executive Officer
CFTC Commodity Futures Trading Commission
CPFF Commercial Paper Funding Facility
CRA credit rating agency
DRC Democratic Republic of the Congo
DSB Dispute Settlement Body
EOI Export-Oriented Industrialization
EU European Union
FDIC Federal Deposit Insurance Corporation
FHFA Federal Housing Finance Agency
GATT General Agreement on Tariffs and Trade
GDP Gross Domestic Product (or GNP Gross National Product)
GE General Electric
GE genetically engineered
GM General Motors Corporation
GMO genetically modified organisms
GNH Gross National Happiness
GPI Genuine Progress Indicator
GSE Government Sponsored Entity
HDI Human Development Index
IMF International Monetary Fund
IP Intellectual Property
ISI Import Substitution Industrialization
LDC Least Developed Countries
MBS Mortgage Backed Securities
MNC multinational corporation
OECD Organization for Economic Cooperation and Development
OPEC Organization of Oil Producing Countries
S & P Standard & Poor's
SEC Securities and Exchange Commission
TARP Troubled Asset Relief Program
TBTF too big to fail
TRIPS Trade-Related Aspects of Intellectual Property Rights
TVA Tennessee Valley Authority
UAW United Auto Workers
UK United Kingdom
U.S. United States
WTO World Trade Organization

About the Author

Denise R. Ames is an educator with over 30 years of teaching experience at secondary schools, two colleges, two universities, adult and outreach educational programs, and professional development workshops. She took her bachelor's degree in history education from Southern Illinois University, master's degree in history from Illinois State University, and doctorate in history, with a focus in world history education, also from Illinois State University. Her teaching topics range from academic subjects such as world history, global issues, United States history, Western Civilization, world humanities, cultural studies, and global business issues, to secondary social studies classes, pedagogy, and current topics such as global issues, globalization, consumerism and worldviews.

Dr. Ames has presented numerous workshops, classes and lectures on her holistic world history model, the global economy, and other topics locally, nationally, and internationally. She is currently founder and President of the Center for Global Awareness, a non-profit organization encouraging greater global awareness for students and educators. She is dedicated to working with teachers, students, and the general public to foster a better understanding of the myriad of global issues we face, a teaching model for world history, and the effects of the global economy on ourselves, the global community, and the environment. She is the author of *Waves of Global Change: A Holistic World History* and its accompanying book for educators: *Waves of Global Change: An Educator's Handbook for Teaching a Holistic World History*. Along with this book, a brief edition of the global economy, she has completed the full edition of the book, *The Global Economy: Connecting the Roots of a Holistic System*, and *Financial Literacy: Wall Street and How it Works*. Dr. Ames' forthcoming book, *Human Rights: A Holistic Approach to a Universal Values System*, is due out in late 2015.

World history has been Dr. Ames' life-long interest and study. Her extensive travels, personal experiences, reflections, and scholarly research have all contributed to her common sense approach to the often overwhelming subject of world history and the global economy. Along with her interest and work in history, the global economy, global issues, and education, Dr. Ames has owned her own small business for eight years, constructed and remodeled eight houses, exhibited and trained Arabian horses, and traveled extensively. She has two grown children, Dennis and Mia and their spouses Kim and Alex, and one grandchild Lilly. She particularly enjoys traveling, hiking, yoga, reading, biking, gardening, and visiting with family and friends. She and her partner Jim currently reside near the campus of the University of New Mexico in sunny Albuquerque, New Mexico.

Index

86430213R00120

Made in the USA
Columbia, SC
14 January 2018